ONE
SOUL

# ONE
# SOUL

by
Ray Fawkes

*Cover design by*
Matt Kindt

*Book design & production by*
Keith Wood

*Edited by*
James Lucas Jones

*To Dorian*
*our beloved son*

born and died
March 13, 2010
*In Memoriam*

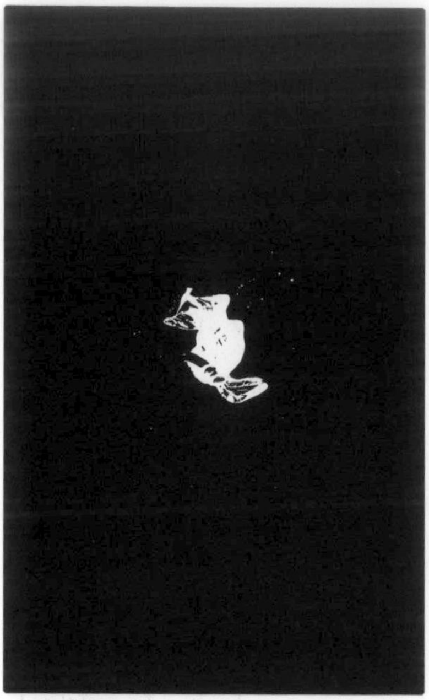
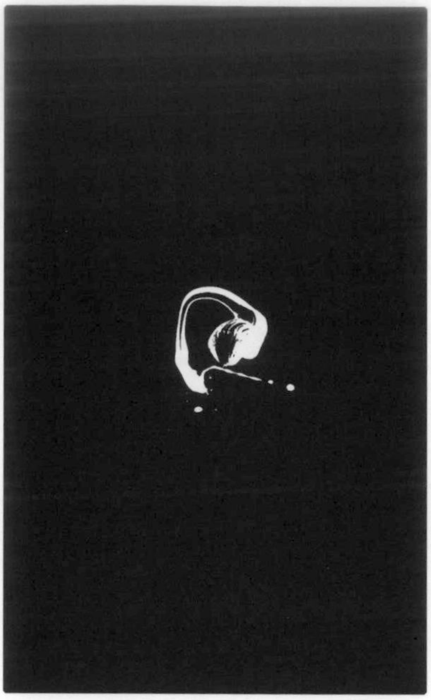
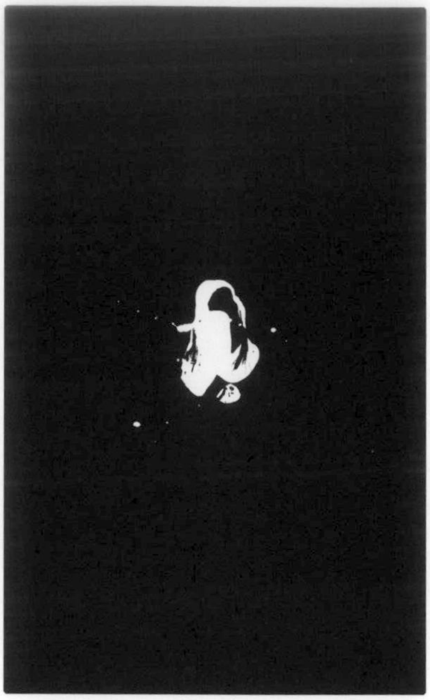
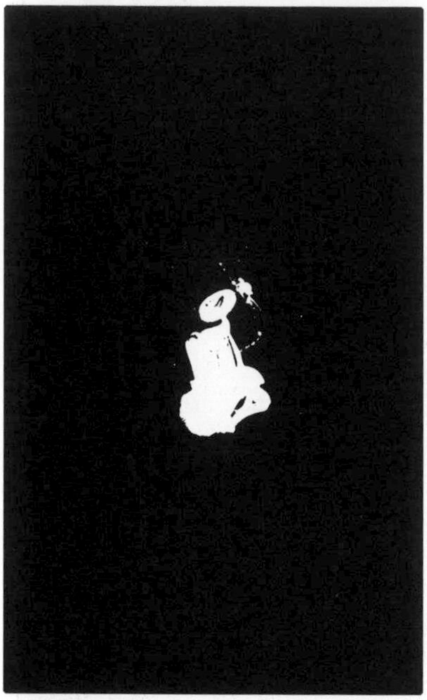
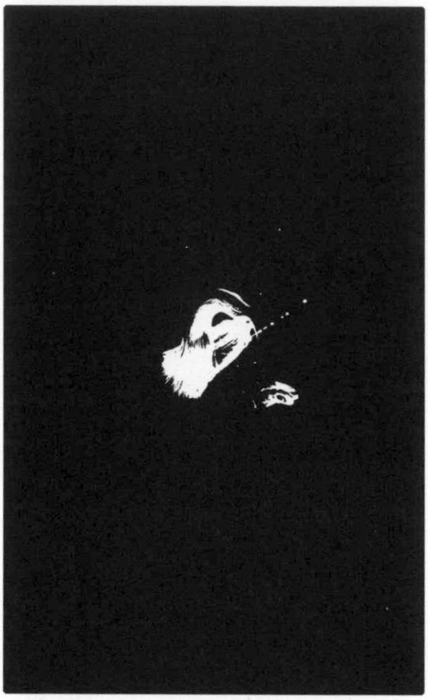
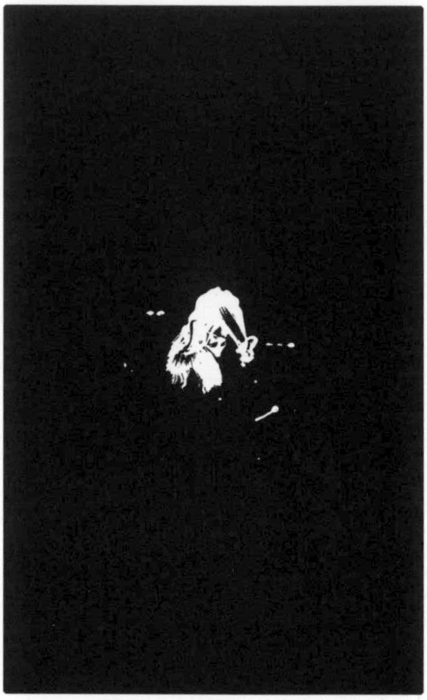
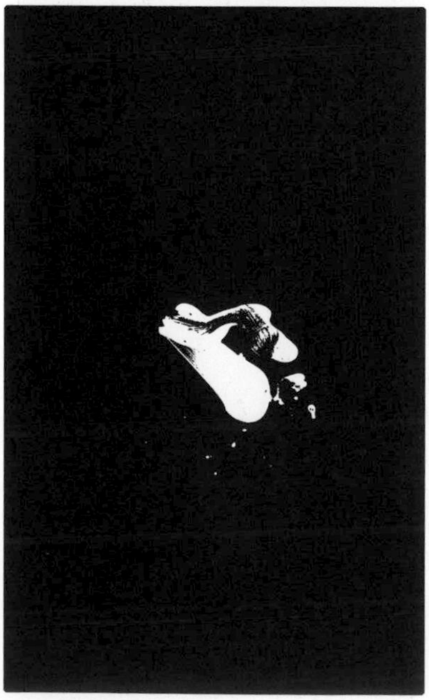
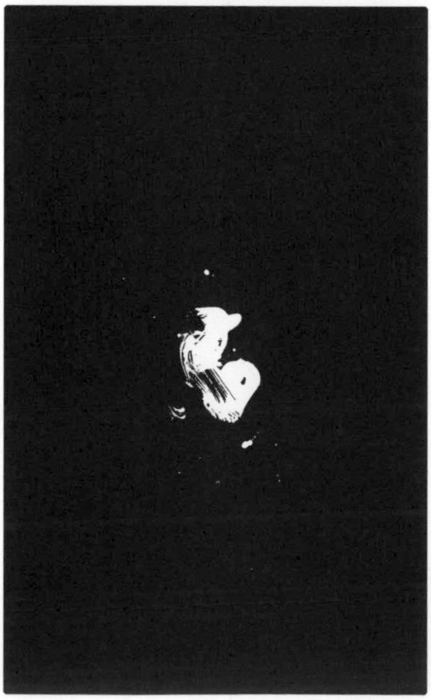
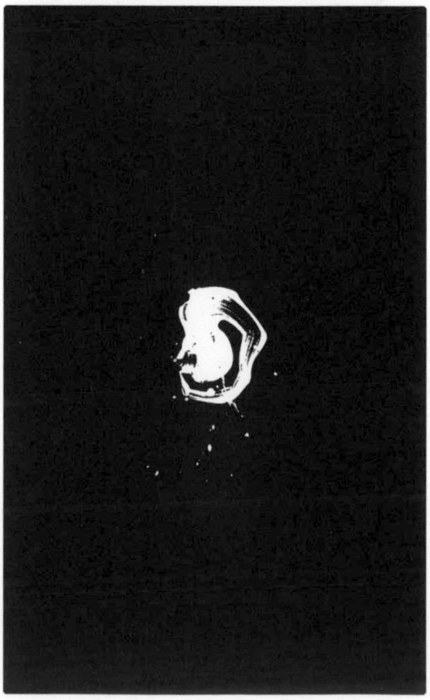

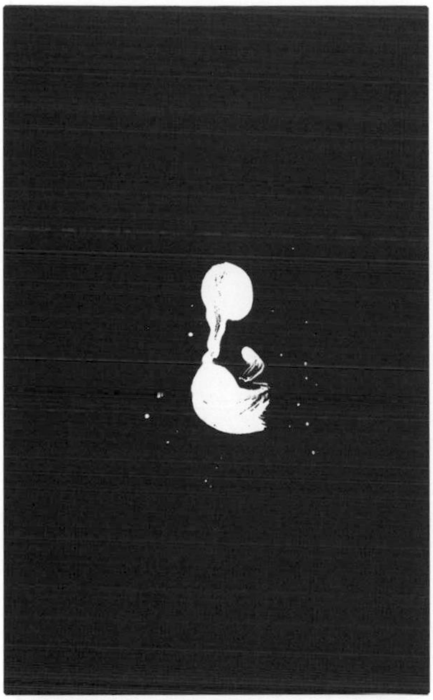
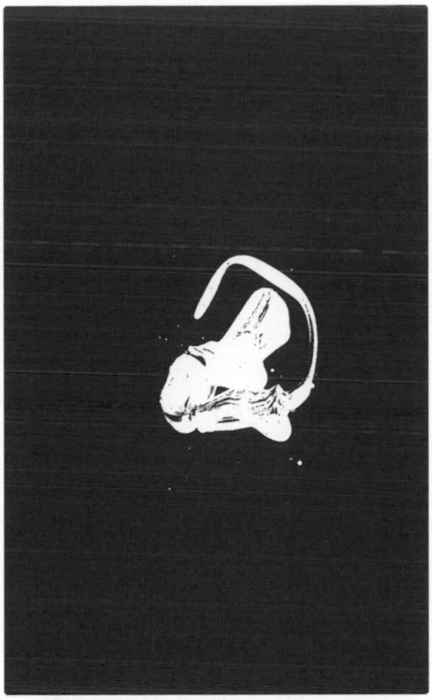
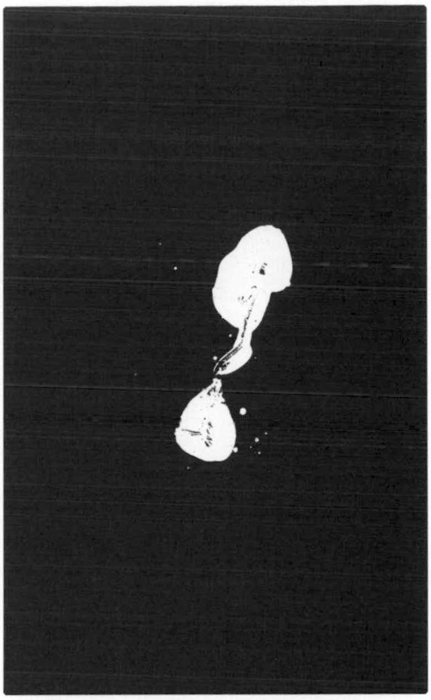
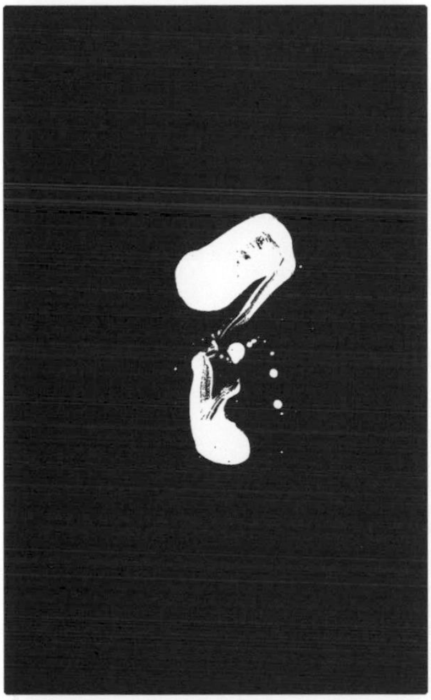
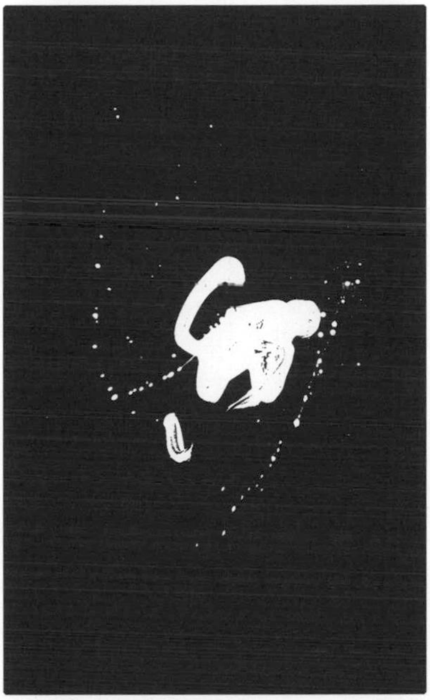
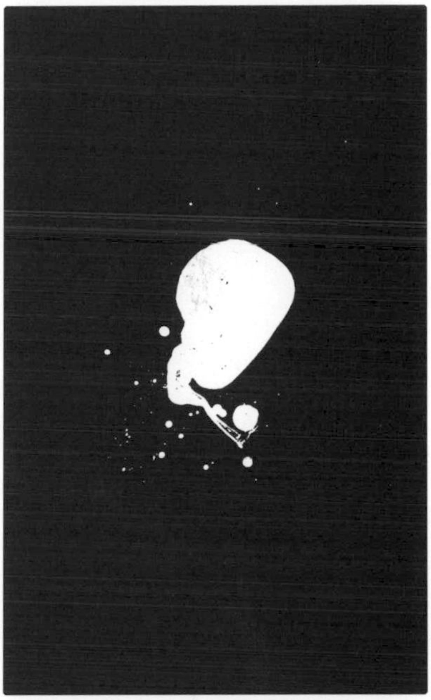
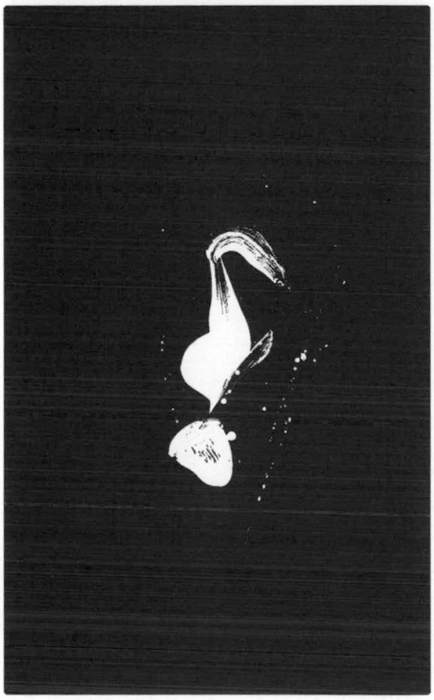
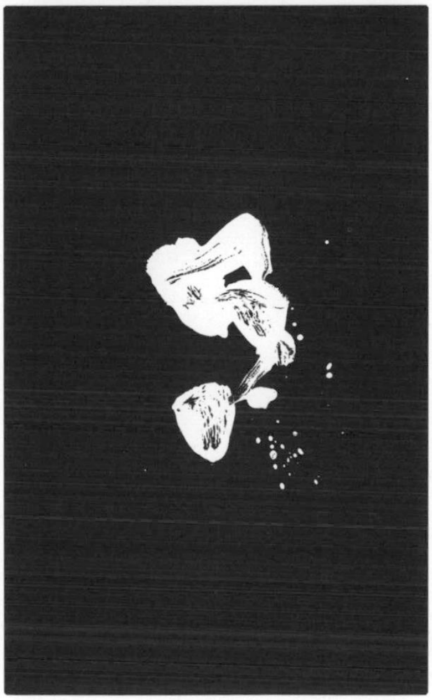
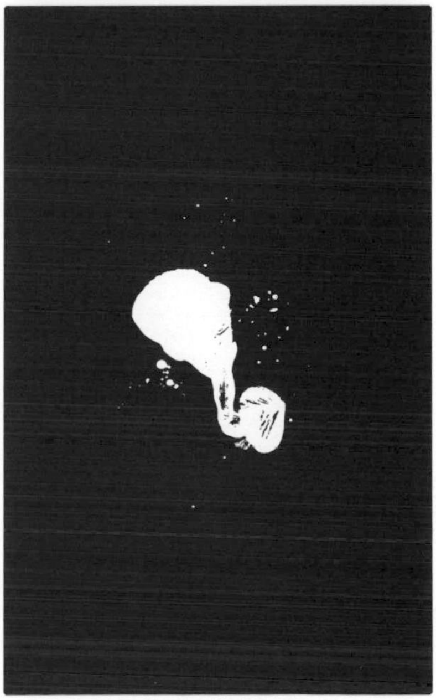

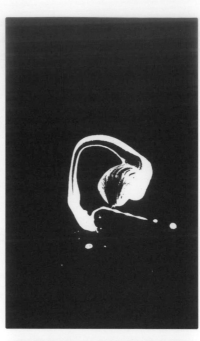

This is me. This and only this.

This is me. This and only this.

This is me. This and only this.

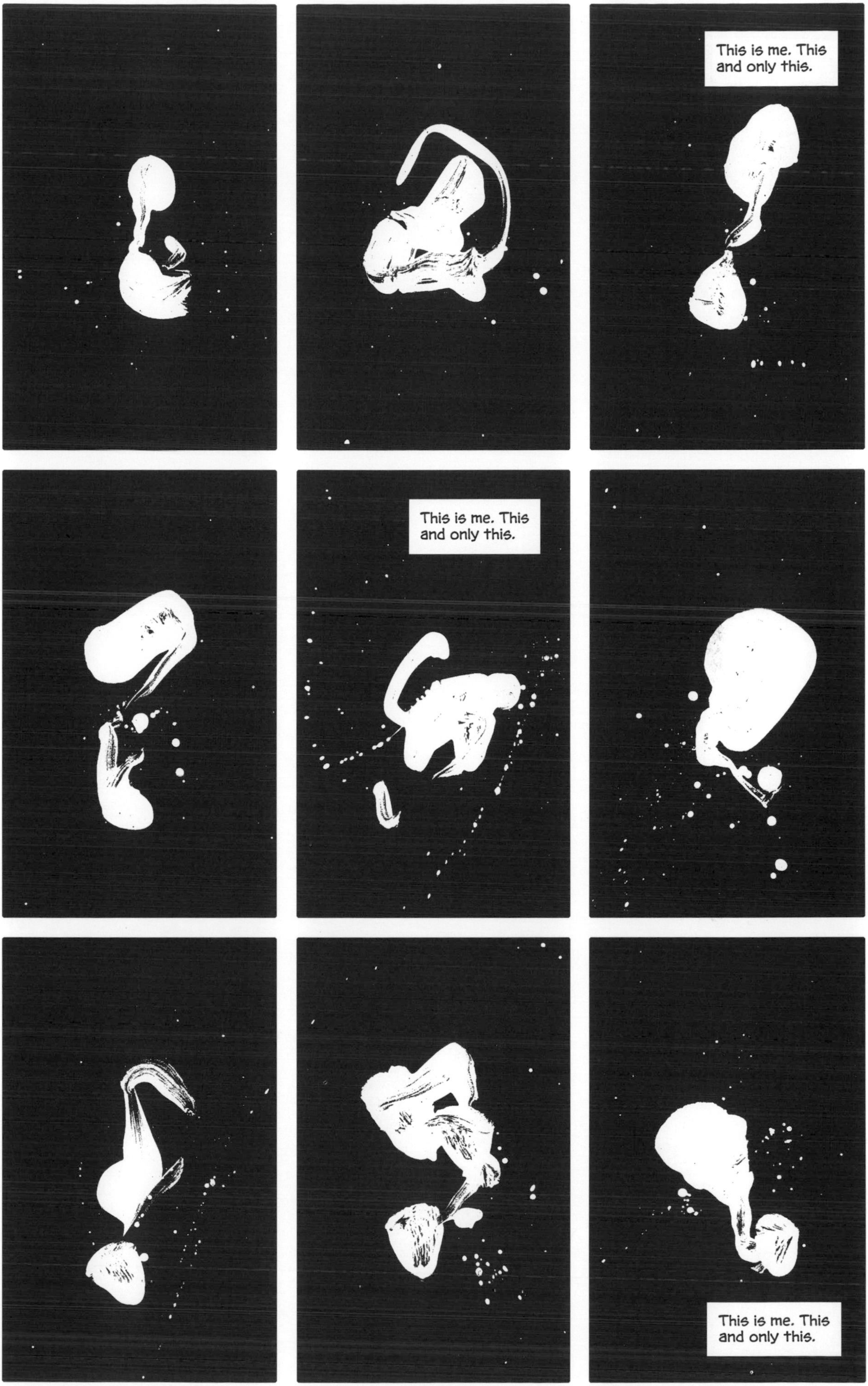
This is me. This and only this.
This is me. This and only this.
This is me. This and only this.

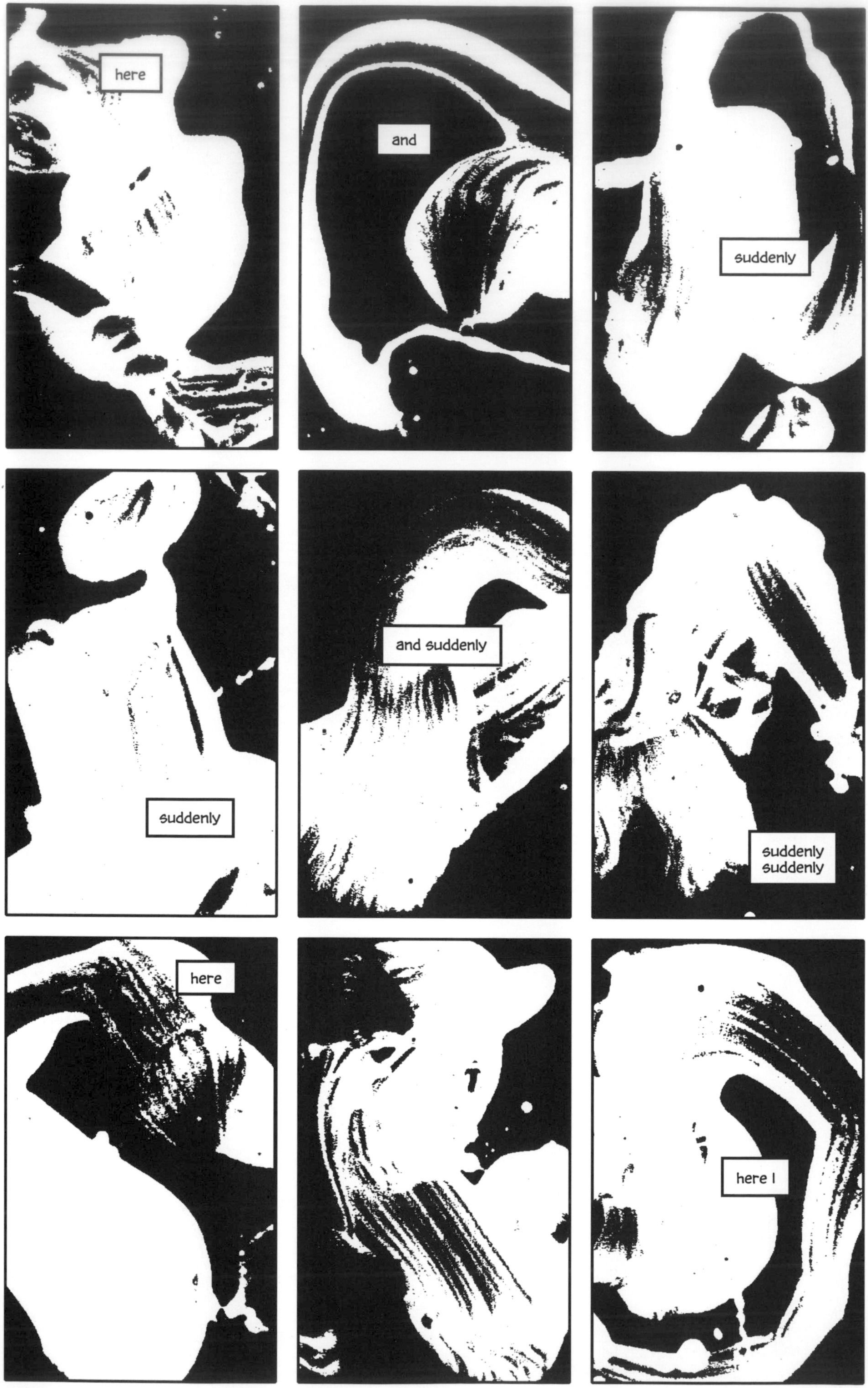
here
and
suddenly
suddenly
and suddenly
suddenly
suddenly
here
here I

here I
and suddenly
suddenly
and I
am
here
and suddenly
and suddenly,
suddenly, here
I am

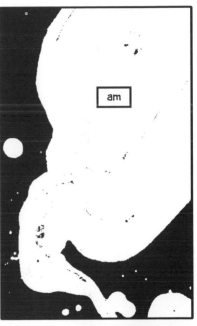

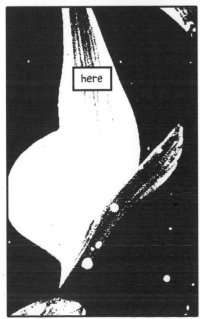

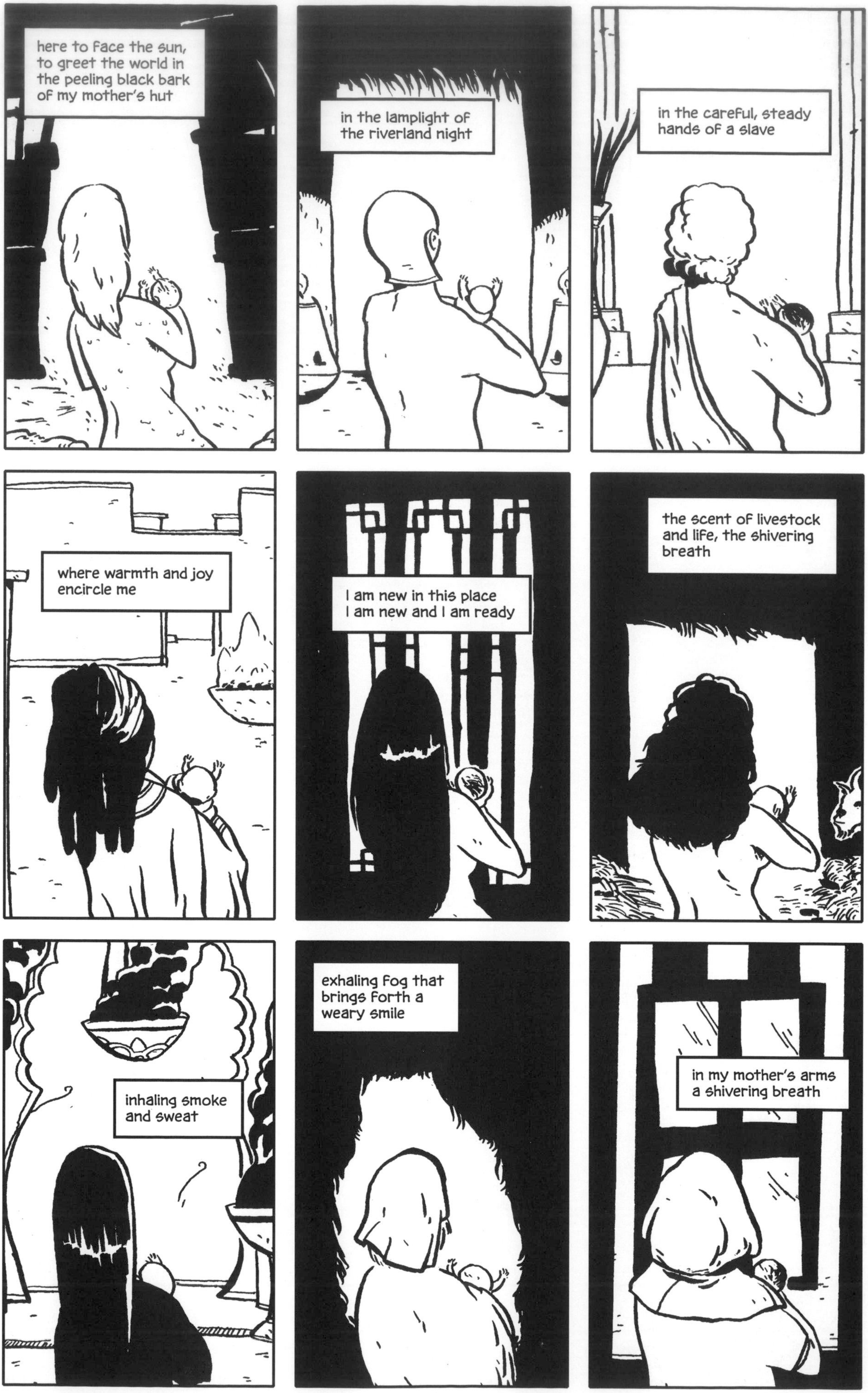
here to face the sun, to greet the world in the peeling black bark of my mother's hut
in the lamplight of the riverland night
in the careful, steady hands of a slave
where warmth and joy encircle me
I am new in this place I am new and I am ready
the scent of livestock and life, the shivering breath
inhaling smoke and sweat
exhaling fog that brings forth a weary smile
in my mother's arms a shivering breath

I clutch at rough cloth

I kick my feet, knotting nerves throughout my flesh, fronds blooming

I feel the bones in my back and my hands

growing with a sound audible to me, a sound I can never name

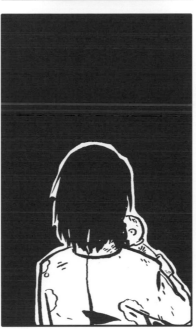

never

I kick and whirl my way into sleep in the careful arms

whirl into sleep

sleep in the warm light

in the damp and dark in wood and soil

dry reeds in a brittle weave crackling in heat

sunlight on white stone

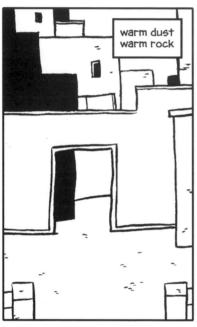

warm dust warm rock

lacquer misted with autumn fog

mud and straw

the glittering, perfumed halls

squat in mud

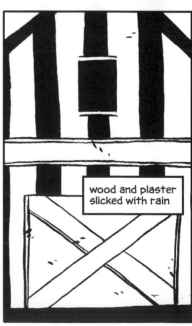

wood and plaster slicked with rain

ribboned tapestries hang on great walls of stone

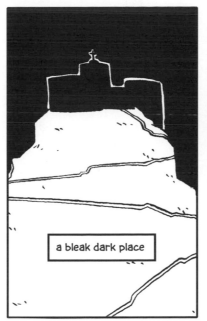

a bleak dark place

aglow in the icy season

clapboard cottage hot like an oven

broken wood with ragged oiled cloth for a door

carved into the corner of a glorious city

chill on the hillside the rooms too big to warm with fire

a green square in front a green square behind

brick and rust

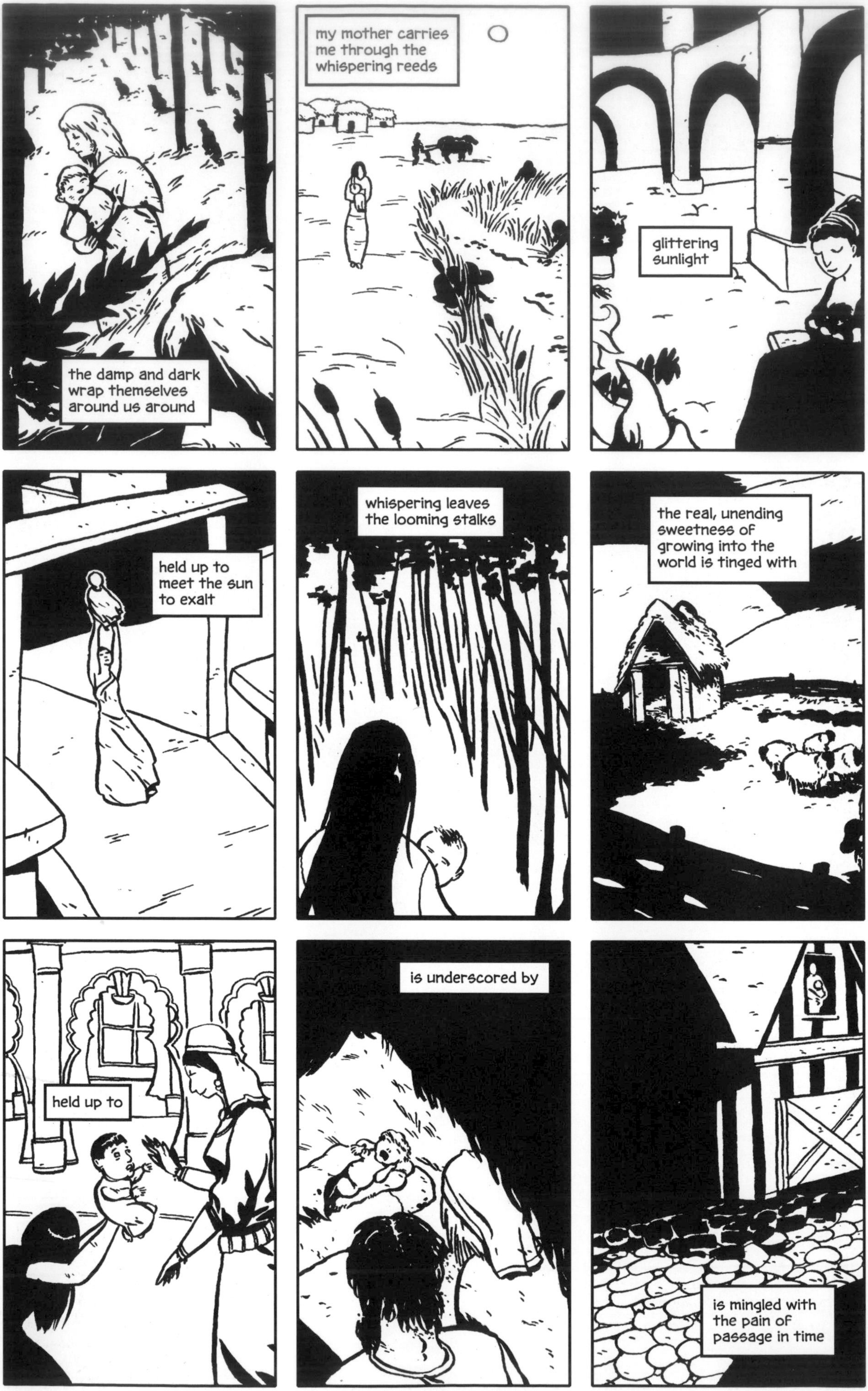
the damp and dark wrap themselves around us around
my mother carries me through the whispering reeds
glittering sunlight
held up to meet the sun to exalt
whispering leaves the looming stalks
the real, unending sweetness of growing into the world is tinged with
held up to
is underscored by
is mingled with the pain of passage in time

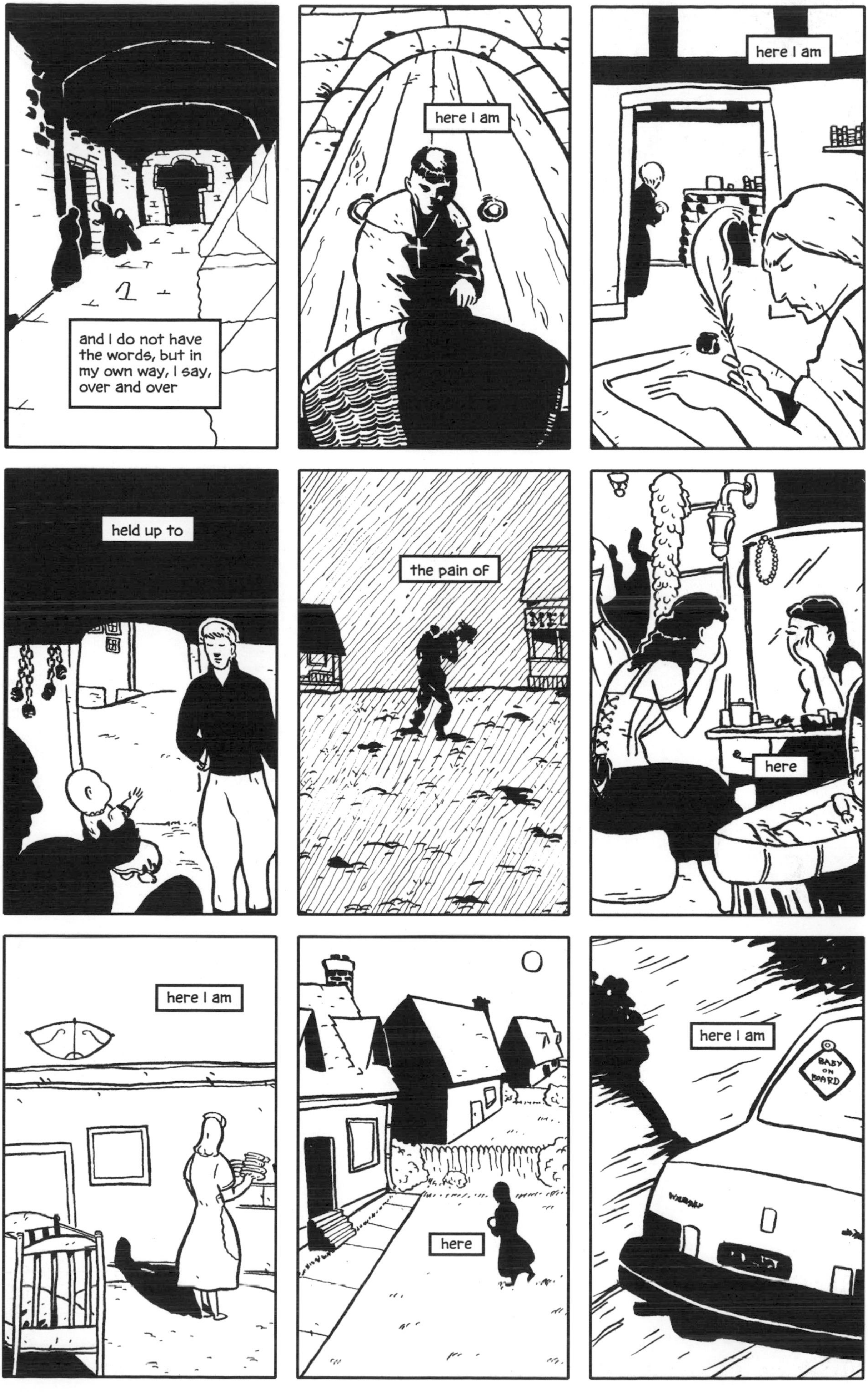
and I do not have the words, but in my own way, I say, over and over
here I am
here I am
held up to
the pain of
here
here I am
here
here I am
BABY ON BOARD

dappled light through the leaves I blink

the lowing of oxen in the distance the warm hands at my back

fragrant blossoms and hissing ferns night-chilled marble in the light of dawn

grit caught in the folds at elbows and knees scorpion husk on arid rock

dappled light through bamboo, hundreds of stalks sway as one

grassland hiss

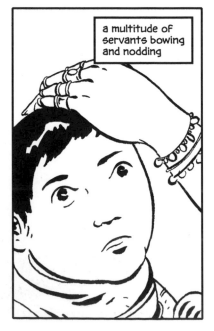

a multitude of servants bowing and nodding

a dank cold hut lost in the mist of moonless night

the scent of bread baking, warmth rising throughout and I smile

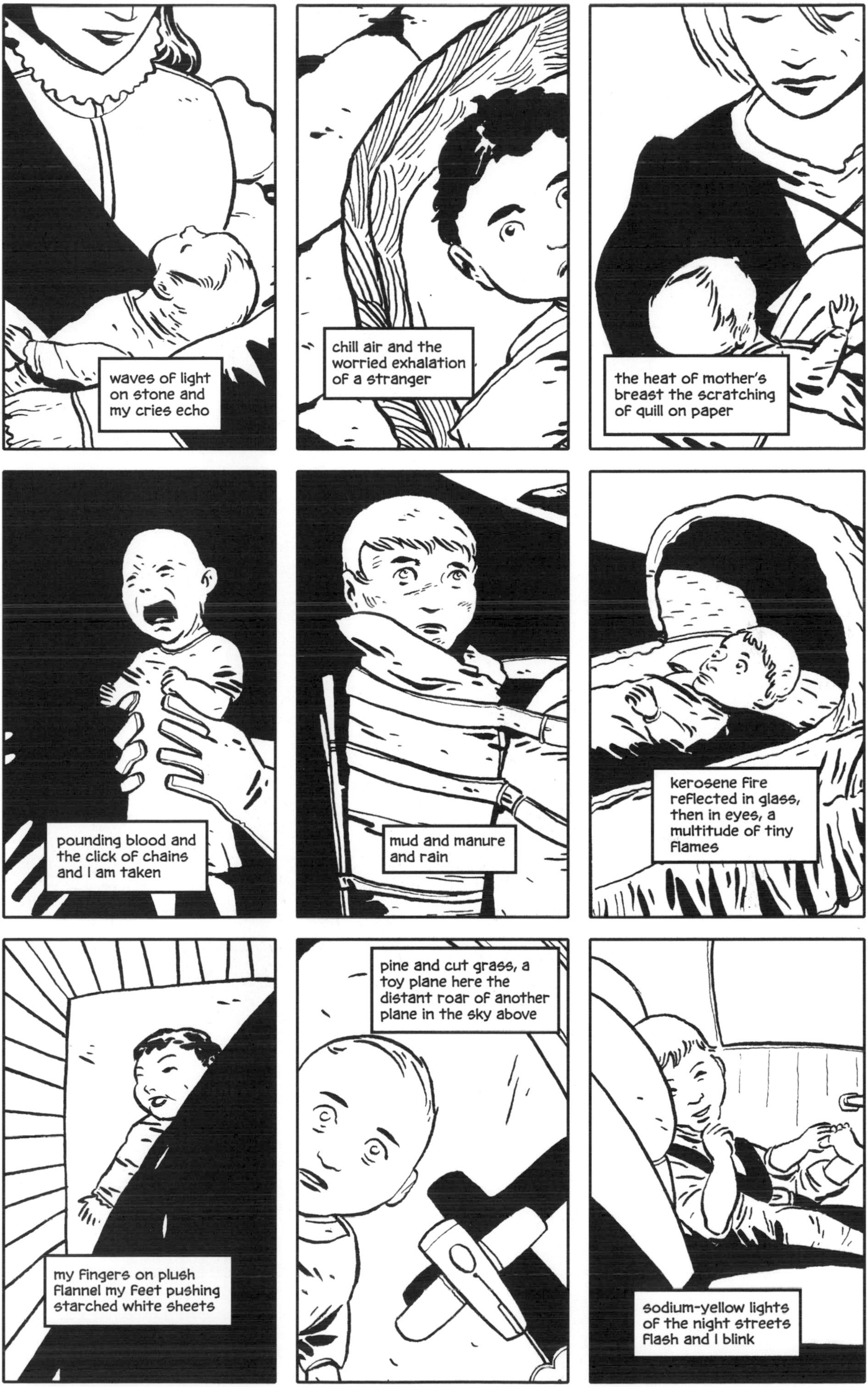
waves of light on stone and my cries echo
chill air and the worried exhalation of a stranger
the heat of mother's breast the scratching of quill on paper
pounding blood and the click of chains and I am taken
mud and manure and rain
kerosene fire reflected in glass, then in eyes, a multitude of tiny flames
my fingers on plush flannel my feet pushing starched white sheets
pine and cut grass, a toy plane here the distant roar of another plane in the sky above
sodium-yellow lights of the night streets flash and I blink

and I look through the standing wood and see the shifting place beyond

behind the reeds

and a blossom opens right before my eyes

beyond the drifting sands

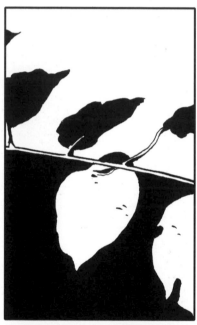

straw in straw under straw over

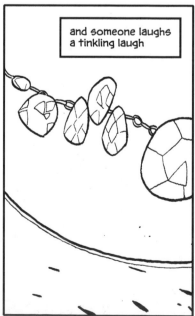

and someone laughs a tinkling laugh

hacking cough

behind the smoke beyond the stone

Frosted panes of rippled glass set in iron

stone thrust up into the sky

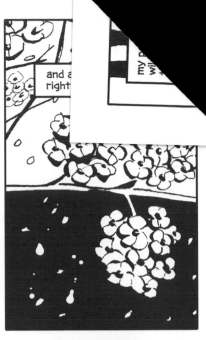

and a
right

my
will

hacking cough horse manure and mud

shell-pink and soft cream

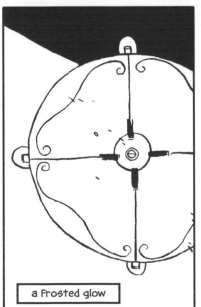

a Frosted glow

shifting, crossing, forming patterns

patterns of light and dark

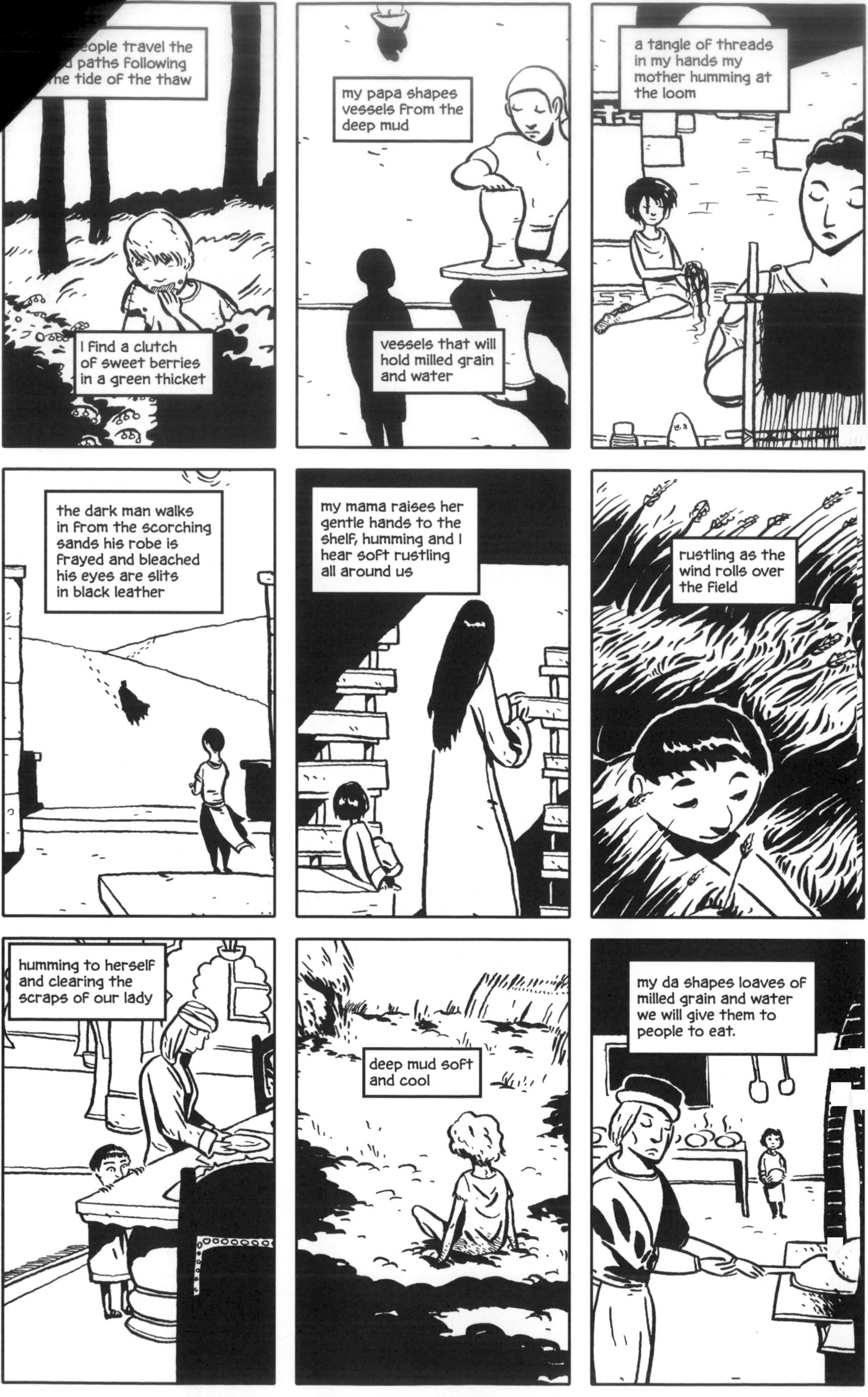
eople travel the
paths following
he tide of the thaw
I find a clutch of sweet berries in a green thicket
my papa shapes vessels from the deep mud
vessels that will hold milled grain and water
a tangle of threads in my hands my mother humming at the loom
the dark man walks in from the scorching sands his robe is frayed and bleached his eyes are slits in black leather
my mama raises her gentle hands to the shelf, humming and I hear soft rustling all around us
rustling as the wind rolls over the field
humming to herself and clearing the scraps of our lady
deep mud soft and cool
my da shapes loaves of milled grain and water we will give them to people to eat.

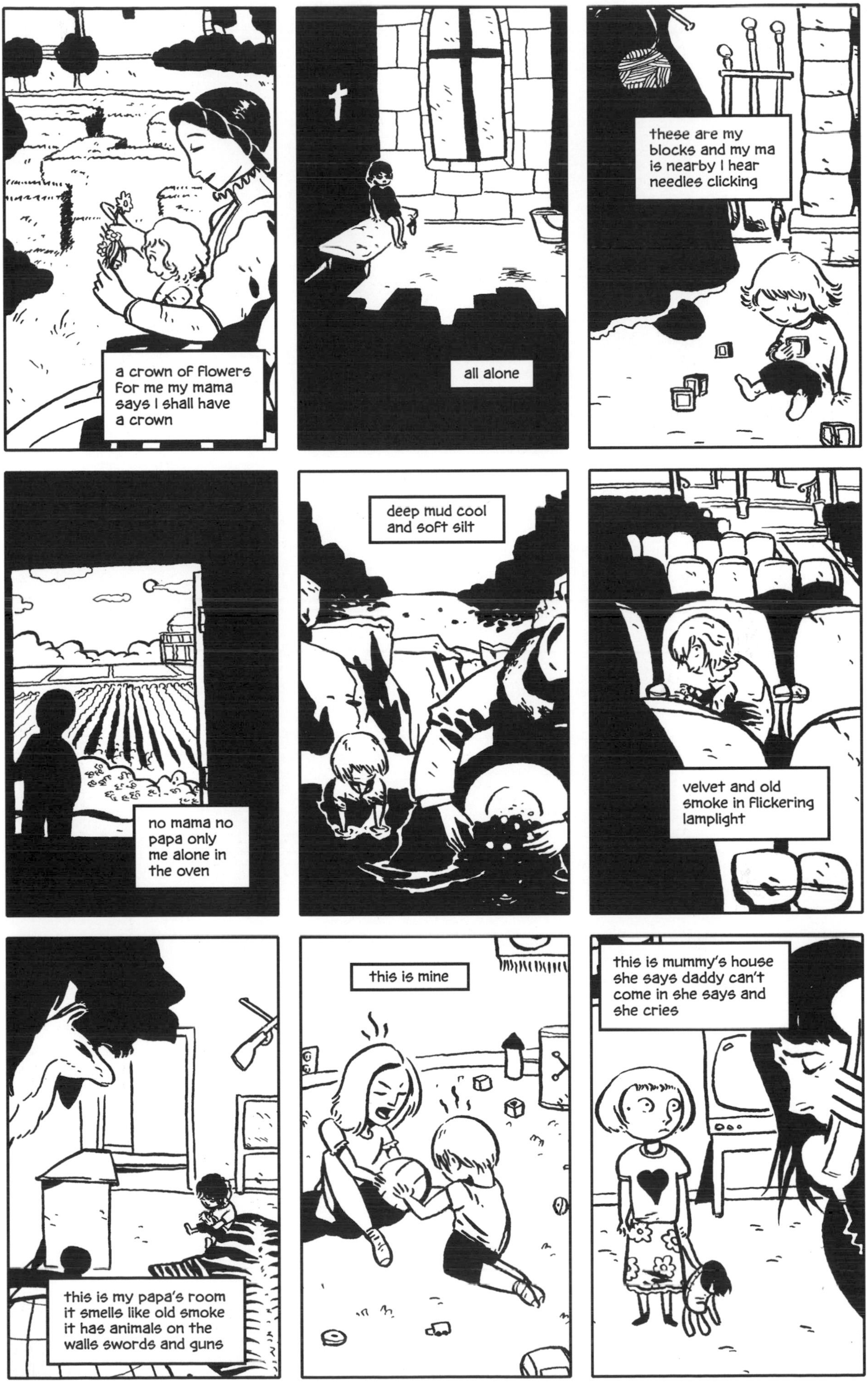
a crown of flowers for me my mama says I shall have a crown
all alone
these are my blocks and my ma is nearby I hear needles clicking
no mama no papa only me alone in the oven
deep mud cool and soft silt
velvet and old smoke in flickering lamplight
this is my papa's room it smells like old smoke it has animals on the walls swords and guns
this is mine
this is mummy's house she says daddy can't come in she says and she cries

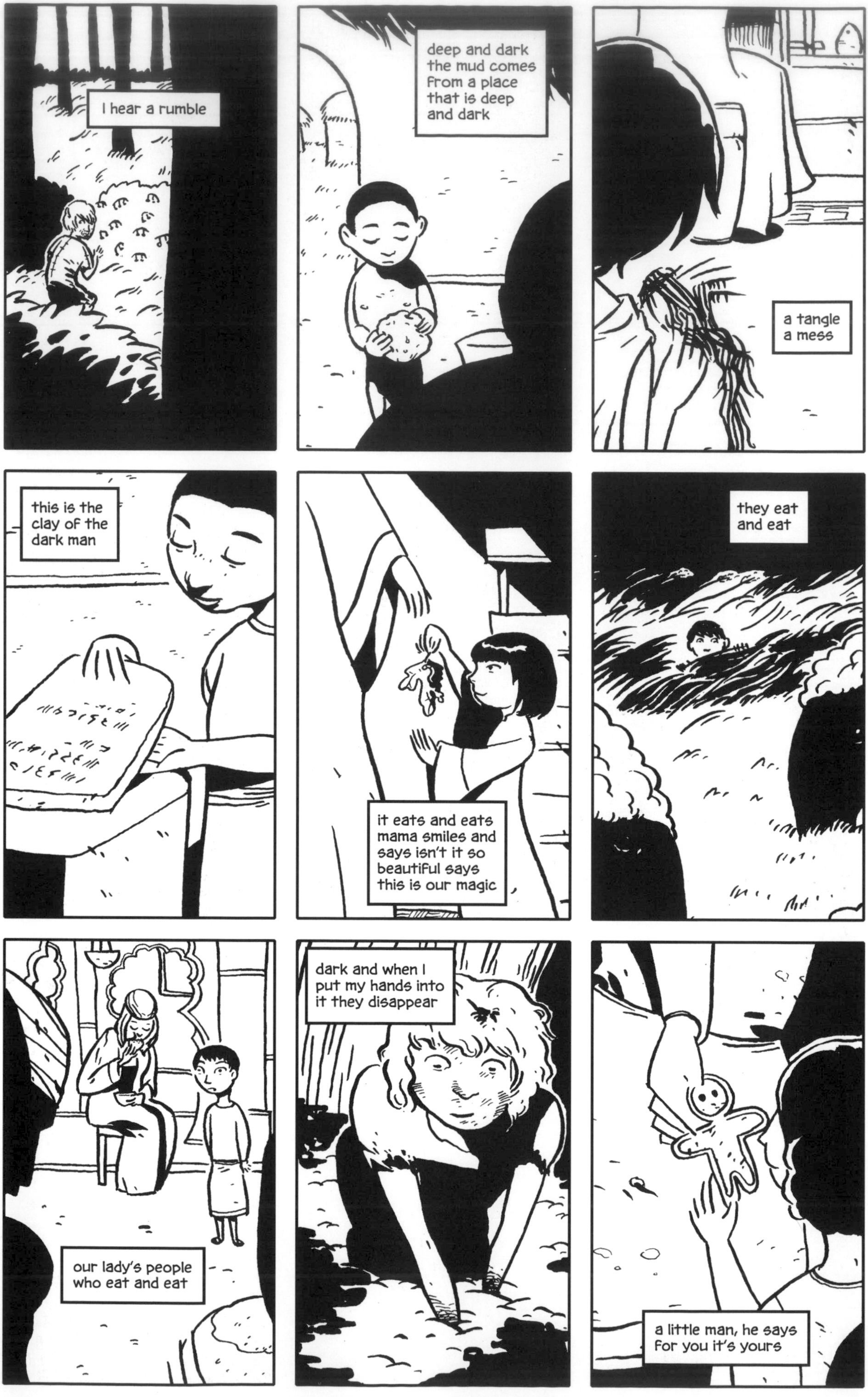
I hear a rumble
deep and dark the mud comes from a place that is deep and dark
a tangle a mess
this is the clay of the dark man
it eats and eats mama smiles and says isn't it so beautiful says this is our magic
they eat and eat
our lady's people who eat and eat
dark and when I put my hands into it they disappear
a little man, he says for you it's yours

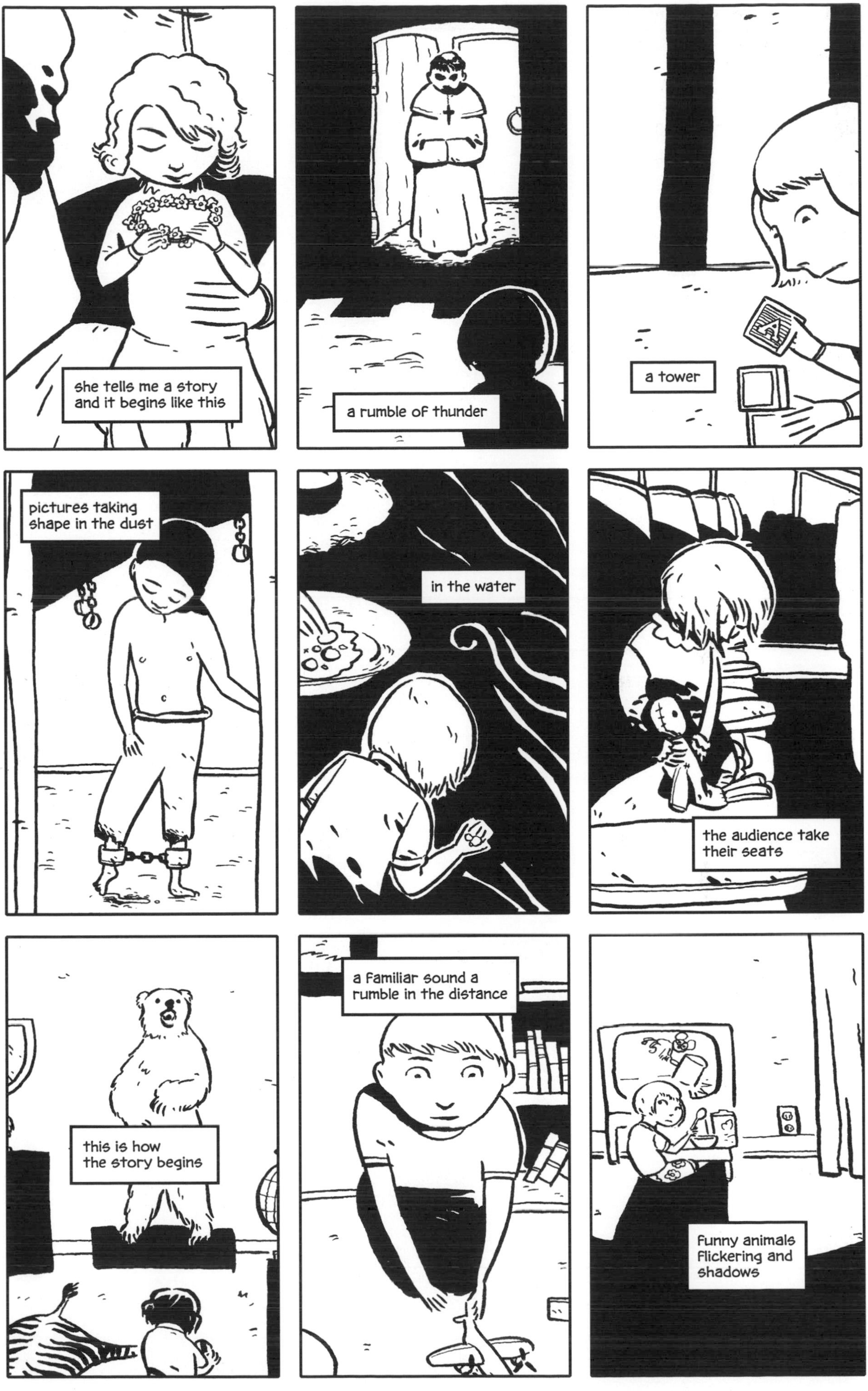
she tells me a story
and it begins like this
a rumble of thunder
a tower
pictures taking
shape in the dust
in the water
the audience take
their seats
this is how
the story begins
a familiar sound a
rumble in the distance
funny animals
flickering and
shadows

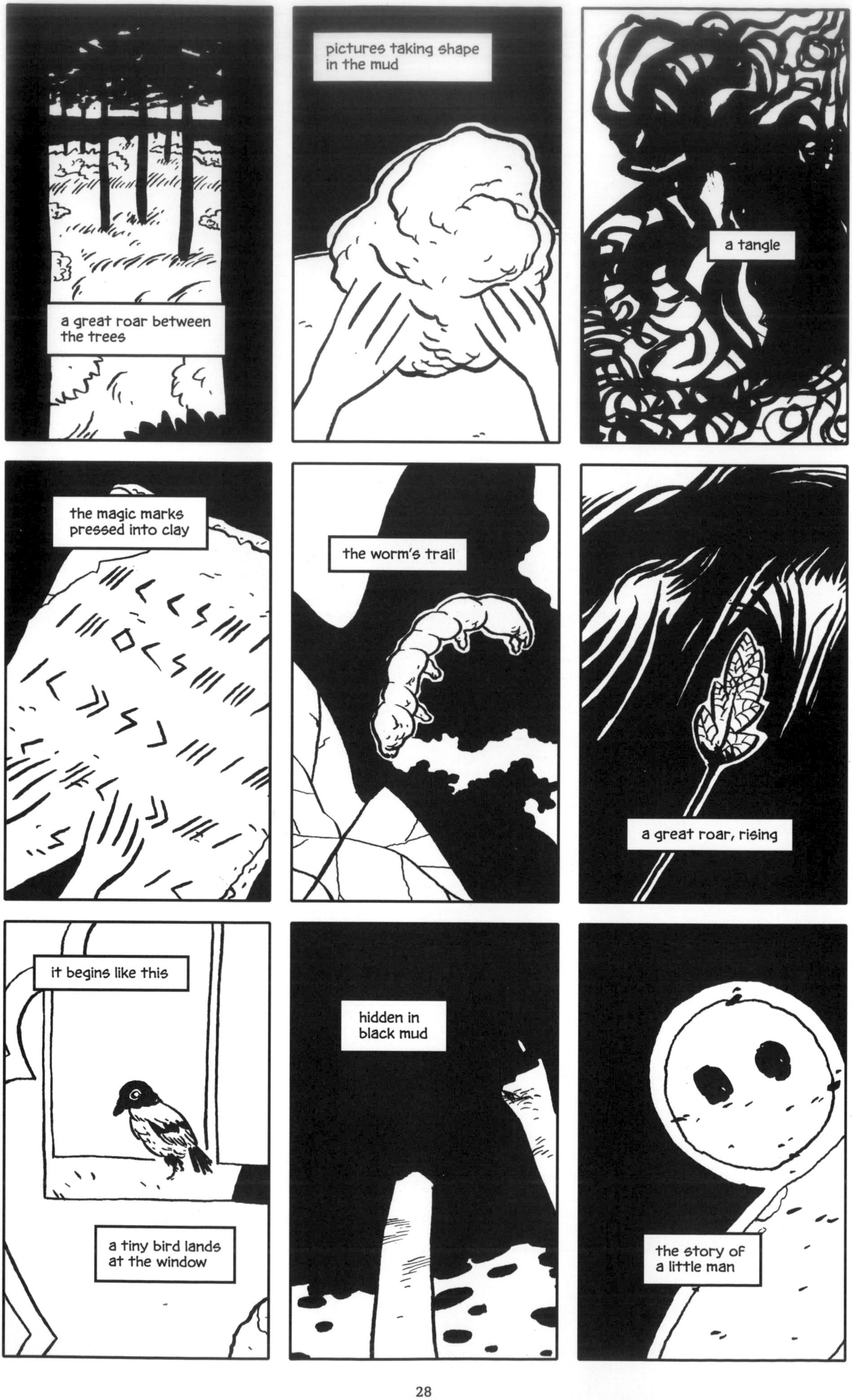
a great roar between the trees
pictures taking shape in the mud
a tangle
the magic marks pressed into clay
the worm's trail
a great roar, rising
it begins like this
a tiny bird lands at the window
hidden in black mud
the story of a little man

a wee girl

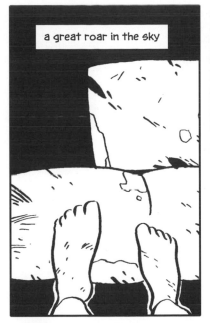

a great roar in the sky

a tower

these marks are magic marks

emerging from the mud my father says we will find the rocks that make us kings

clap your hands and that is called applause

a great roar

and the hero takes to the skies

bang and I clap my hands

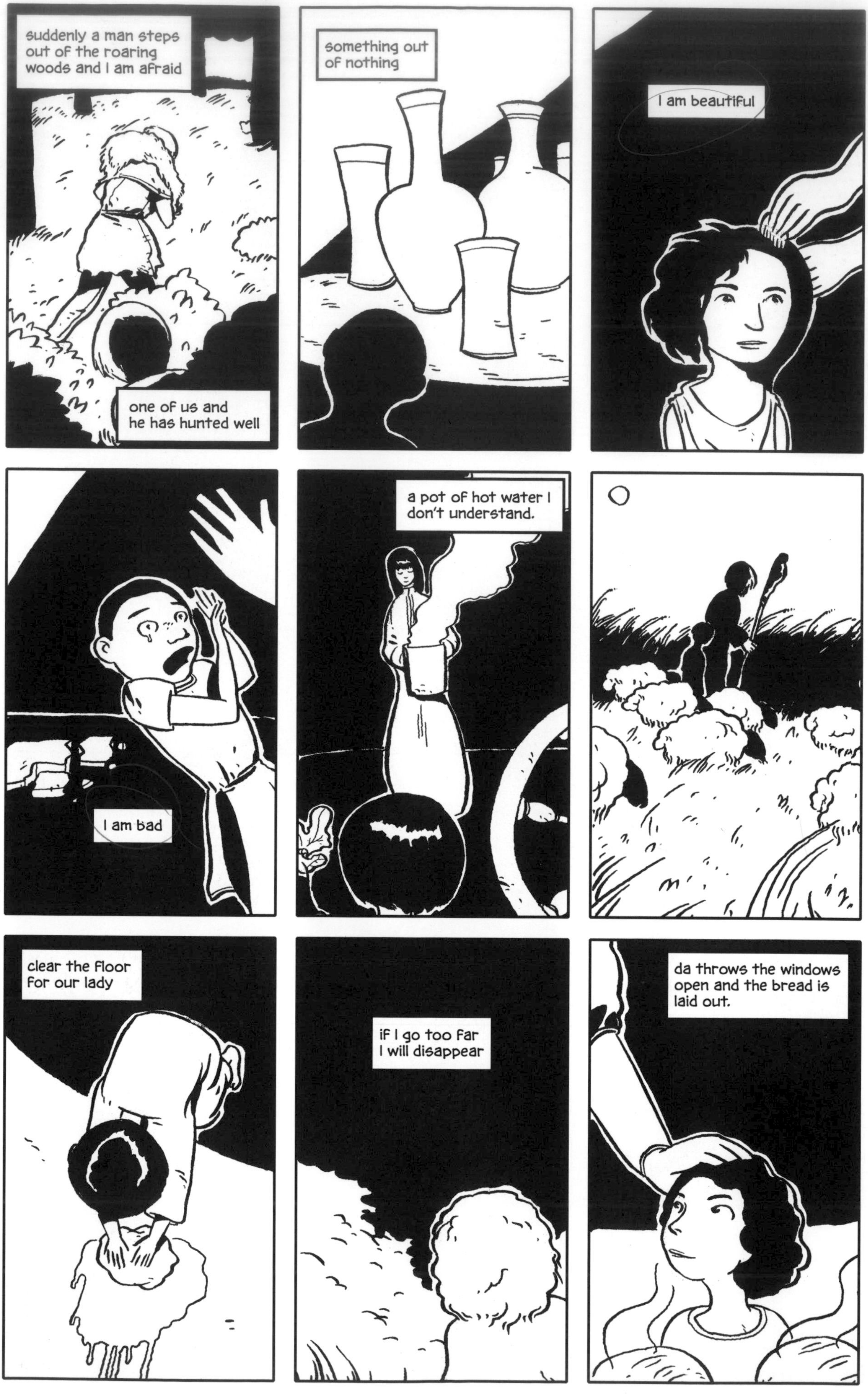
suddenly a man steps out of the roaring woods and I am afraid
one of us and he has hunted well
something out of nothing
I am beautiful
I am bad
a pot of hot water I don't understand.
clear the floor for our lady
if I go too far I will disappear
da throws the windows open and the bread is laid out.

REPINION

I am beautiful

I am bad

this is when
builds he k
to put th
iron hoo

all arou
men o
we w
we

rough and heavy

he knows how to put
the wood in the stream
he knows how to find
what everybody wants

mama knows how
to dance and sing

hot water I slap
it with my hands
and laugh

our feet in
the sand

I am strong

31

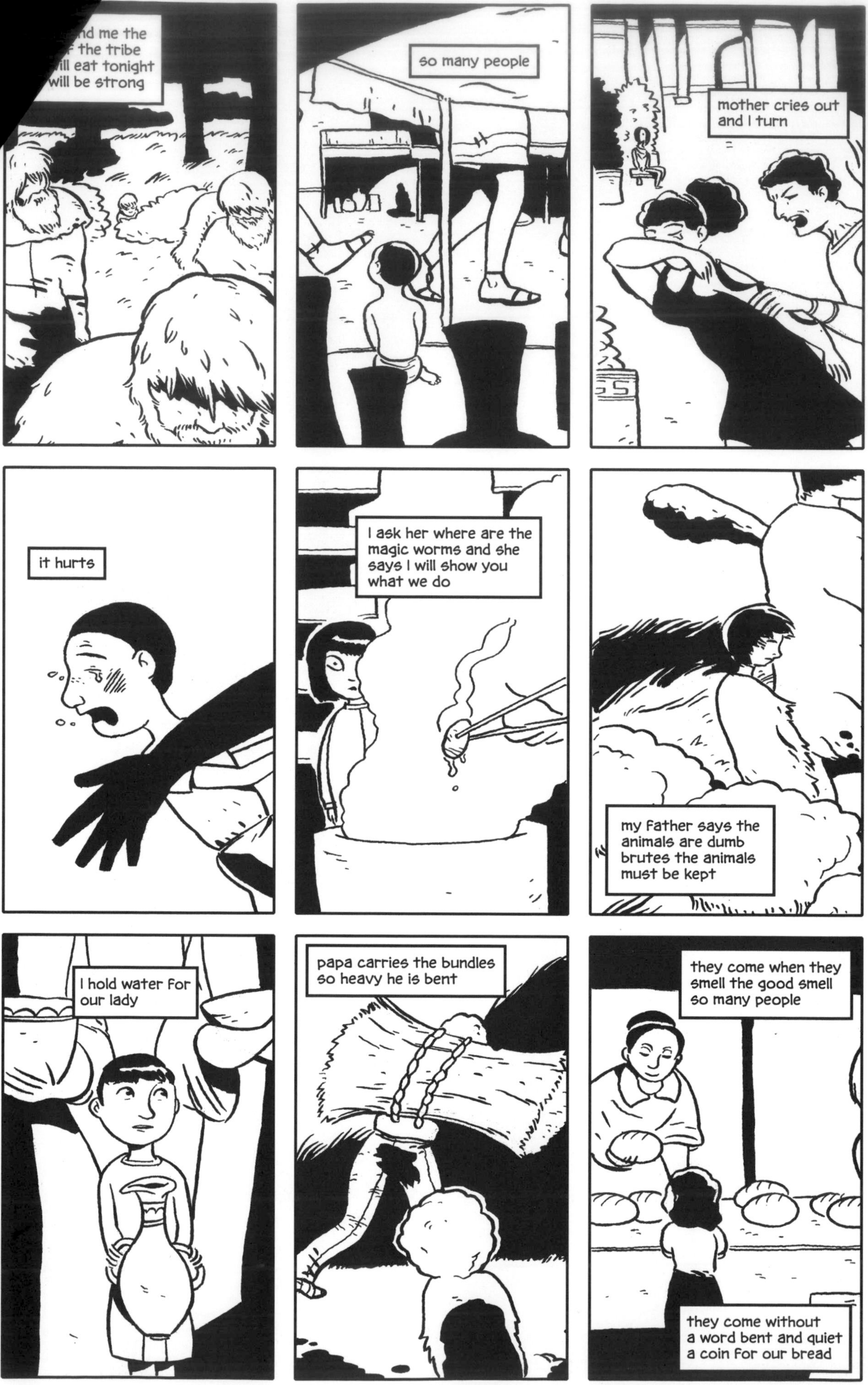
nd me the
f the tribe
ill eat tonight
will be strong
so many people
mother cries out and I turn
it hurts
I ask her where are the magic worms and she says I will show you what we do
my father says the animals are dumb brutes the animals must be kept
I hold water for our lady
papa carries the bundles so heavy he is bent
they come when they smell the good smell so many people
they come without a word bent and quiet a coin for our bread

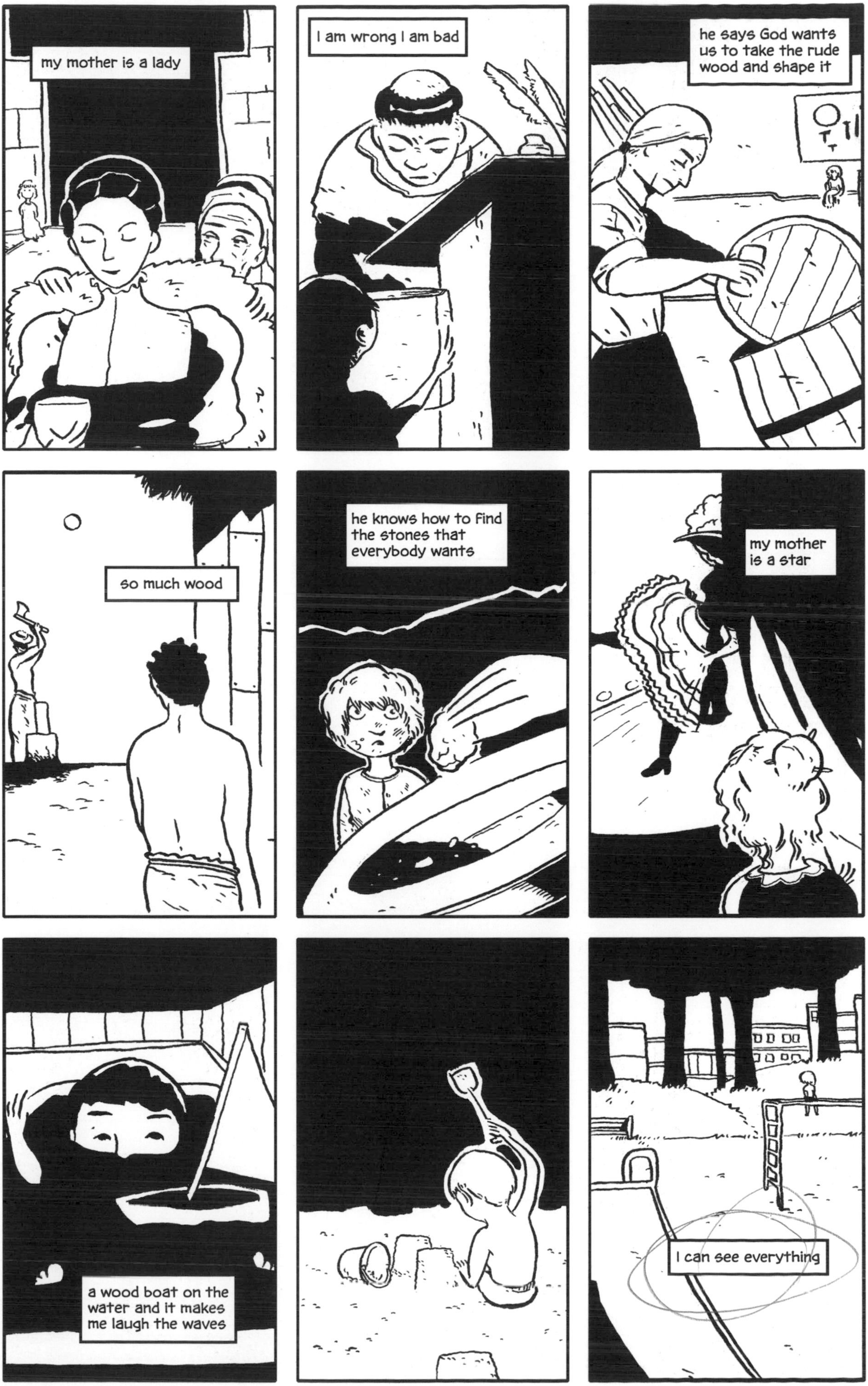
my mother is a lady
I am wrong I am bad
he says God wants us to take the rude wood and shape it
so much wood
he knows how to find the stones that everybody wants
my mother is a star
a wood boat on the water and it makes me laugh the waves
I can see everything

one of them is wounded

blood

this is how it works

he hit her

it hurts

this is how it works

you see, he says

this is what we do

this is how we live

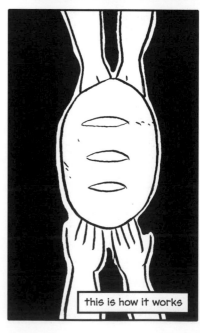

this is how it works

This is how... repitition, learning about lifestyle

a kiss on the hand
wet lips touch
this is how it works
this is how we live
this is it
this is how we live
the boat rolls in the water
a wave
I can see everything

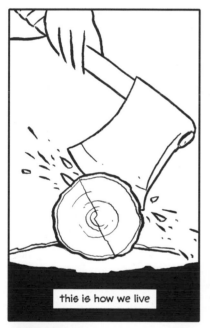

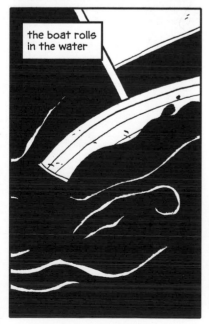

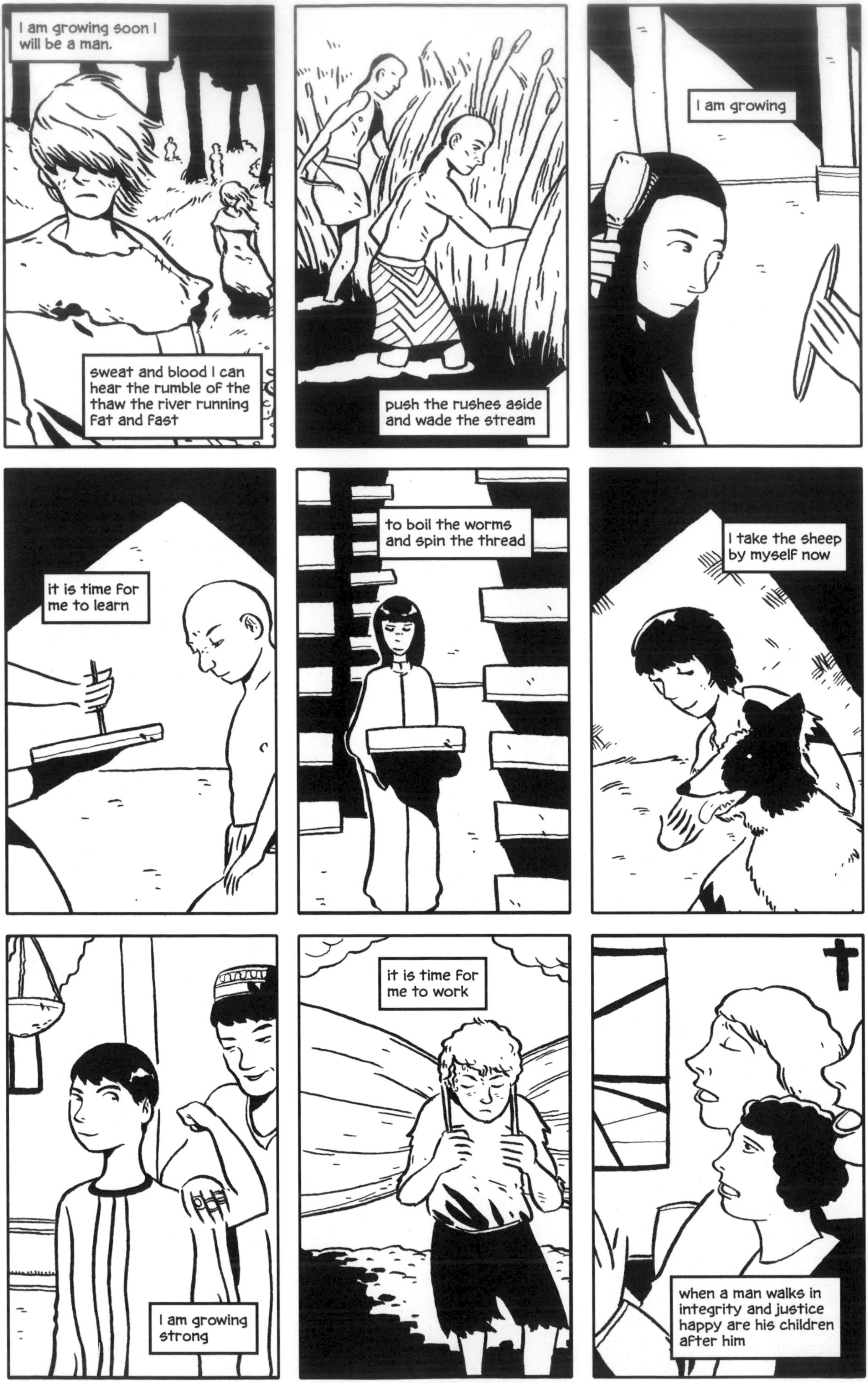
I am growing soon I will be a man.
sweat and blood I can hear the rumble of the thaw the river running fat and fast
push the rushes aside and wade the stream
I am growing
it is time for me to learn
to boil the worms and spin the thread
I take the sheep by myself now
I am growing strong
it is time for me to work
when a man walks in integrity and justice happy are his children after him

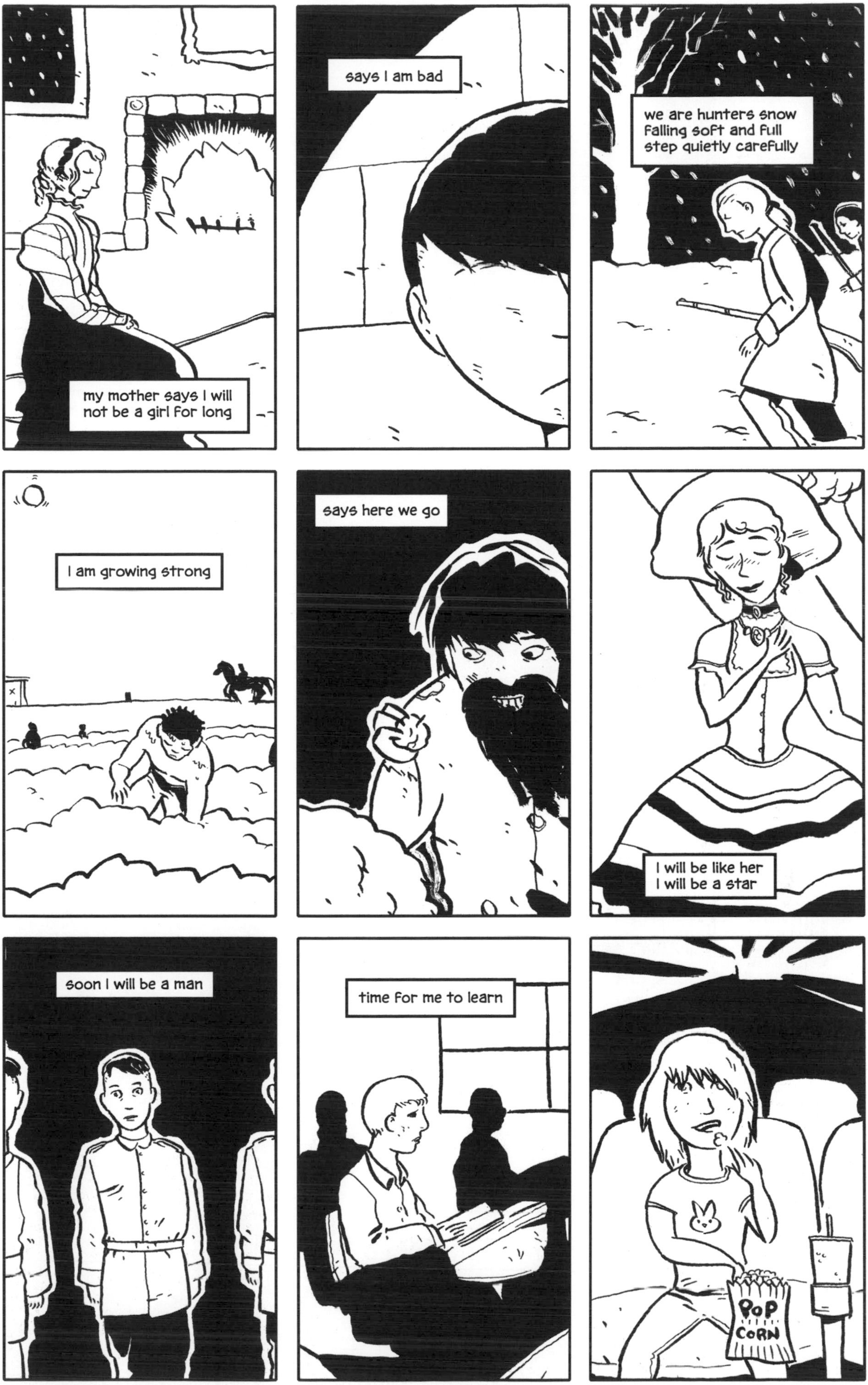
my mother says I will not be a girl for long
says I am bad
we are hunters snow falling soft and full step quietly carefully
I am growing strong
says here we go
I will be like her I will be a star
soon I will be a man
time for me to learn
POP CORN

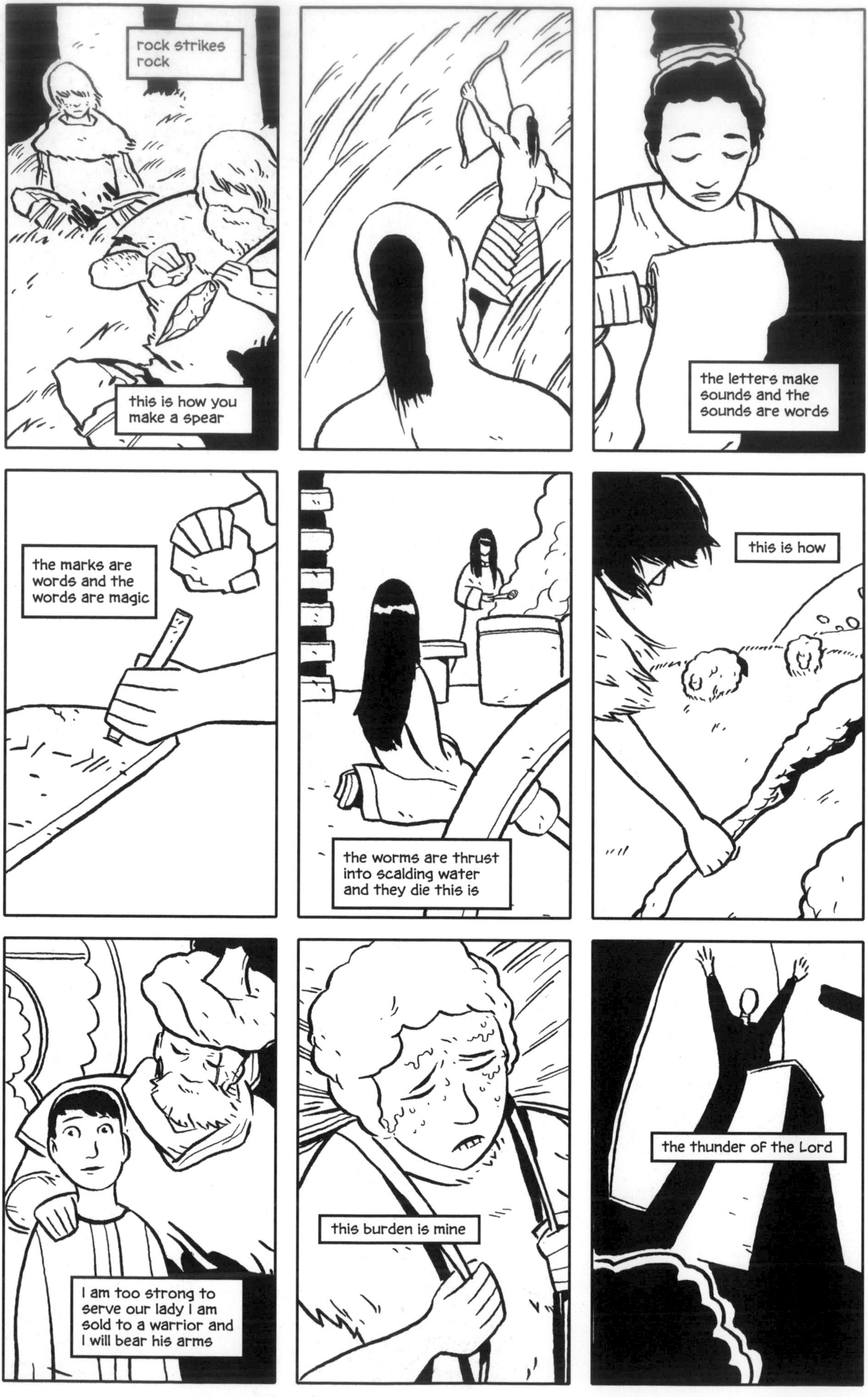
rock strikes rock
this is how you make a spear
the letters make sounds and the sounds are words
the marks are words and the words are magic
the worms are thrust into scalding water and they die this is
this is how
I am too strong to serve our lady I am sold to a warrior and I will bear his arms
this burden is mine
the thunder of the Lord

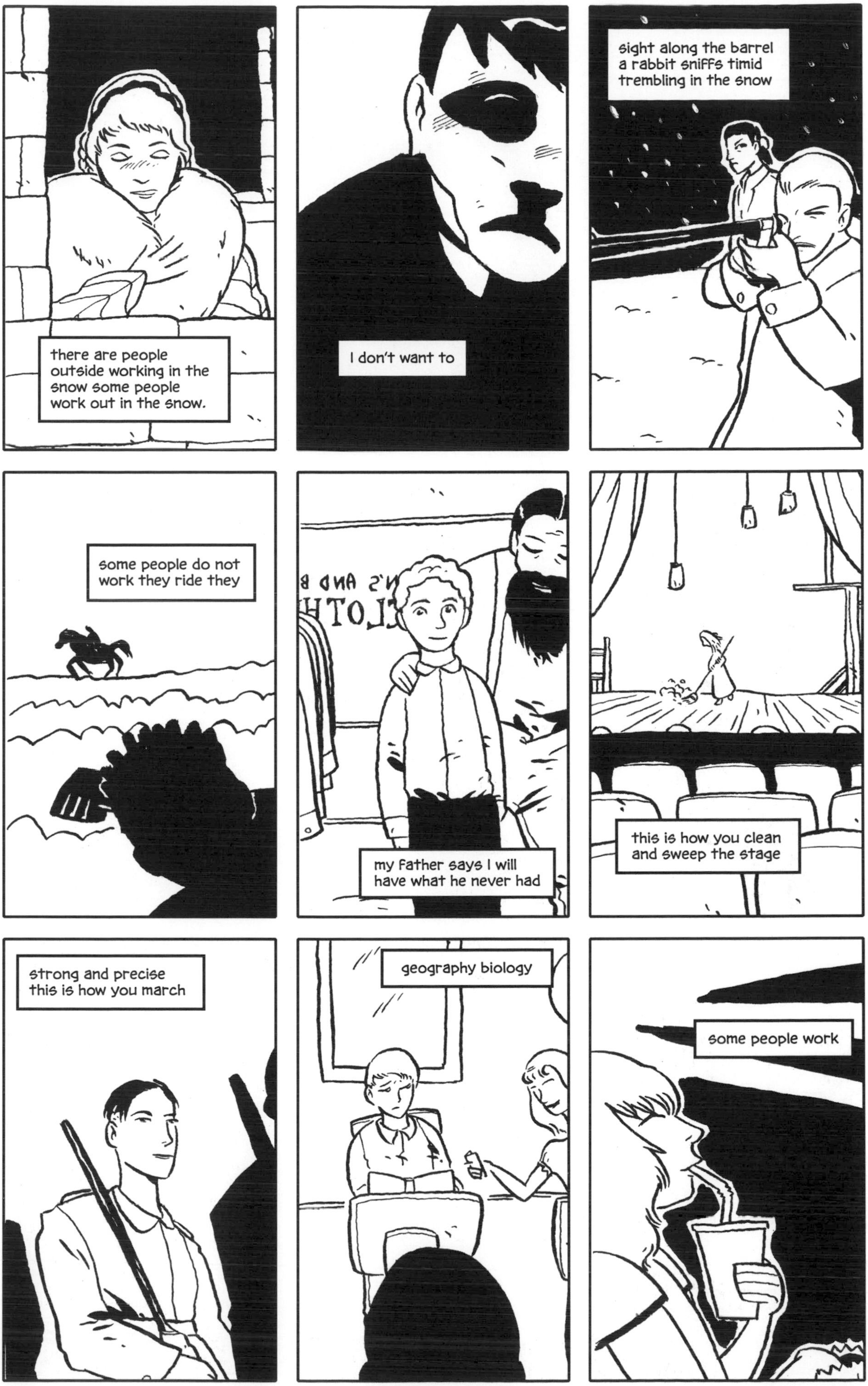
there are people outside working in the snow some people work out in the snow.
I don't want to
sight along the barrel a rabbit sniffs timid trembling in the snow
some people do not work they ride they
N'S AND B
CLOTH
my father says I will have what he never had
this is how you clean and sweep the stage
strong and precise this is how you march
geography biology
some people work

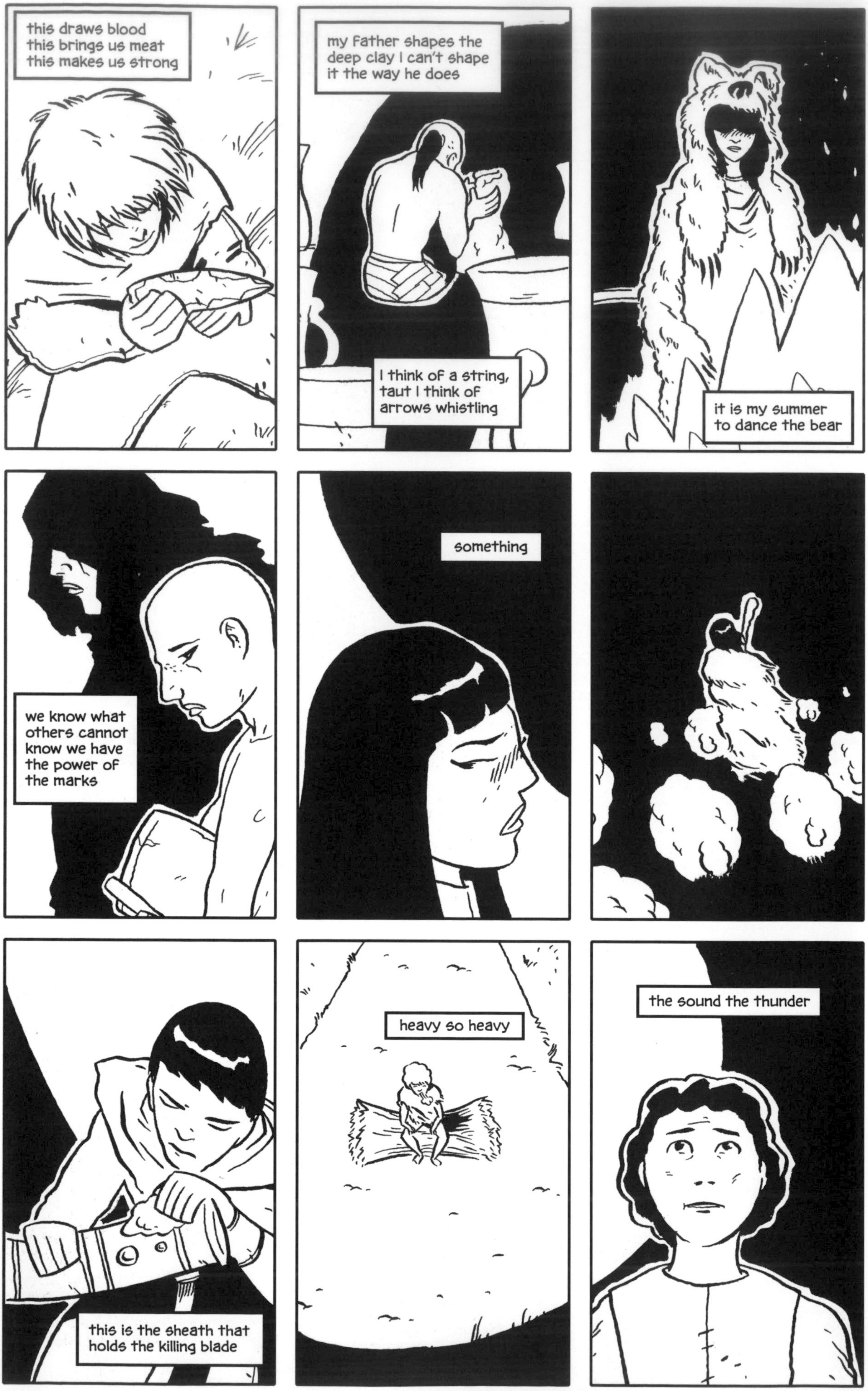
this draws blood
this brings us meat
this makes us strong
my father shapes the deep clay I can't shape it the way he does
I think of a string, taut I think of arrows whistling
it is my summer to dance the bear
we know what others cannot know we have the power of the marks
something
this is the sheath that holds the killing blade
heavy so heavy
the sound the thunder

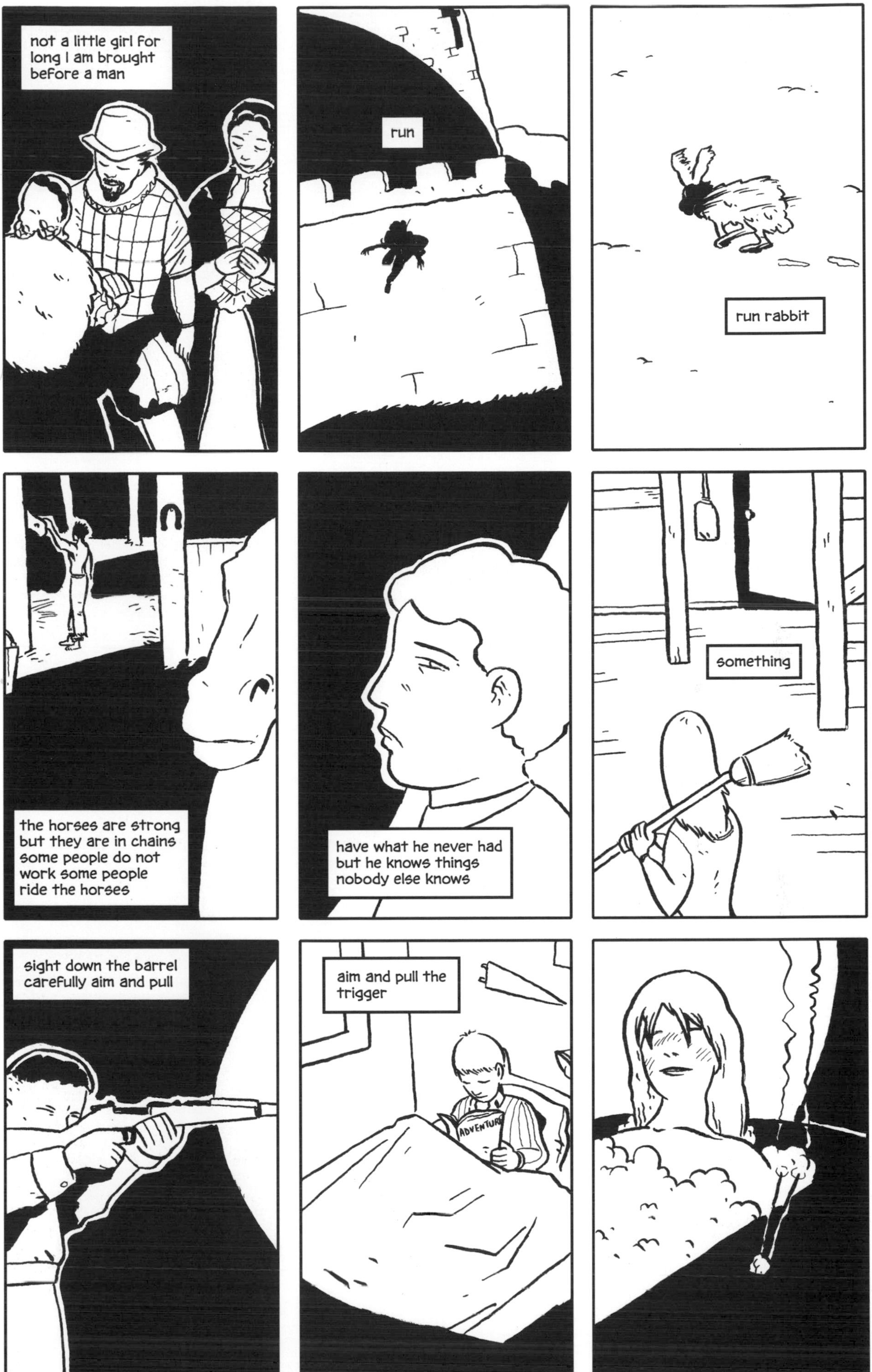
not a little girl for long I am brought before a man
run
run rabbit
the horses are strong but they are in chains some people do not work some people ride the horses
have what he never had but he knows things nobody else knows
something
sight down the barrel carefully aim and pull
aim and pull the trigger
ADVENTURE

a sudden sound and we look

dark clouds gather the reeds bow to the ground

I dance the bear

a muddy stream the water a feeble trickle

sound like thunder we step out to see

thunder

skies gone black and the warrior awaits the order

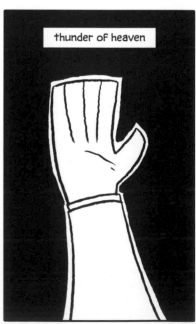

thunder of heaven

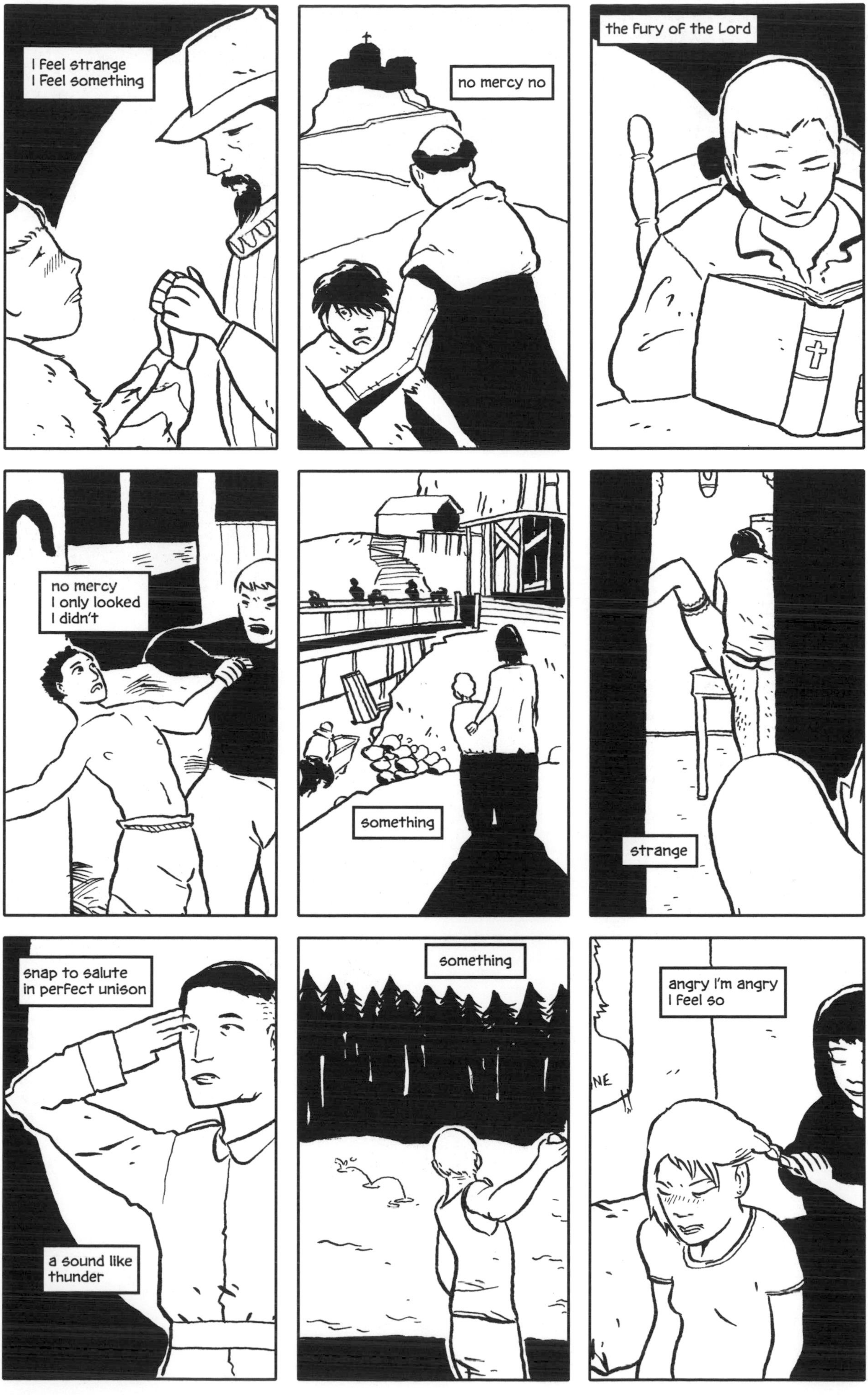
I feel strange
I feel something
no mercy no
the fury of the Lord
no mercy
I only looked
I didn't
something
strange
snap to salute
in perfect unison
a sound like
thunder
something
angry I'm angry
I feel so

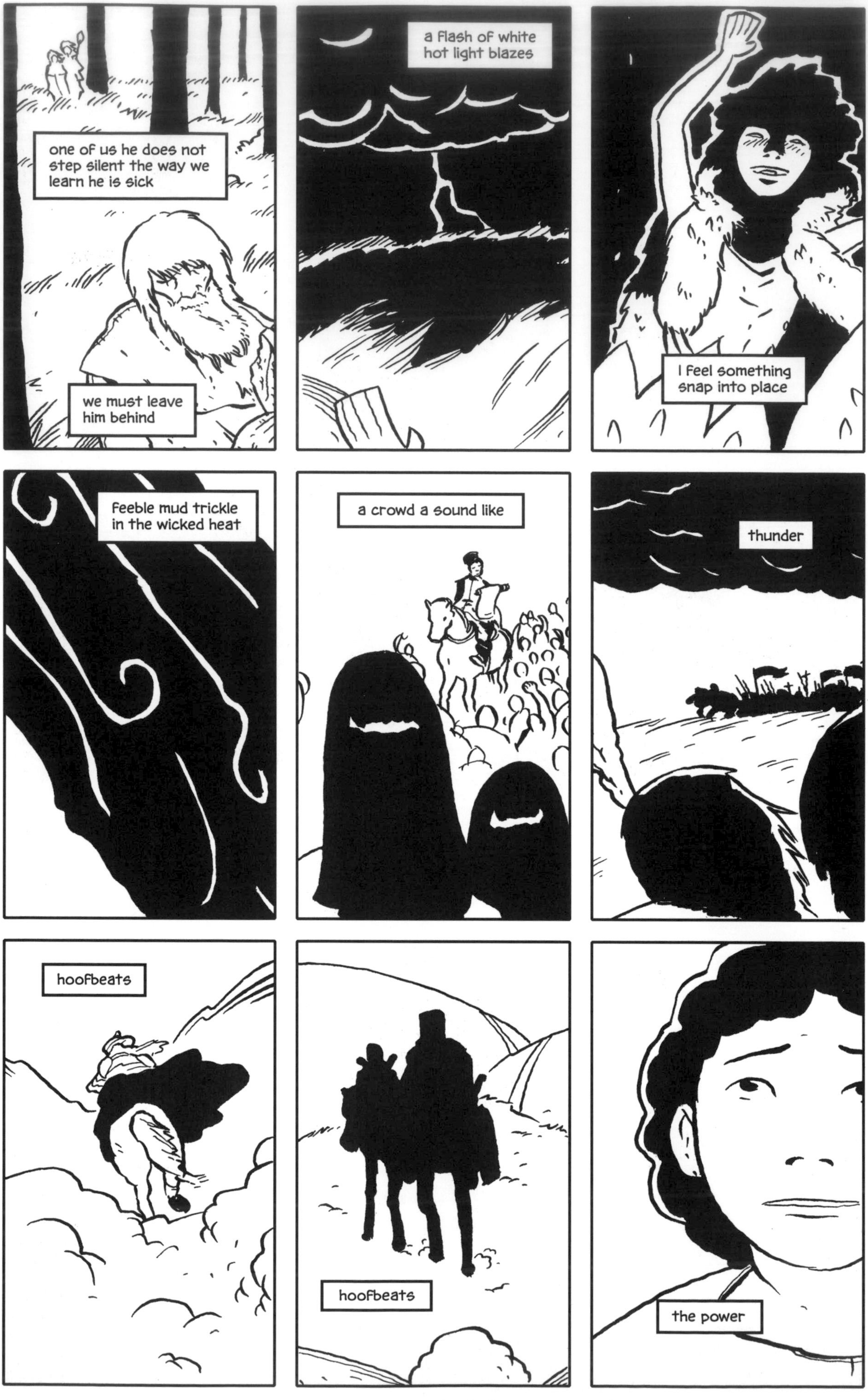
one of us he does not step silent the way we learn he is sick
we must leave him behind
a flash of white hot light blazes
I feel something snap into place
feeble mud trickle in the wicked heat
a crowd a sound like
thunder
hoofbeats
hoofbeats
the power

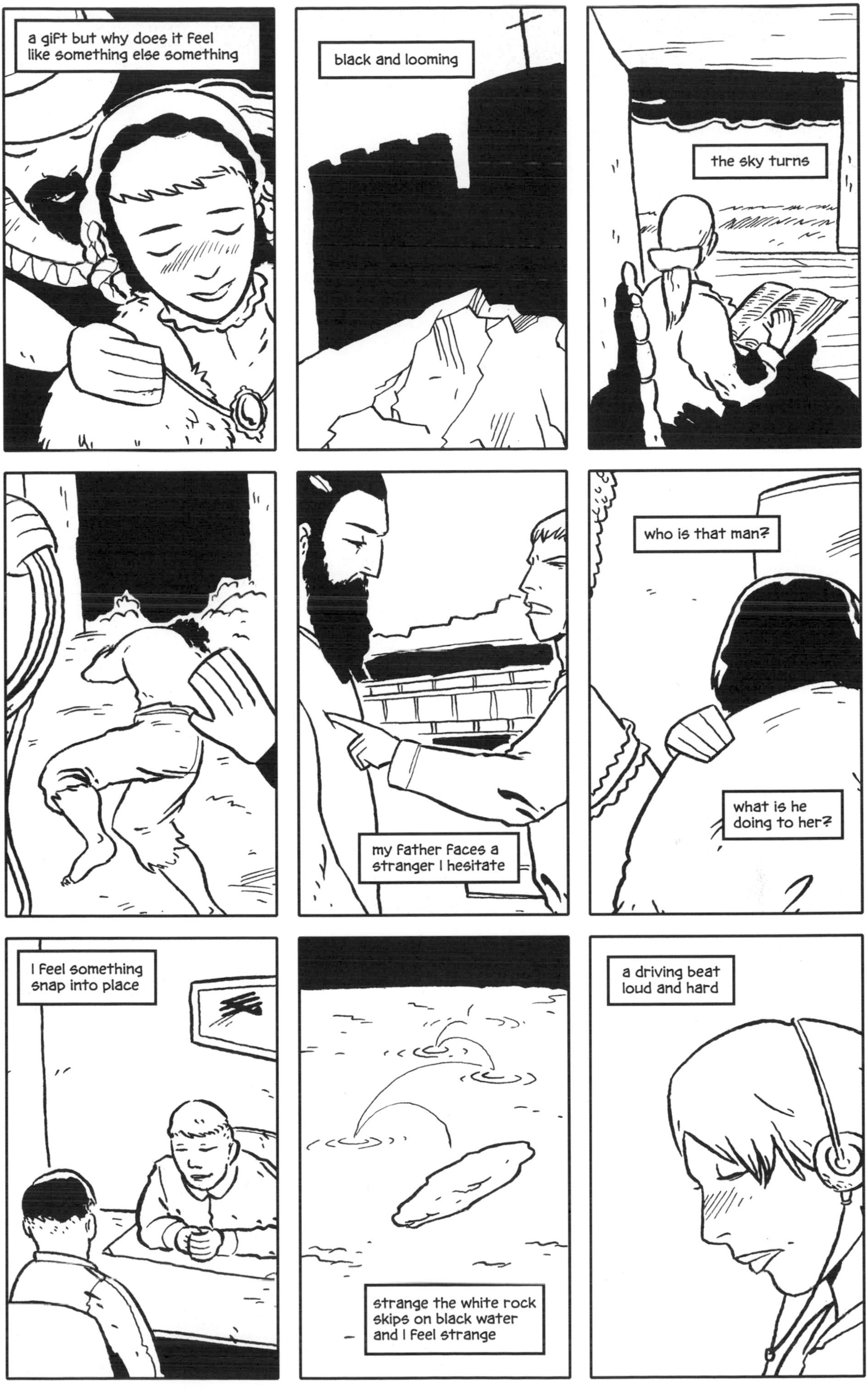

a gift but why does it feel like something else something
black and looming
the sky turns
my father faces a stranger I hesitate
who is that man?
what is he doing to her?
I feel something snap into place
strange the white rock skips on black water and I feel strange
a driving beat loud and hard

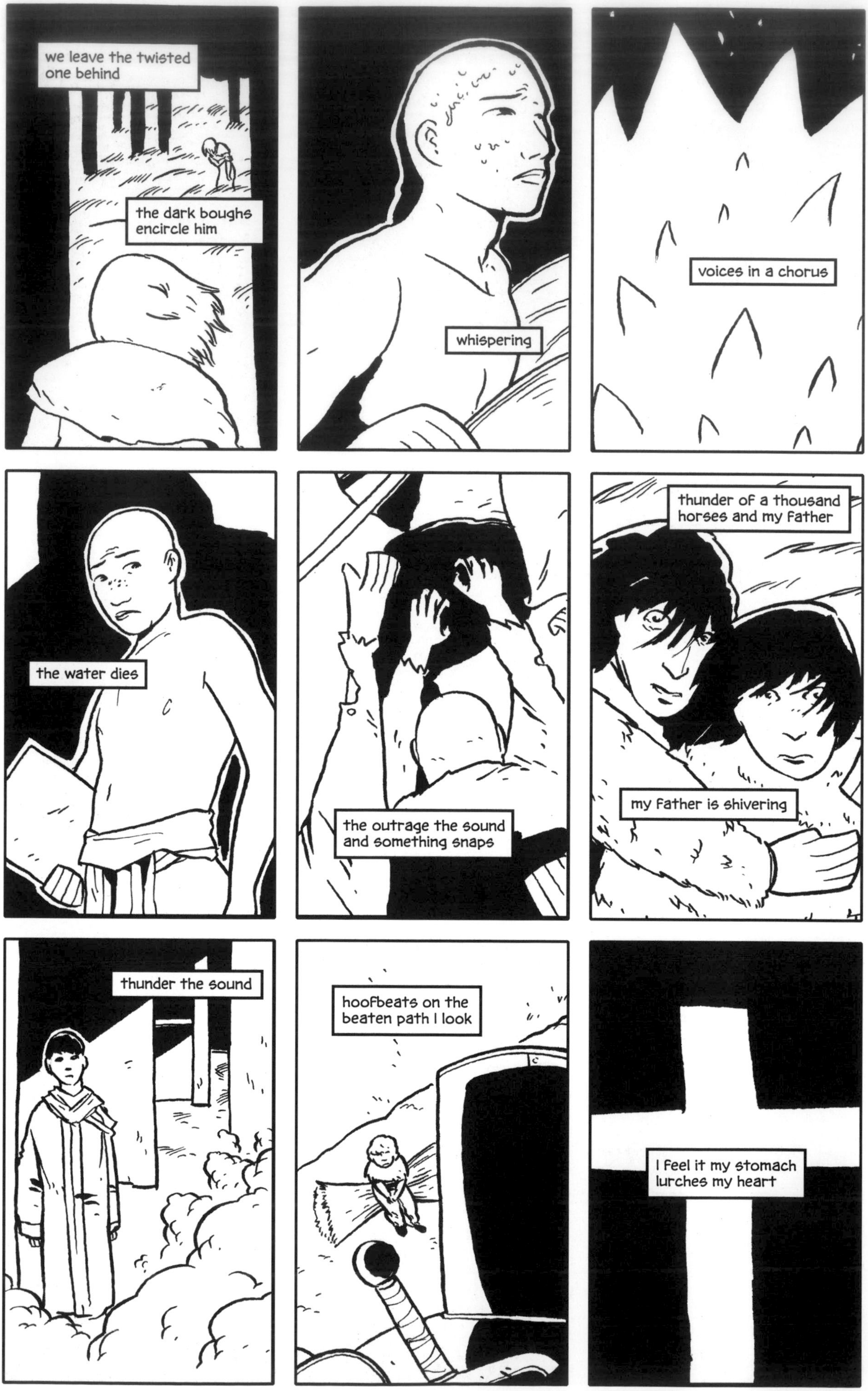
we leave the twisted one behind
the dark boughs encircle him
whispering
voices in a chorus
the water dies
the outrage the sound and something snaps
thunder of a thousand horses and my father
my father is shivering
thunder the sound
hoofbeats on the beaten path I look
I feel it my stomach lurches my heart

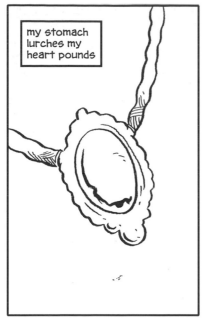

my stomach lurches my heart pounds

the sound

a flash of white-hot light

white-hot

my stomach lurches

love he loves her I will sing like my

I look up

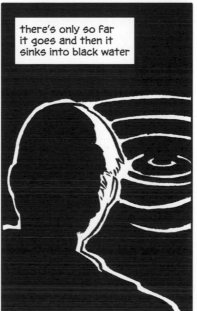

there's only so far it goes and then it sinks into black water

disappearing into the sound

dark wood closing

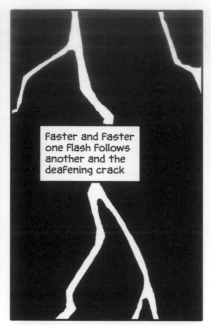

faster and faster one flash follows another and the deafening crack

a black shape flies

the water dies

steel flashes

deafening

the skies turn black

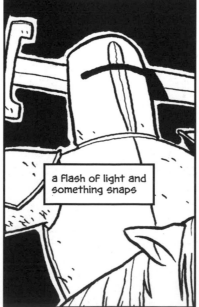

a flash of light and something snaps

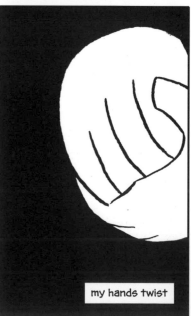

my hands twist

all experiencing similar emotions/events

louder and louder
blood pounding in my ears a great roar and I spit
bang
pain and pain
the man draws
everything so slow my father draws
blood pounding snap of silk
a black wave
louder and louder my fingers grip the bottle and something snaps

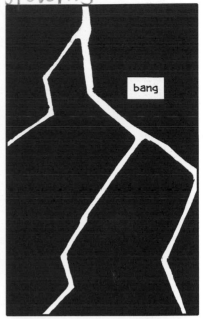

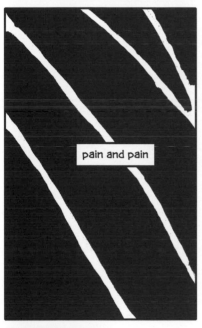

the air itself

it strikes

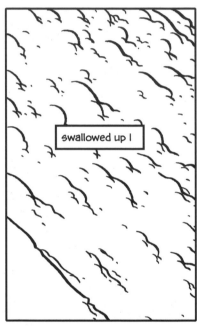

swallowed up I

shake

the ground shakes
my father shakes

the timbers shake

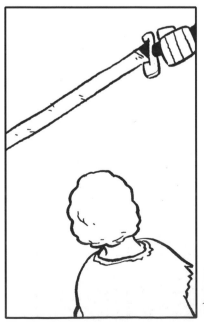

I look up

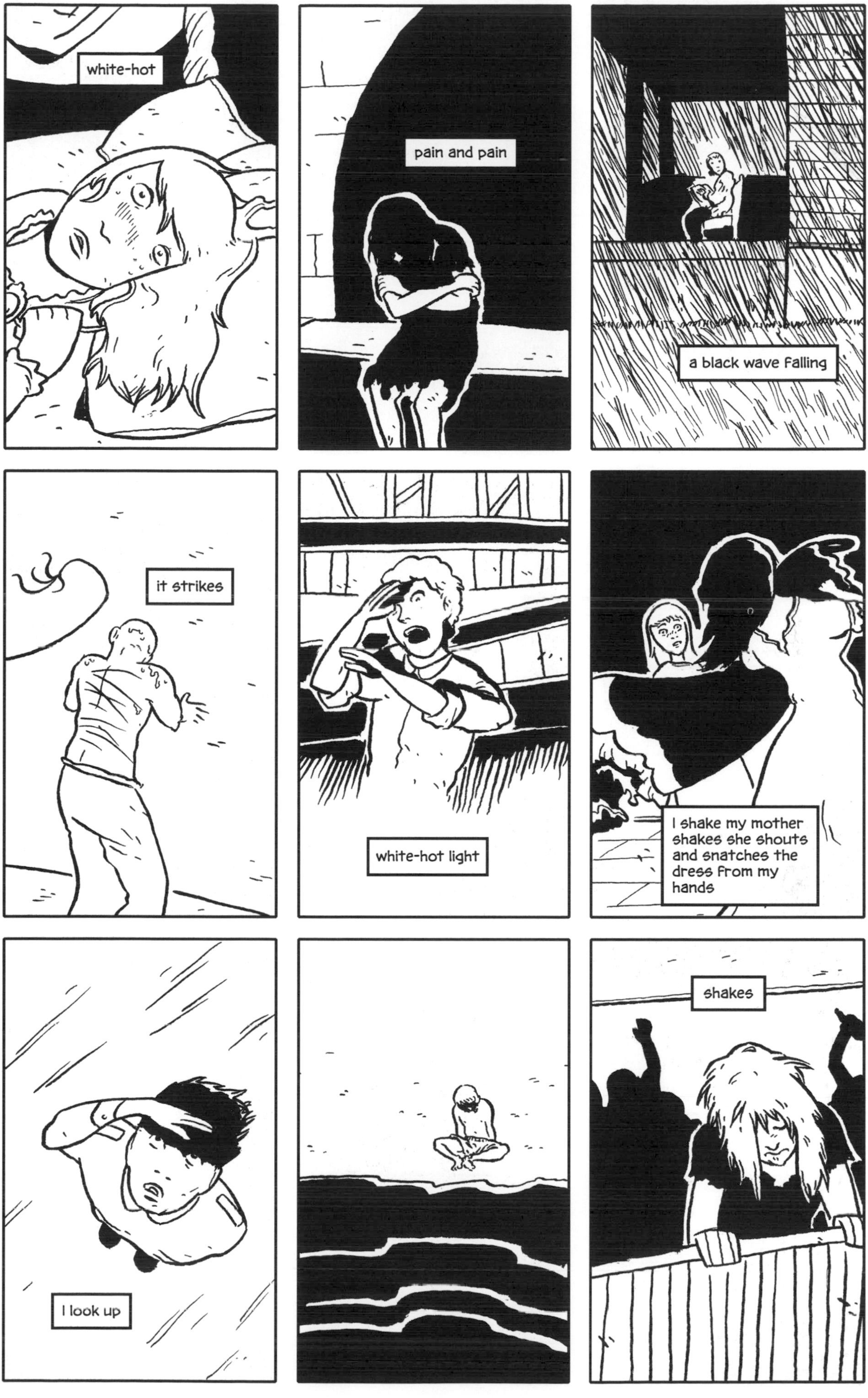
white-hot
pain and pain
a black wave falling
it strikes
white-hot light
I shake my mother shakes she shouts and snatches the dress from my hands
I look up
shakes

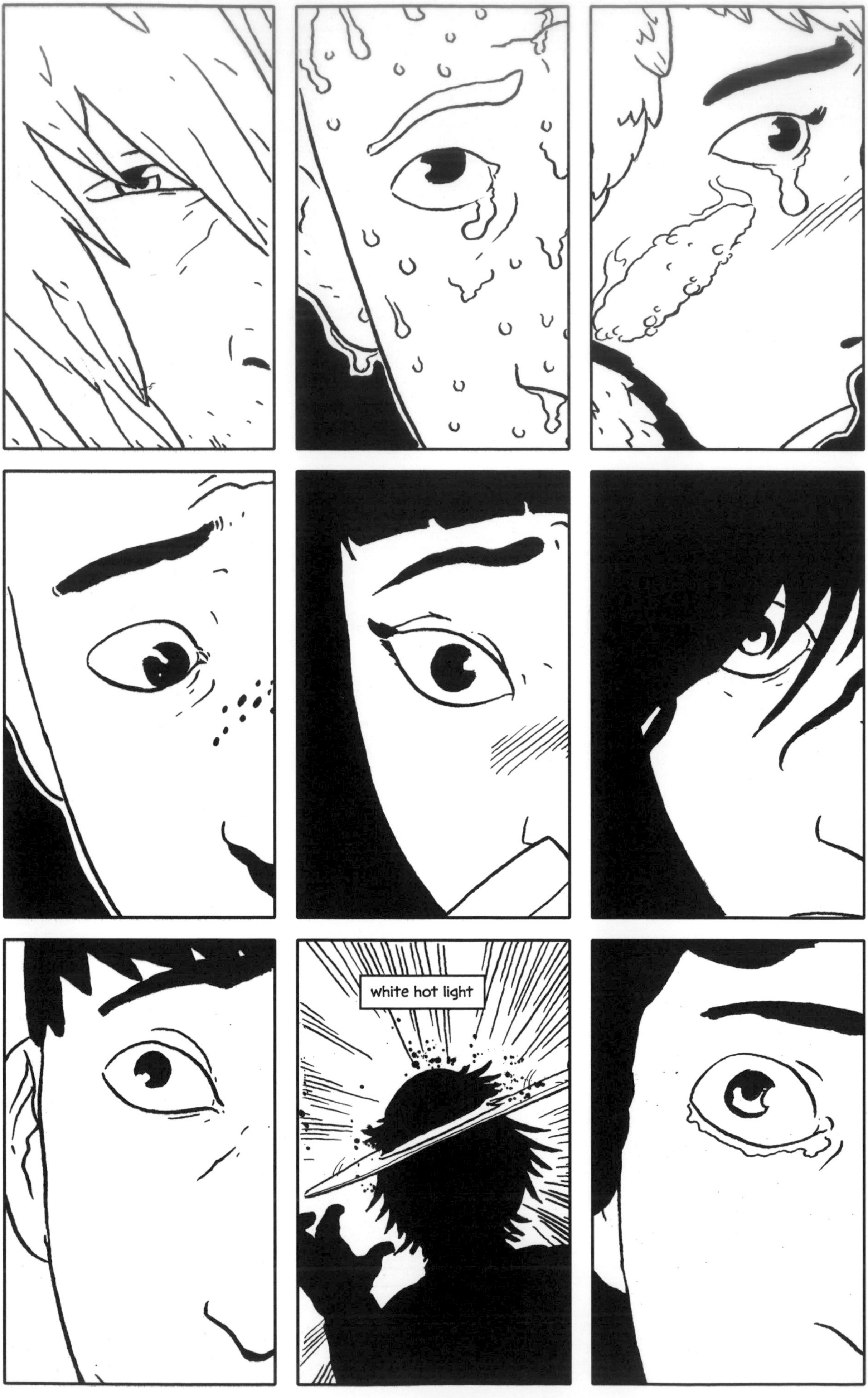
white hot light

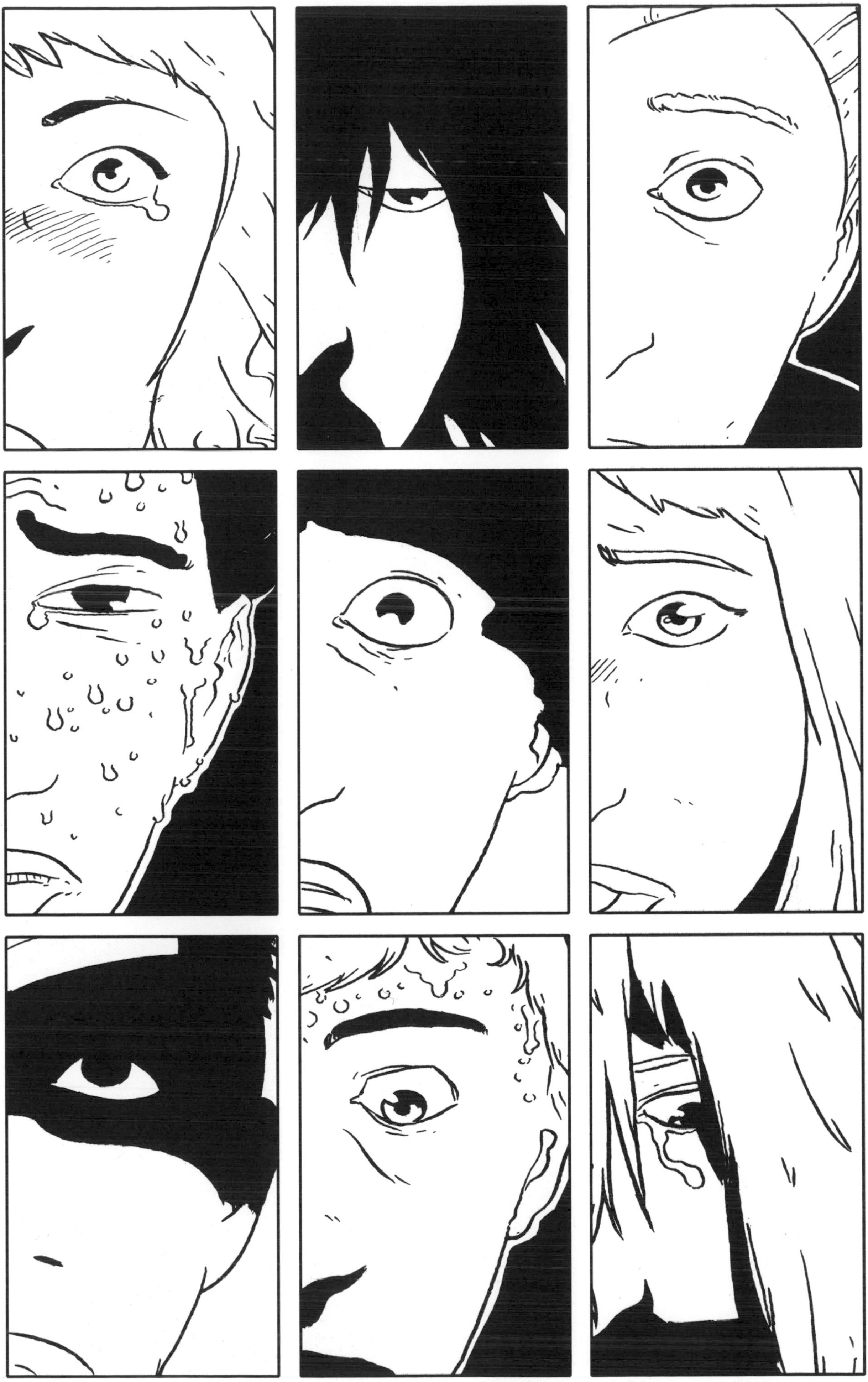

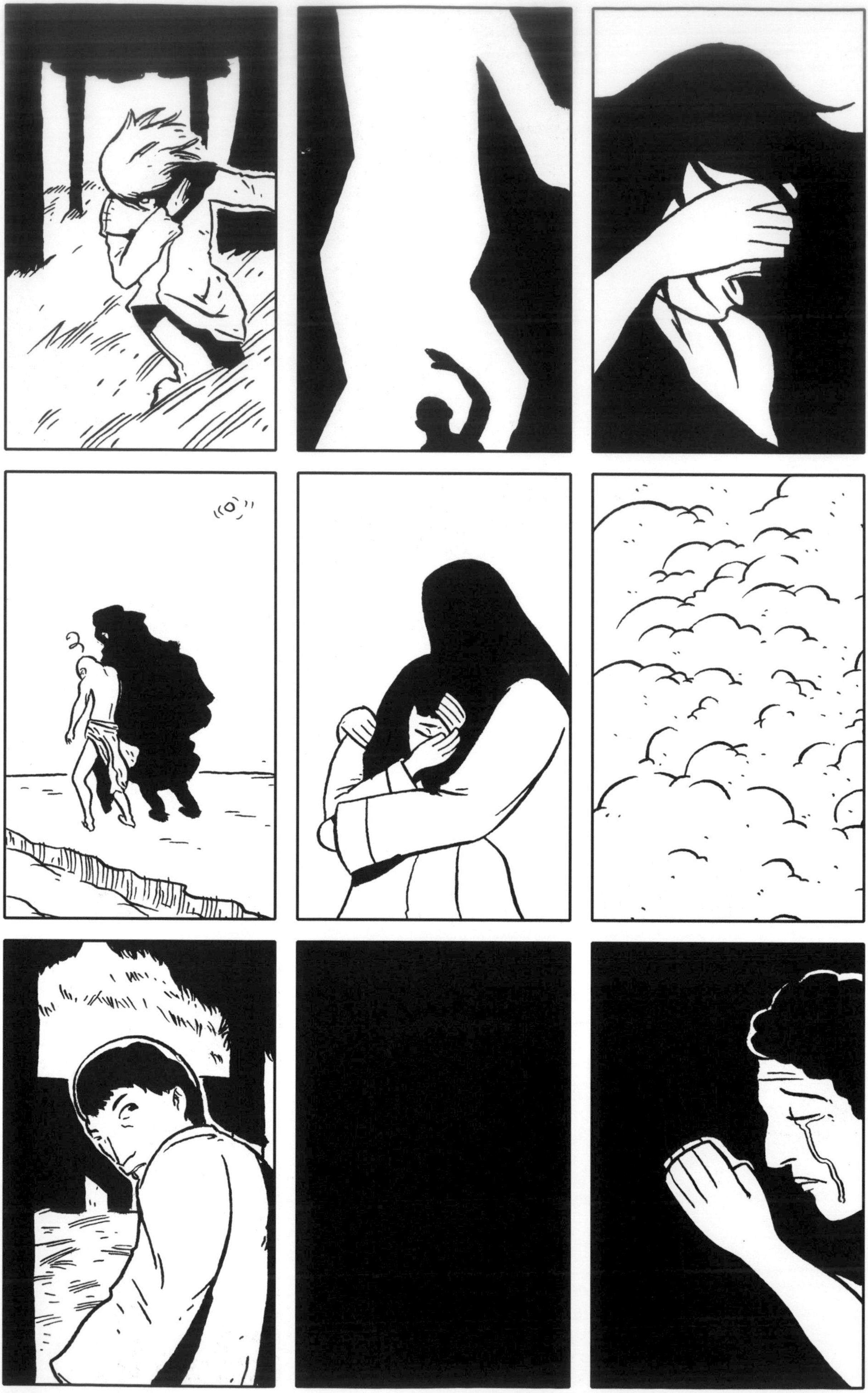

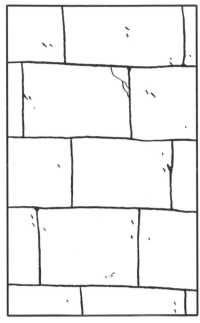

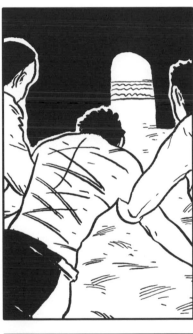

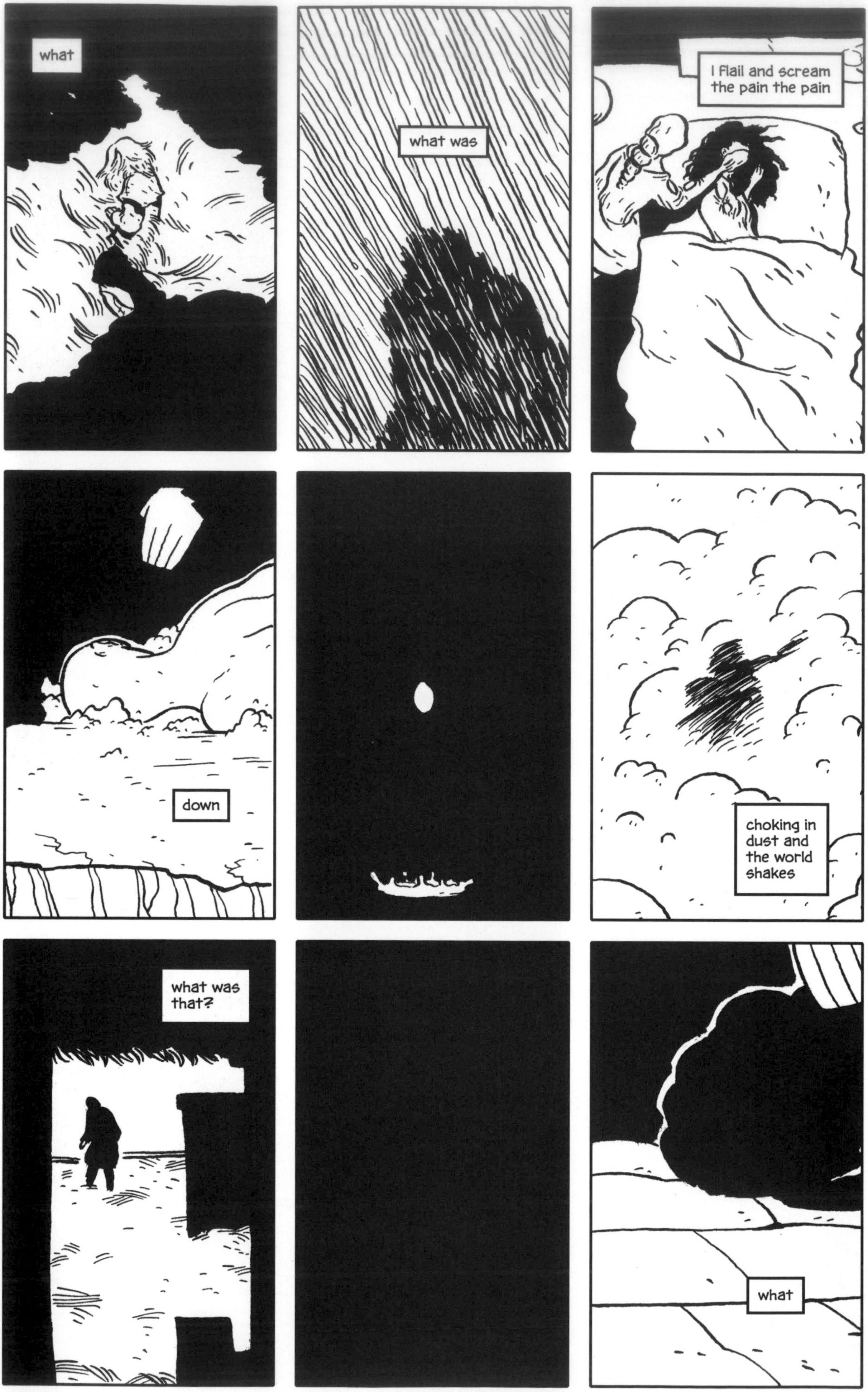
what
what was
I flail and scream
the pain the pain
down
choking in
dust and
the world
shakes
what was
that?
what

Flail and choke

Flail and run

the pain the

what happened?

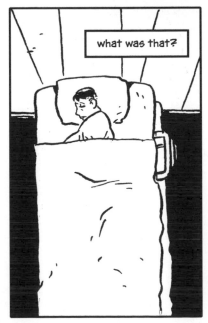

what was that?

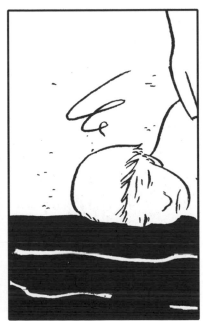

what just happened?

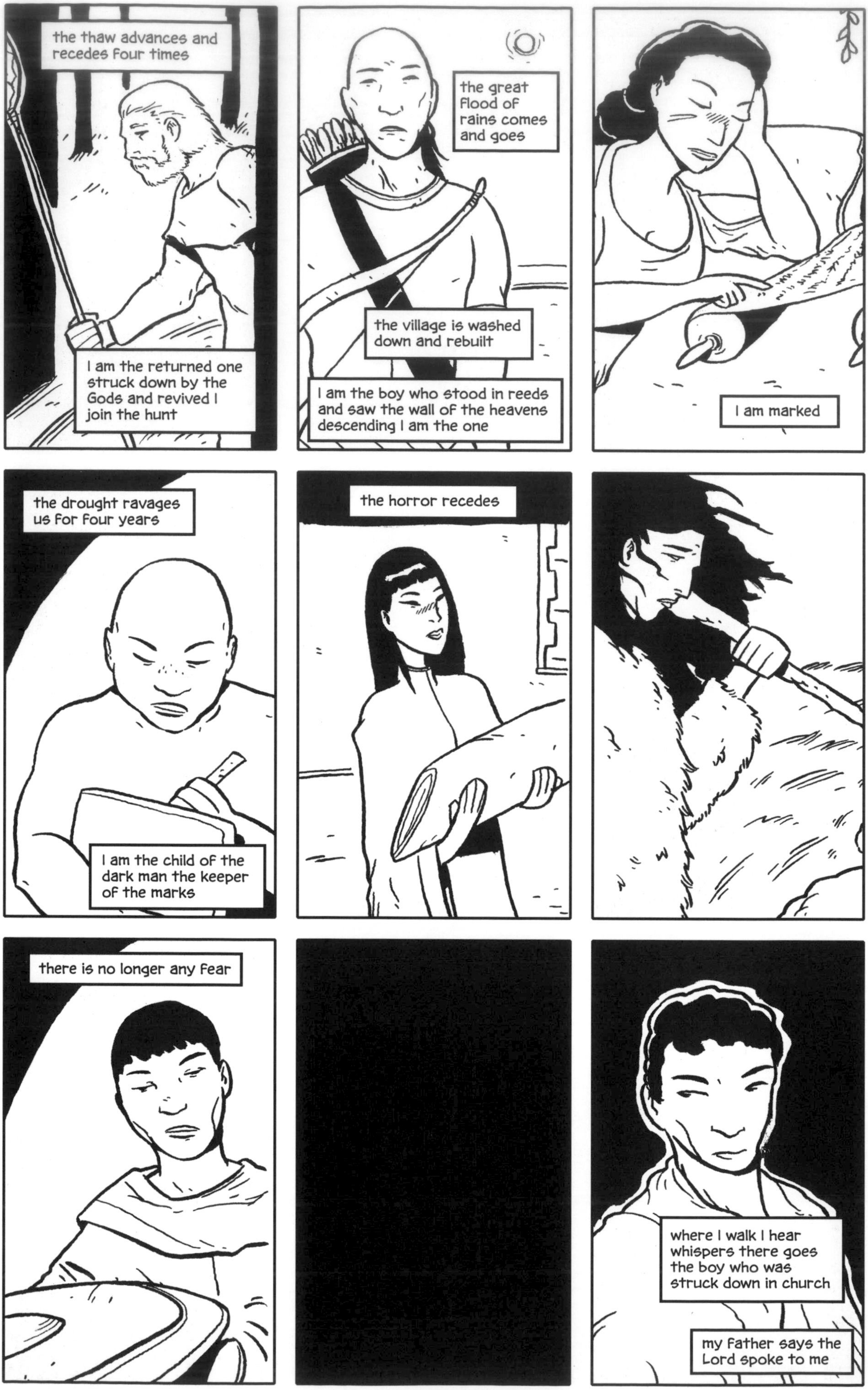

the thaw advances and recedes four times
I am the returned one struck down by the Gods and revived I join the hunt
the great flood of rains comes and goes
the village is washed down and rebuilt
I am the boy who stood in reeds and saw the wall of the heavens descending I am the one
I am marked
the drought ravages us for four years
I am the child of the dark man the keeper of the marks
the horror recedes
there is no longer any fear
where I walk I hear whispers there goes the boy who was struck down in church
my father says the Lord spoke to me

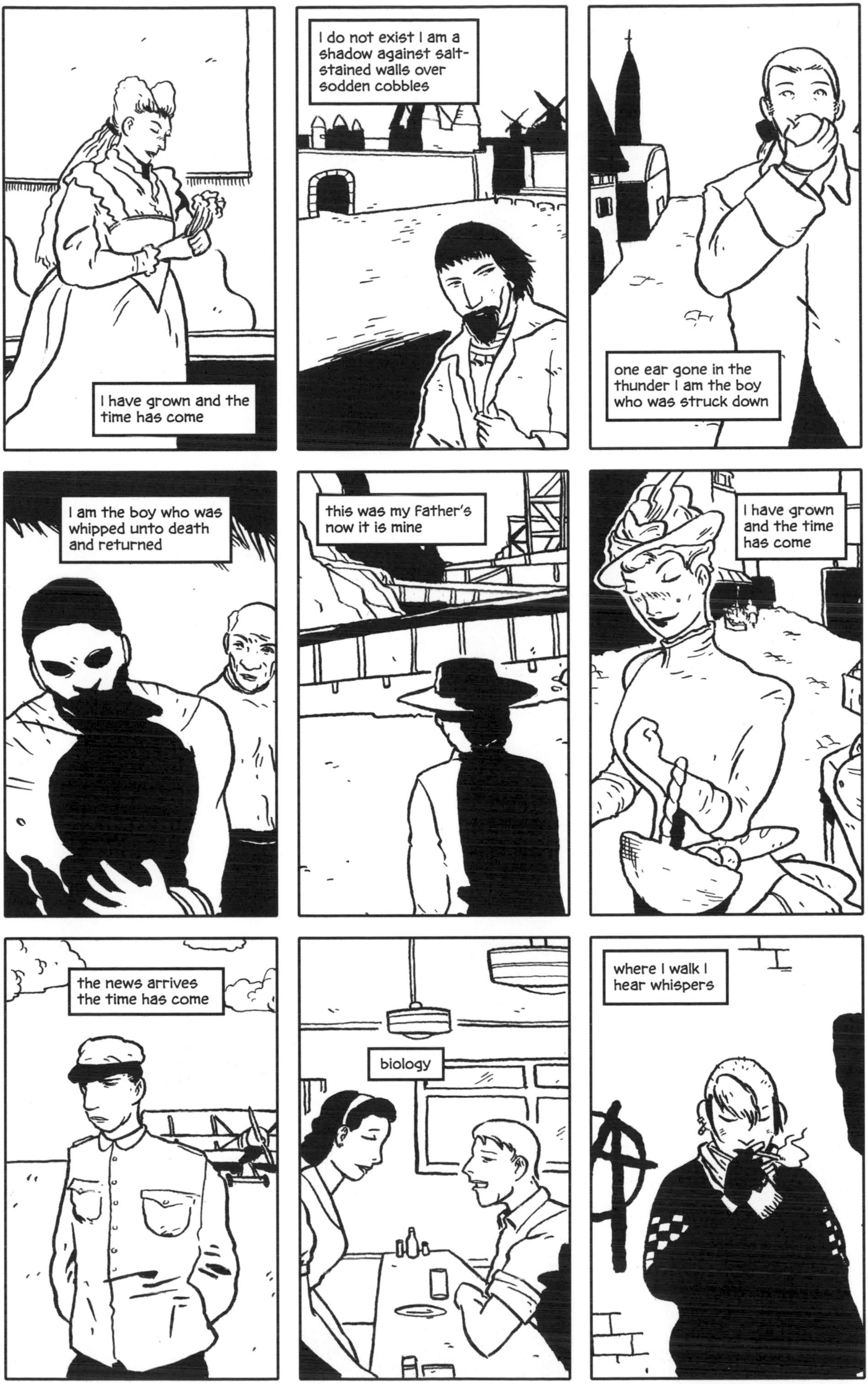
I have grown and the time has come
I do not exist I am a shadow against salt-stained walls over sodden cobbles
one ear gone in the thunder I am the boy who was struck down
I am the boy who was whipped unto death and returned
this was my Father's now it is mine
I have grown and the time has come
the news arrives the time has come
biology
where I walk I hear whispers

not a sound of warning

my hand

my hand releases an arrow flies

a priestess of Artemis and questions do I read? do I know the tales? yes yes

the marks are words and the words are what is true

in whispering fields the herd roves and I see a boy

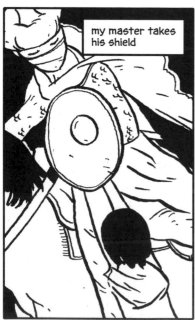

my master takes his shield

and suddenly

suddenly

my master reluctantly teaches me the ways of the leech

he says he will teach me but not for the Lord, sour face

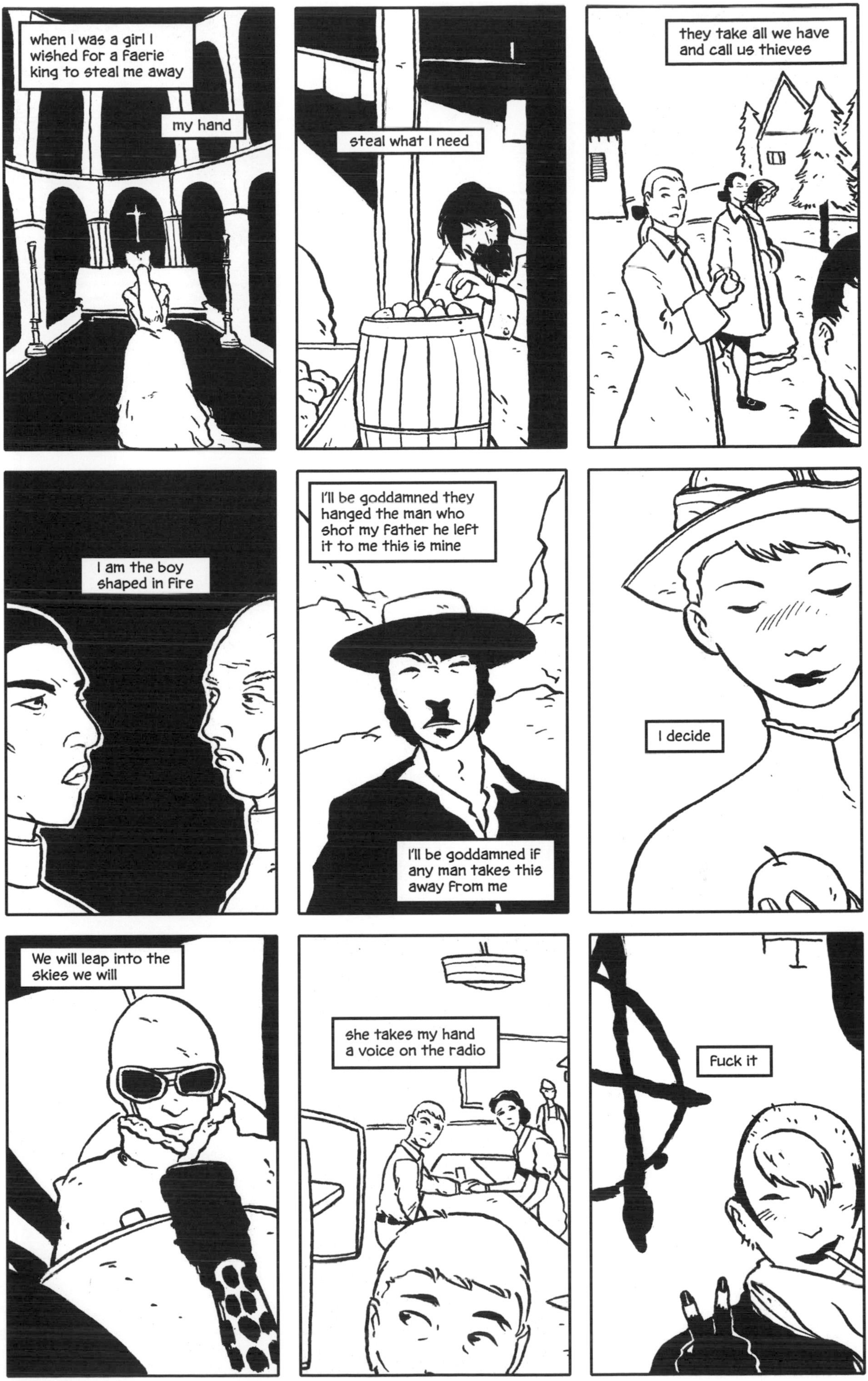
when I was a girl I wished for a faerie king to steal me away
my hand
steal what I need
they take all we have and call us thieves
I am the boy shaped in fire
I'll be goddamned they hanged the man who shot my father he left it to me this is mine
I'll be goddamned if any man takes this away from me
I decide
We will leap into the skies we will
she takes my hand a voice on the radio
Fuck it

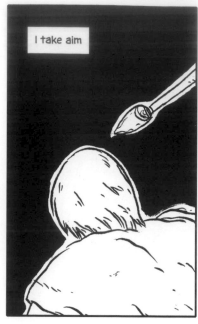

I take aim

a killing shot

in the chill of the temple

the dread Goddess watches over us and I walk head bowed

I am marked

the marks are truth

they may spin honey words but I only mark the ones that are true

I am of the age

beautiful

here

I do not tell my father that my master blasphemes

the master says that God is a madman grinning and drooling in his own filth

father says the master is blessed a great man

this is only a man

where is my king?

oh ships come disgorge your crews and I'll gently relieve them of their gold.

I'll not hurt a soul

I stand

I'll be goddamned

I am the boy shaped in fire

barking orders like a man

hard and cold my father worked alone I'll be goddamned if I lose what he gave me

hard strong arms and sweat

beautiful

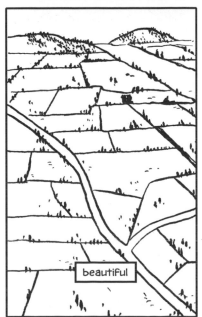

beautiful

a voice hard and cold and it says war it says war

the men around me stand from their seats

and I stand

I stand

I won't be coming back

in between heartbeats

my prey takes a step I leap

I release

under the gaze of the Goddess

with my power with my truth

I take what I want and I make it true

I am given away

beautiful I want him

somewhere the battle rages somewhere steel rings on steel

my master will return

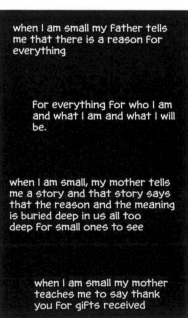

when I am small my father tells me that there is a reason for everything

For everything for who I am and what I am and what I will be.

when I am small, my mother tells me a story and that story says that the reason and the meaning is buried deep in us all too deep for small ones to see

when I am small my mother teaches me to say thank you for gifts received

he blasphemes and he heals

he rails against God and he heals God's creatures with his hands

I learn and I pray

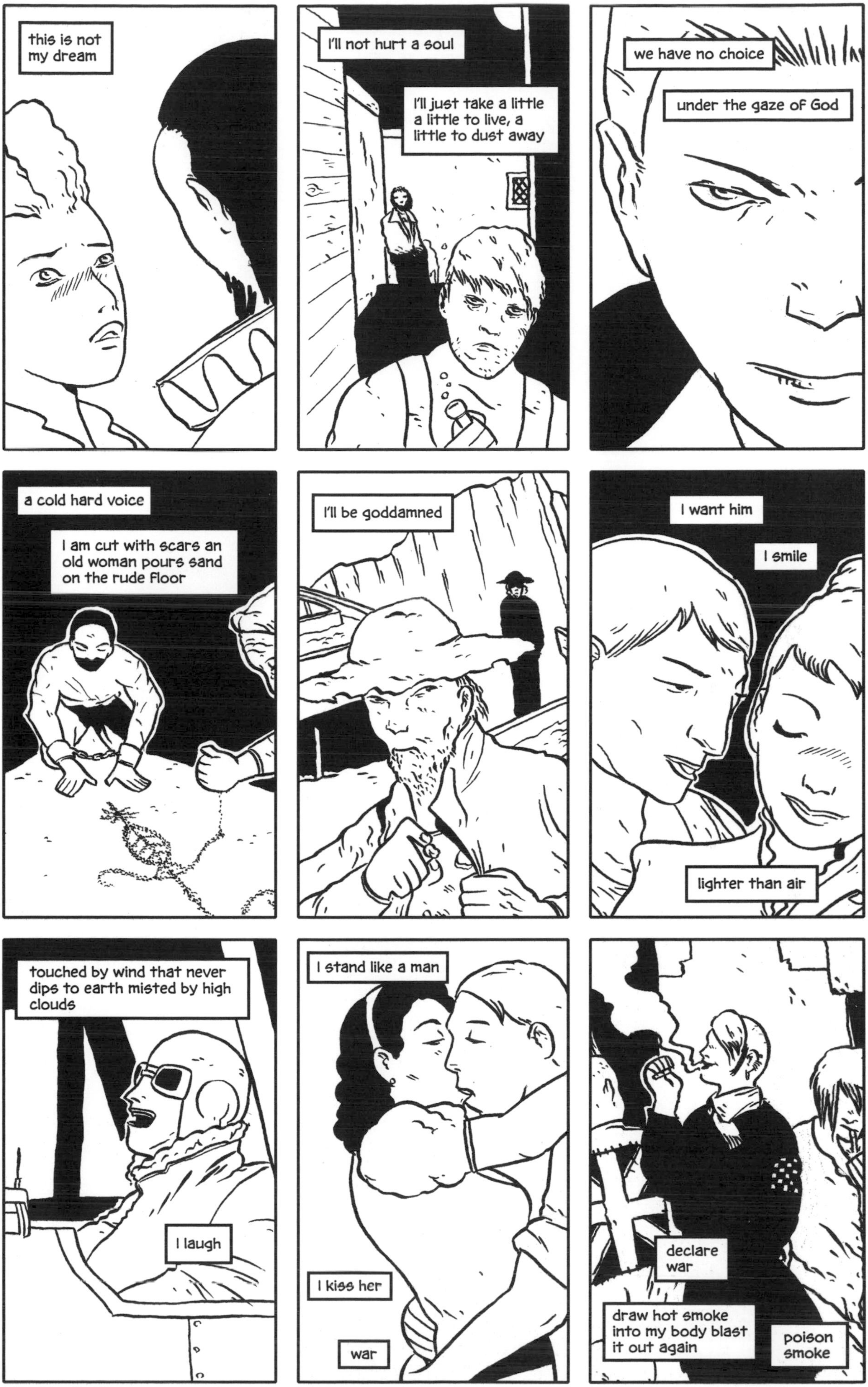
this is not my dream
I'll not hurt a soul
I'll just take a little a little to live, a little to dust away
we have no choice
under the gaze of God
a cold hard voice
I am cut with scars an old woman pours sand on the rude floor
I'll be goddamned
I want him
I smile
lighter than air
touched by wind that never dips to earth misted by high clouds
I laugh
I stand like a man
I kiss her
war
declare war
draw hot smoke into my body blast it out again
poison smoke

blood and skin slick I bring my kill back to the tribe and I am flush with my victory with my power

tonight I will drink the blood of the kill

a perfect shot

honored

numbered with the holy priestesses in the eyes of the Goddess

I take what I want

with my power

not a girl but a gift

my heart pounds

flush with

heat

my master will return

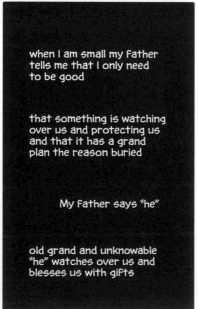

when I am small my Father tells me that I only need to be good

that something is watching over us and protecting us and that it has a grand plan the reason buried

My Father says "he"

old grand and unknowable "he" watches over us and blesses us with gifts

a mouth so foul a mind so blessed

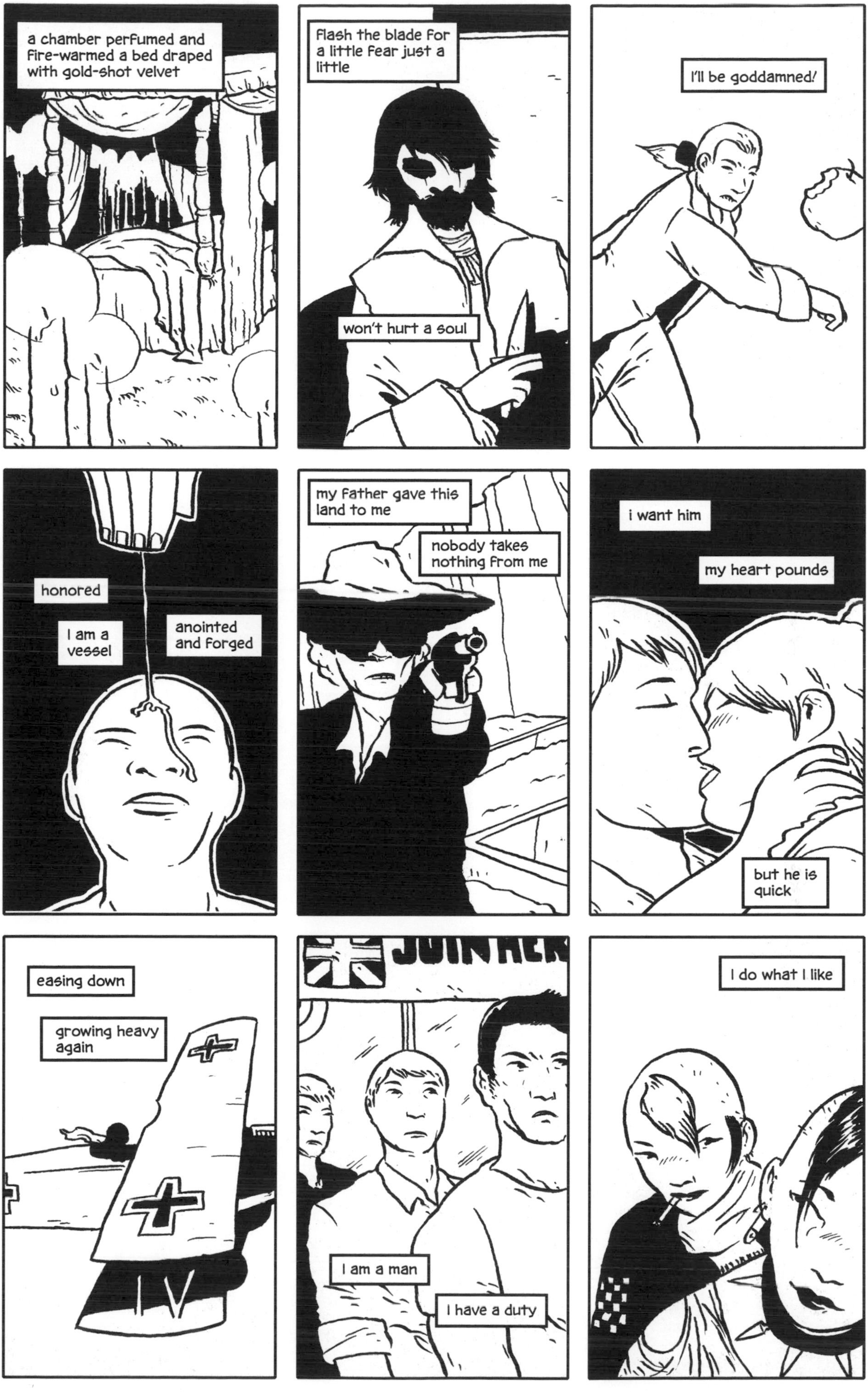
a chamber perfumed and fire-warmed a bed draped with gold-shot velvet
Flash the blade for a little fear just a little
won't hurt a soul
I'll be goddamned!
honored
I am a vessel
anointed and forged
my father gave this land to me
nobody takes nothing from me
i want him
my heart pounds
but he is quick
easing down
growing heavy again
IV
JOIN HER
I am a man
I have a duty
I do what I like

I am powerful

I am the best of the best

I am marked

nobody stands unbent before me

I am bought and sold

I am his

my blood runs cold

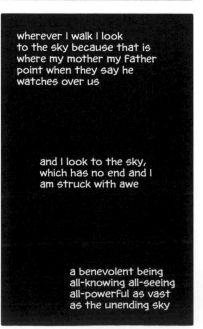

wherever I walk I look to the sky because that is where my mother my father point when they say he watches over us

and I look to the sky, which has no end and I am struck with awe

a benevolent being all-knowing all-seeing all-powerful as vast as the unending sky

I am a conduit

I am revealed
I am a ghost
I am a breaking wave
I am a horse
in this moment
I let him try again
the call is in
I leap to the sky
the call is in
JOI
in this moment

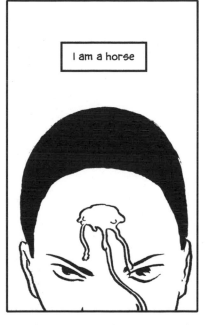

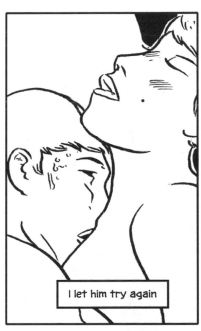

hot blood and skin slick

a world of courage and glory
I bow before the living God.

I stand at the sacrifice

In this place none
will deny me

I am unfettered
unstoppable

traded

taken

I say yes

I say no

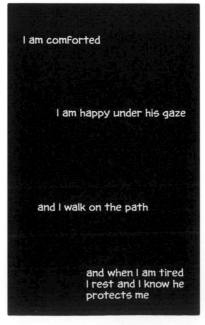

I am comforted

I am happy under his gaze

and I walk on the path

and when I am tired
I rest and I know he
protects me

my father is happy
my father praises God

he says I have
found my calling

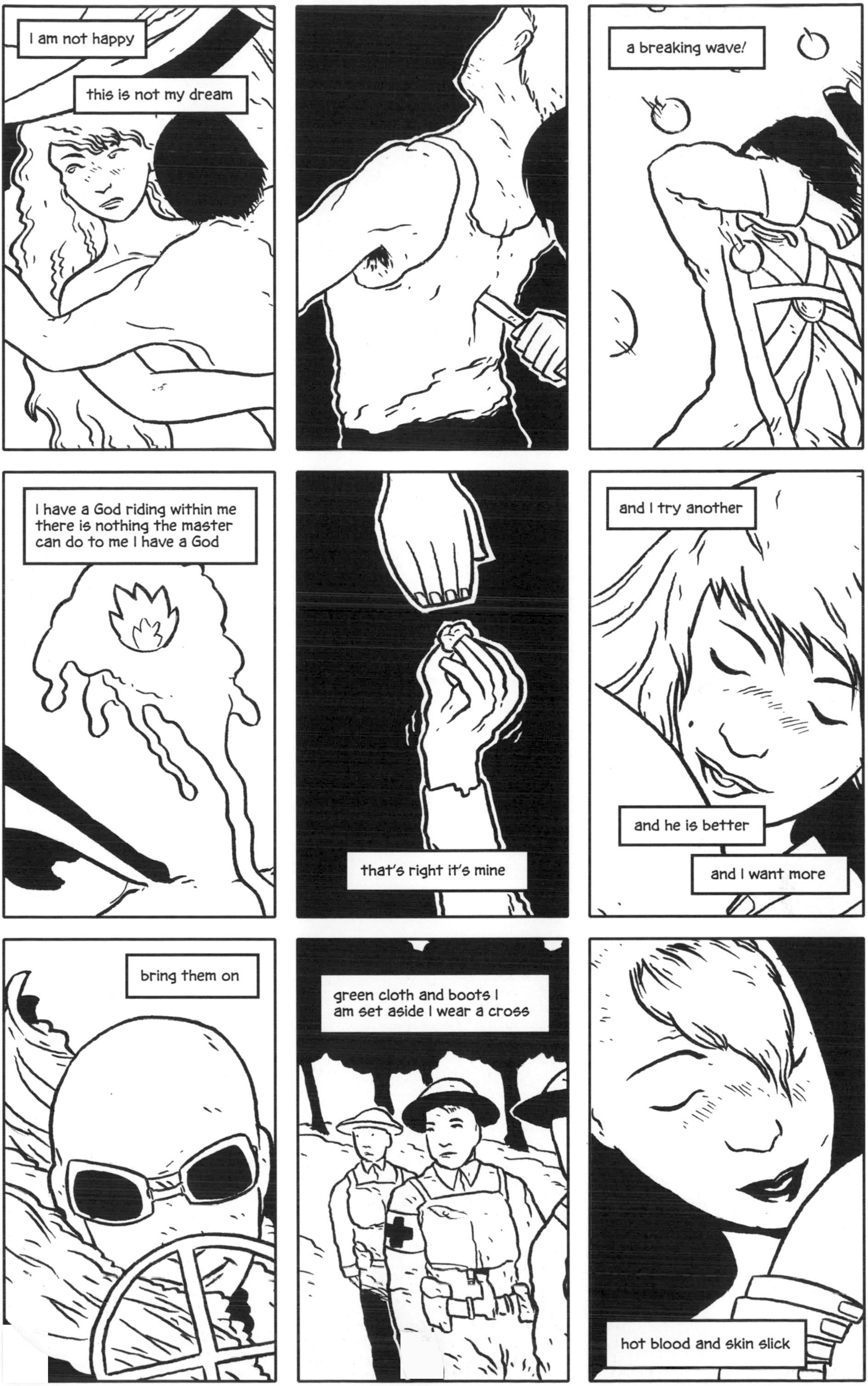
I am not happy
this is not my dream
a breaking wave!
I have a God riding within me there is nothing the master can do to me I have a God
that's right it's mine
and I try another
and he is better
and I want more
bring them on
green cloth and boots I am set aside I wear a cross
hot blood and skin slick

we follow the tide of the thaw frost cracks underfoot and I creep forward with the tribe

shadows flicker under creaking boughs

a single body of fifty thousand men marching

I am a weapon

my year has come and gone but I choose to stay hands outstretched in the marble hall the Goddess above

I count my property

silkworms rustle in their beds of leaves the little one turns in my belly

hands clasped in prayer

he knows what I am

my master is dead and I am drafted into the ranks

I am nothing now

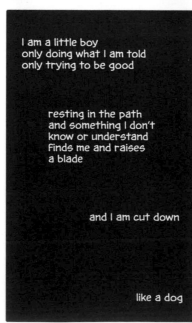

I am a little boy only doing what I am told only trying to be good

resting in the path and something I don't know or understand finds me and raises a blade

and I am cut down

like a dog

one day I am approached

a priest addresses me in low hushed tones

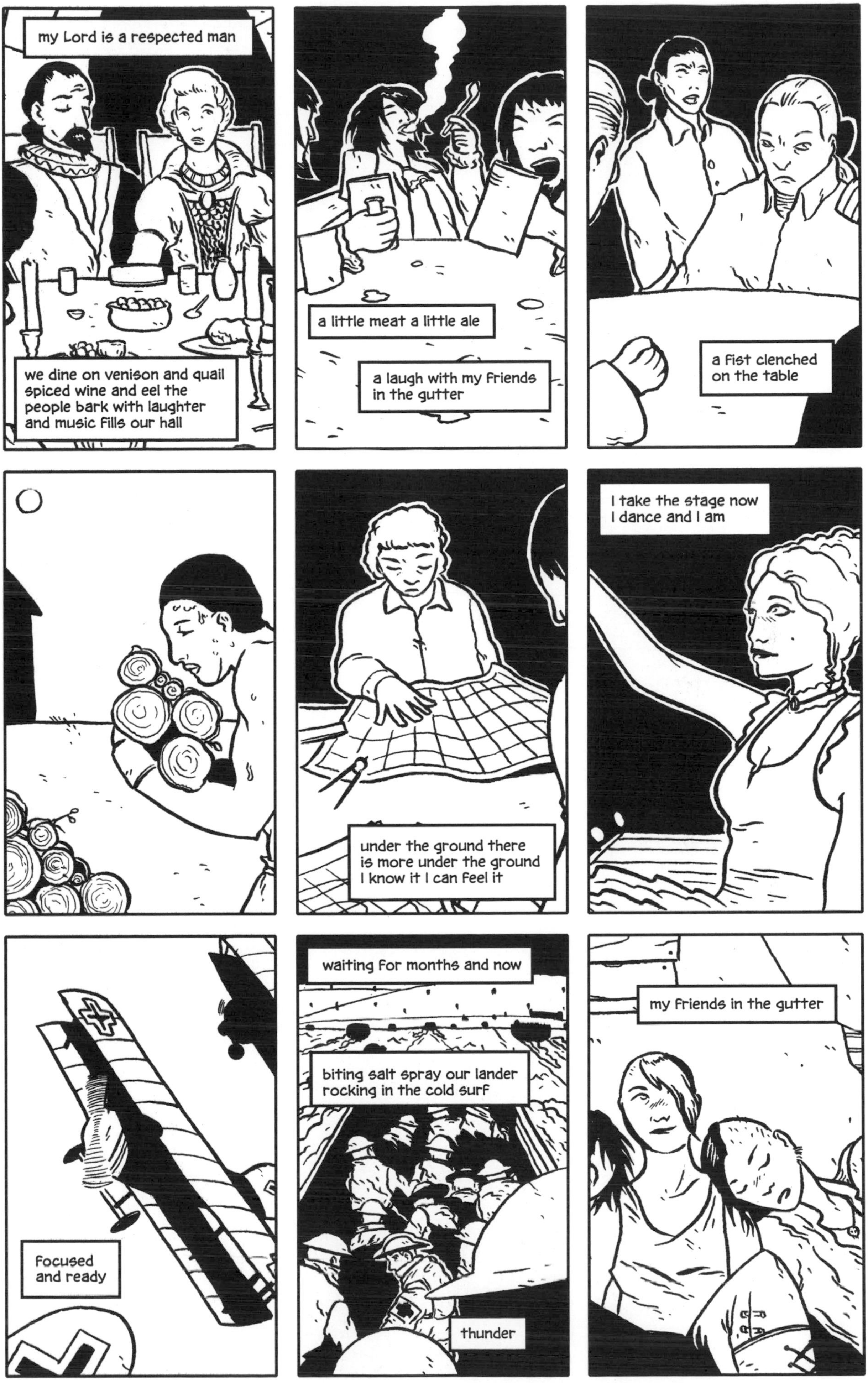
my Lord is a respected man
we dine on venison and quail spiced wine and eel the people bark with laughter and music fills our hall
a little meat a little ale
a laugh with my friends in the gutter
a fist clenched on the table
under the ground there is more under the ground I know it I can feel it
I take the stage now I dance and I am
focused and ready
waiting for months and now
biting salt spray our lander rocking in the cold surf
thunder
my friends in the gutter

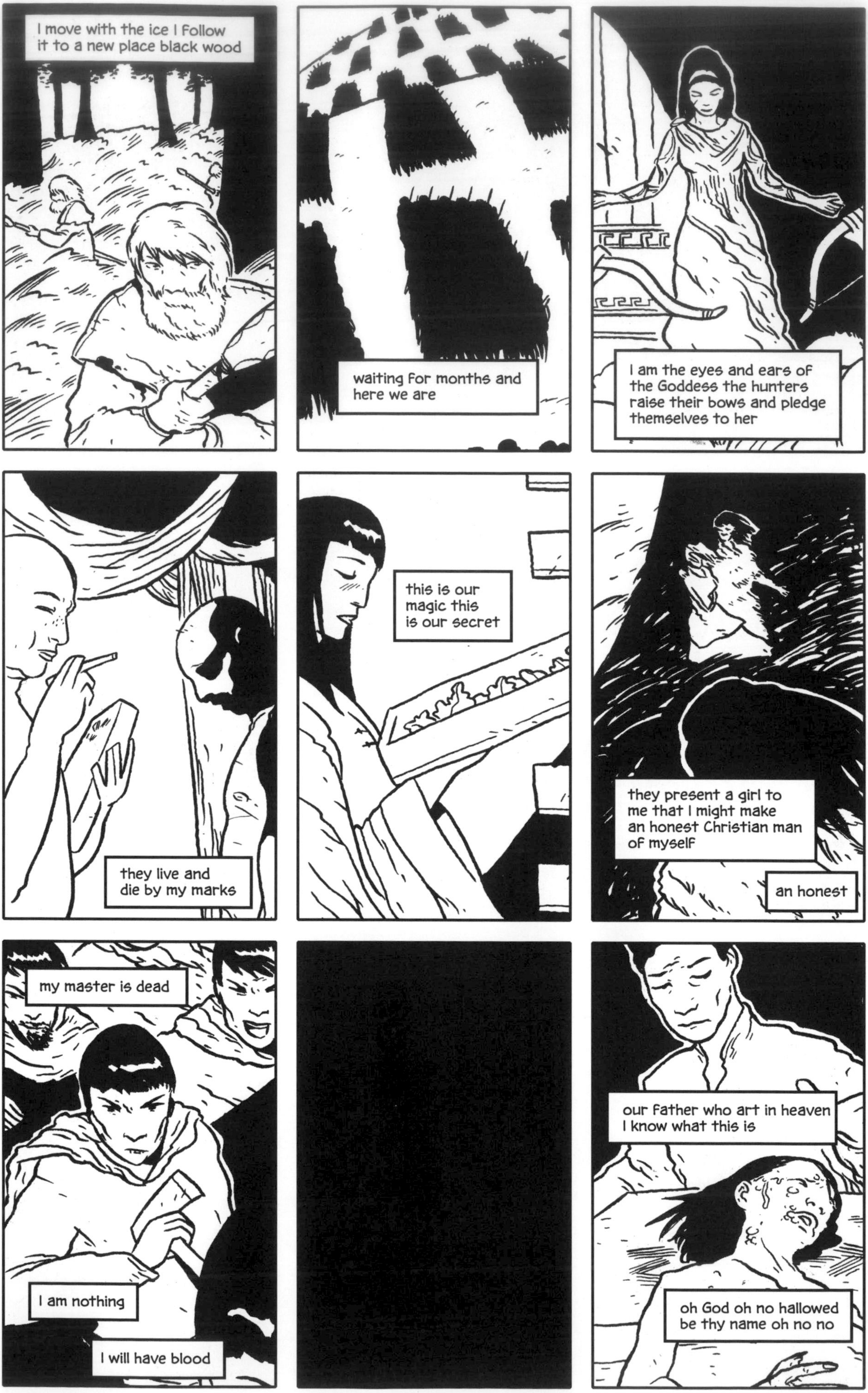
I move with the ice I Follow it to a new place black wood
waiting for months and here we are
I am the eyes and ears of the Goddess the hunters raise their bows and pledge themselves to her
they live and die by my marks
this is our magic this is our secret
they present a girl to me that I might make an honest Christian man of myself
an honest
my master is dead
I am nothing
I will have blood
our father who art in heaven I know what this is
oh God oh no hallowed be thy name oh no no

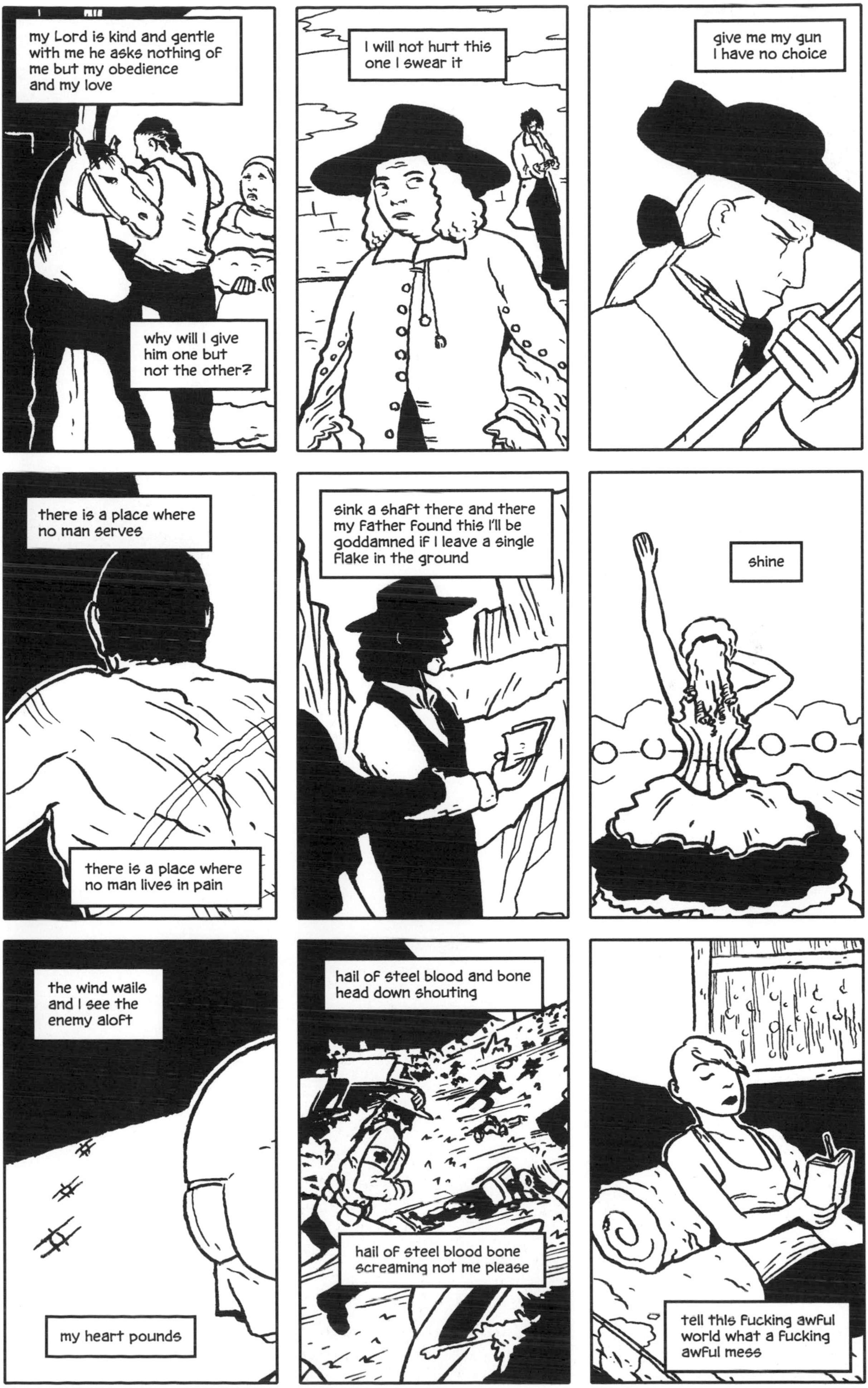
my Lord is kind and gentle with me he asks nothing of me but my obedience and my love
why will I give him one but not the other?
I will not hurt this one I swear it
give me my gun I have no choice
there is a place where no man serves
there is a place where no man lives in pain
sink a shaft there and there my father found this I'll be goddamned if I leave a single flake in the ground
shine
the wind wails and I see the enemy aloft
my heart pounds
hail of steel blood and bone head down shouting
hail of steel blood bone screaming not me please
tell this fucking awful world what a fucking awful mess

a new place
another
tribe's place

one hundred thousand men
clash my heart pounds

I say a
prayer

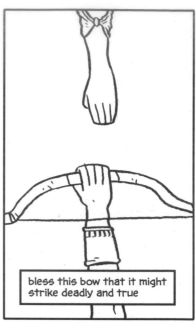

bless this bow that it might
strike deadly and true

arrogant fool

lives and dies
by my marks

wedded
before God

an honest
Christian man

the enemy wears a cross

I will have blood

I want to know

why

plague we are in the valley
of the shadow black death

we are in the valley of
the shadow of death

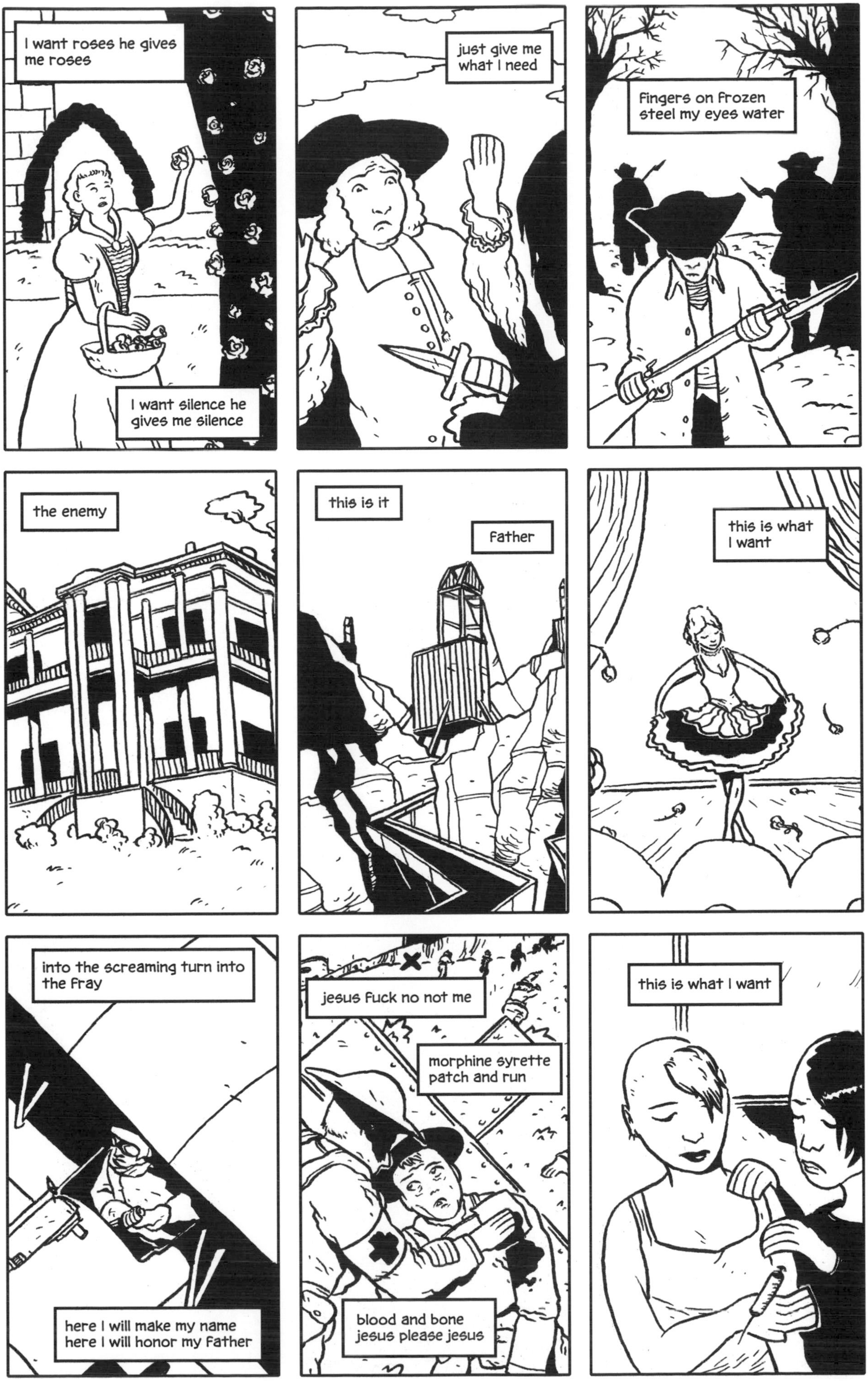
I want roses he gives me roses
I want silence he gives me silence
just give me what I need
Fingers on frozen steel my eyes water
the enemy
this is it
Father
this is what I want
into the screaming turn into the Fray
here I will make my name here I will honor my Father
jesus Fuck no not me
morphine syrette patch and run
blood and bone jesus please jesus
this is what I want

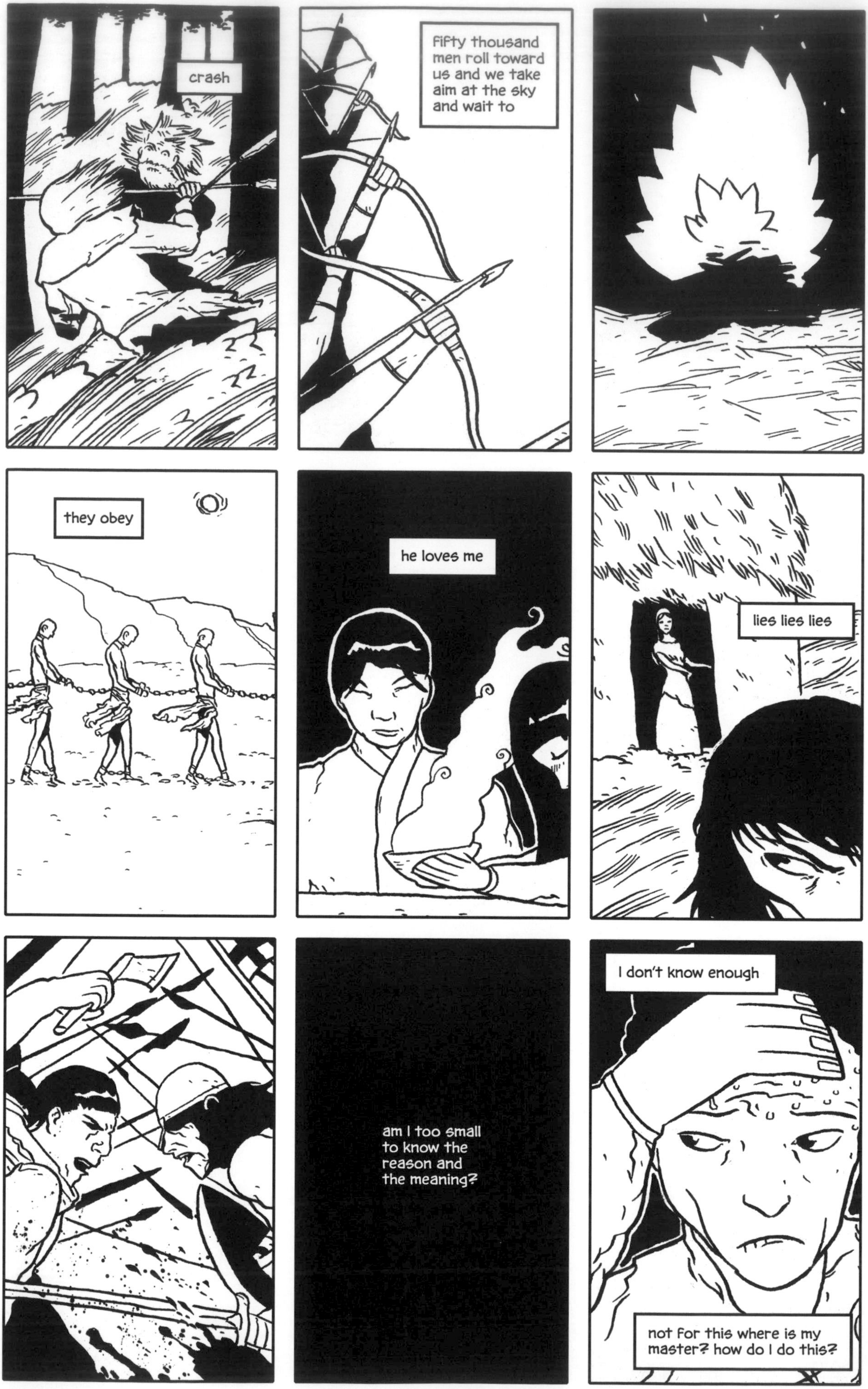
crash
Fifty thousand men roll toward us and we take aim at the sky and wait to
they obey
he loves me
lies lies lies
am I too small to know the reason and the meaning?
I don't know enough
not for this where is my master? how do I do this?

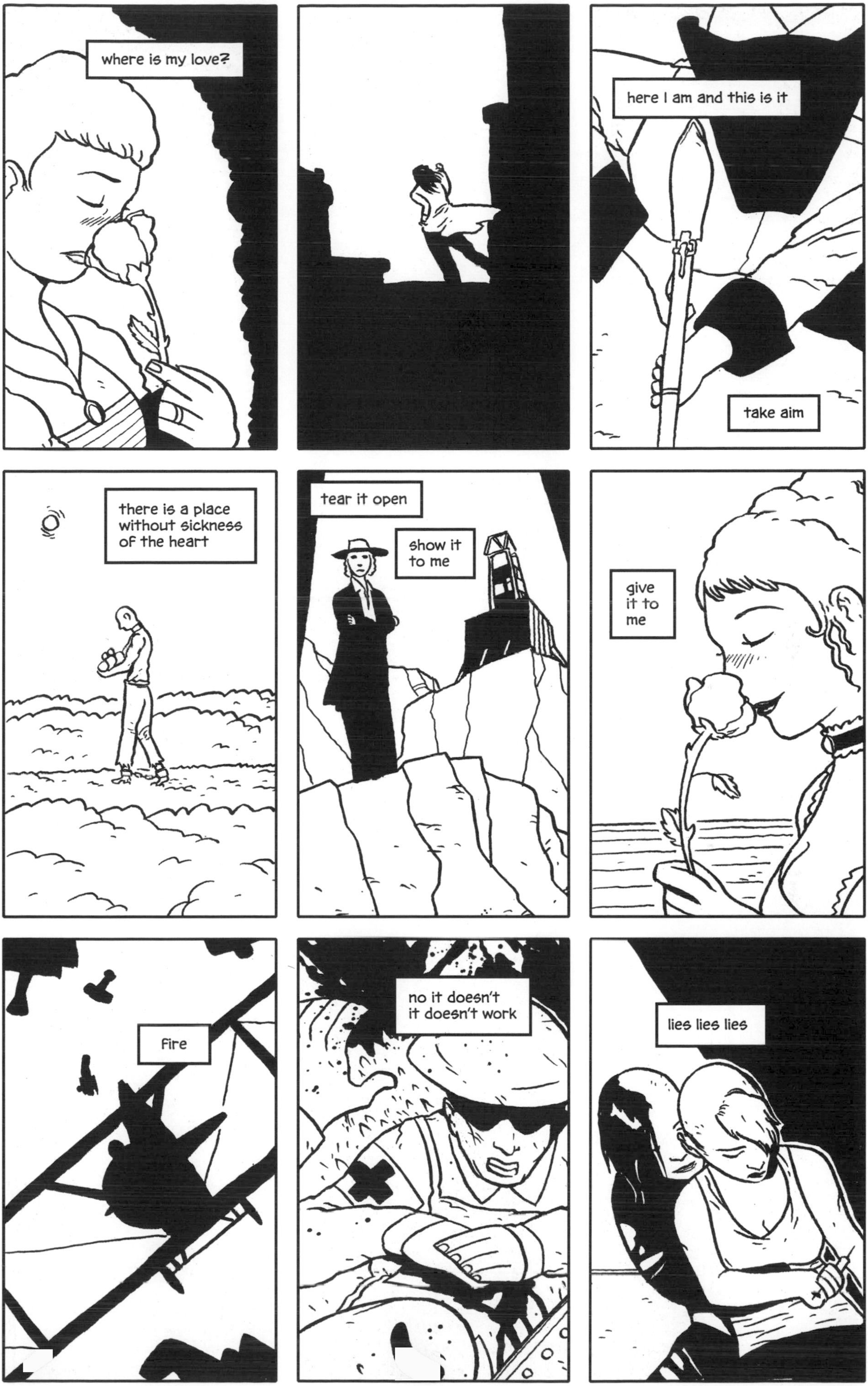
where is my love?
here I am and this is it
take aim
there is a place without sickness of the heart
tear it open
show it to me
give it to me
fire
no it doesn't it doesn't work
lies lies lies

whispering leaves
roaring blood

watching over the fire
and the young girls who
dance the bear this year

sweet memory

sweet words for me
flattery honey

nothing is free

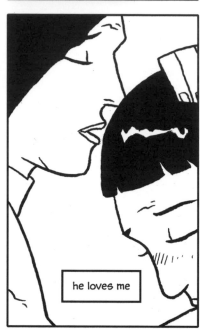

he loves me

he is waiting

I am not an honest
Christian man

I love him

yes!

I am not strong
enough for this

I am not

the dead multiply. my
master dies my father
dies a rude cross on
the doors

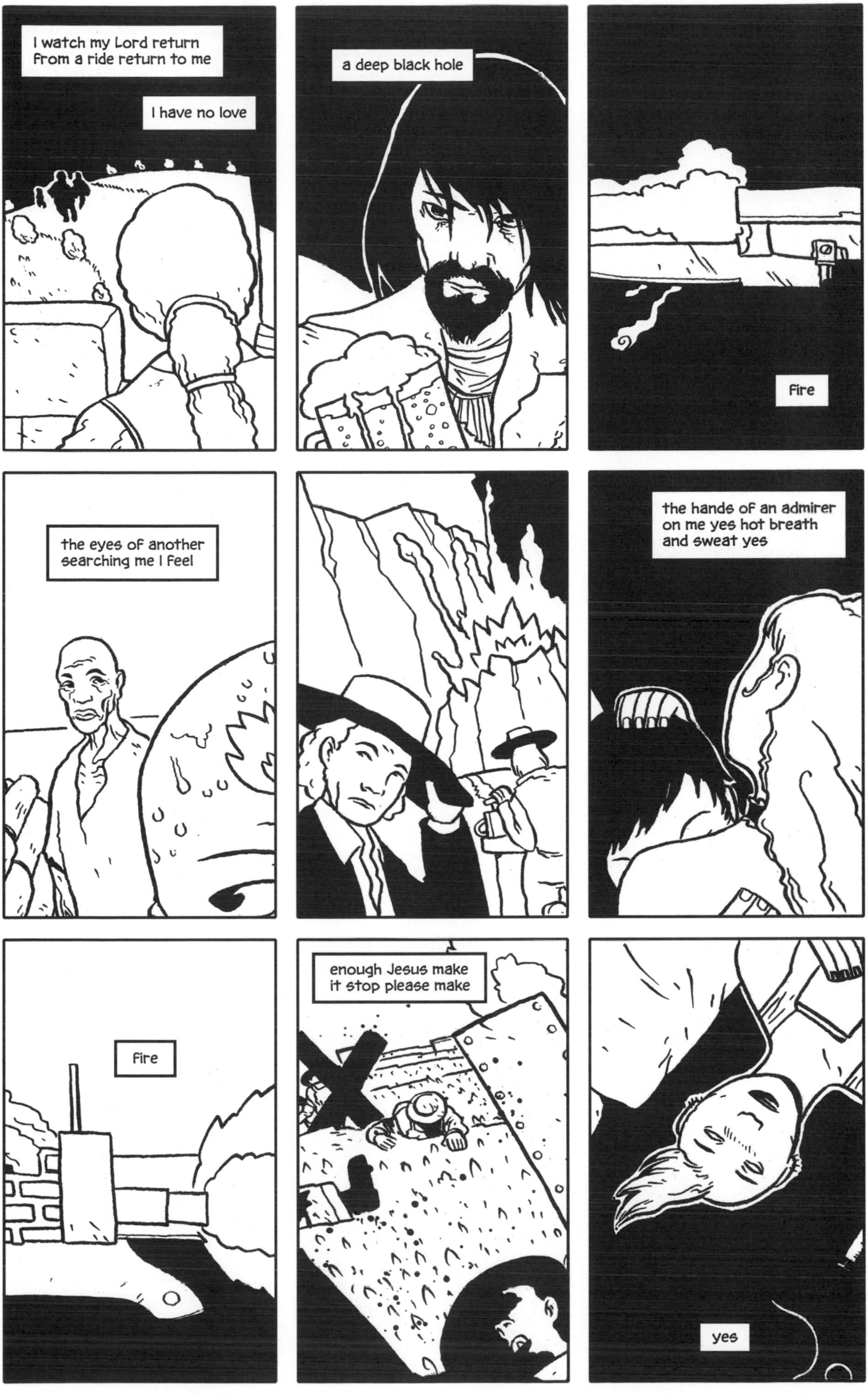
I watch my Lord return from a ride return to me
I have no love
a deep black hole
fire
the eyes of another searching me I feel
the hands of an admirer on me yes hot breath and sweat yes
fire
enough Jesus make it stop please make
yes

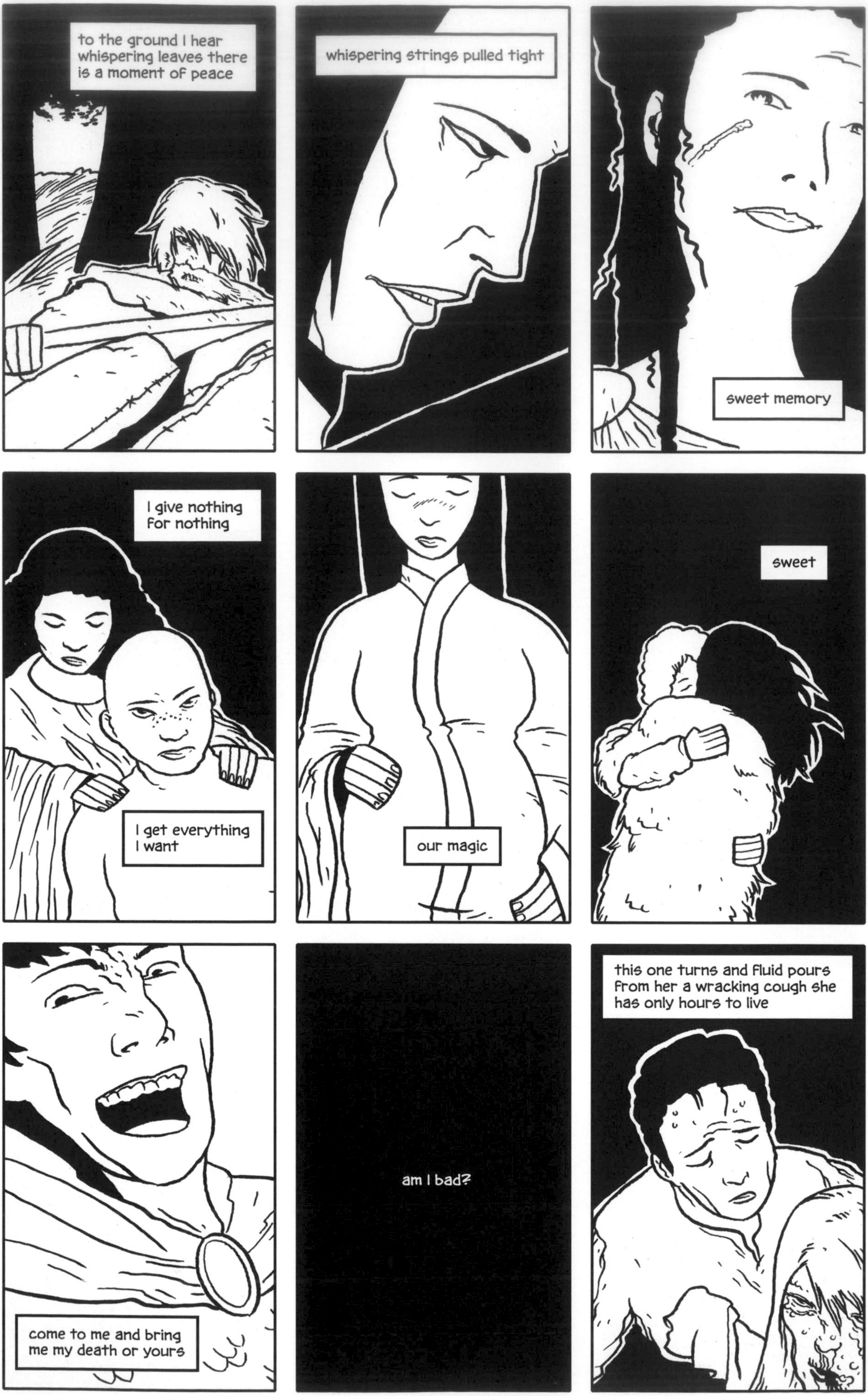
to the ground I hear whispering leaves there is a moment of peace
whispering strings pulled tight
sweet memory
I give nothing for nothing
I get everything I want
our magic
sweet
come to me and bring me my death or yours
am I bad?
this one turns and fluid pours from her a wracking cough she has only hours to live

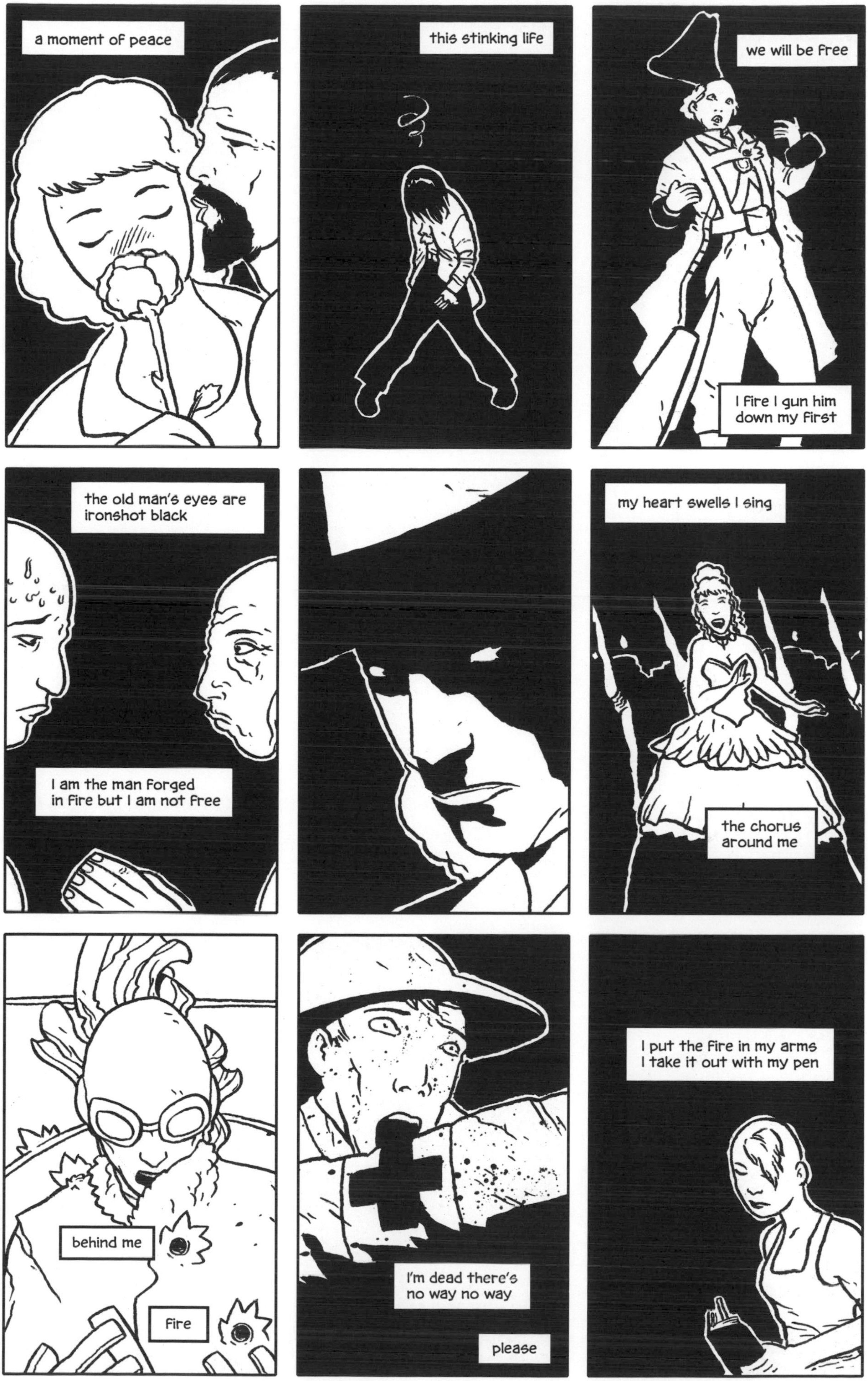
a moment of peace
this stinking life
we will be free
I fire I gun him down my first
the old man's eyes are ironshot black
I am the man forged in fire but I am not free
my heart swells I sing
the chorus around me
behind me
fire
I'm dead there's no way no way
please
I put the fire in my arms I take it out with my pen

and then a searing pain flares along my side brings me back

and I fight

and I draw again

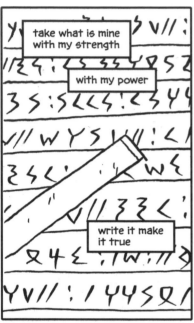

take what is mine with my strength

with my power

write it make it true

I run the jade comb through my hair I hear him in the house and

I love him

I fight

I live he dies

I am a little boy run down on the path

but why

I only need to be good

run down like a dog

why

she dies in agony

I am powerless in the face of this I am nothing

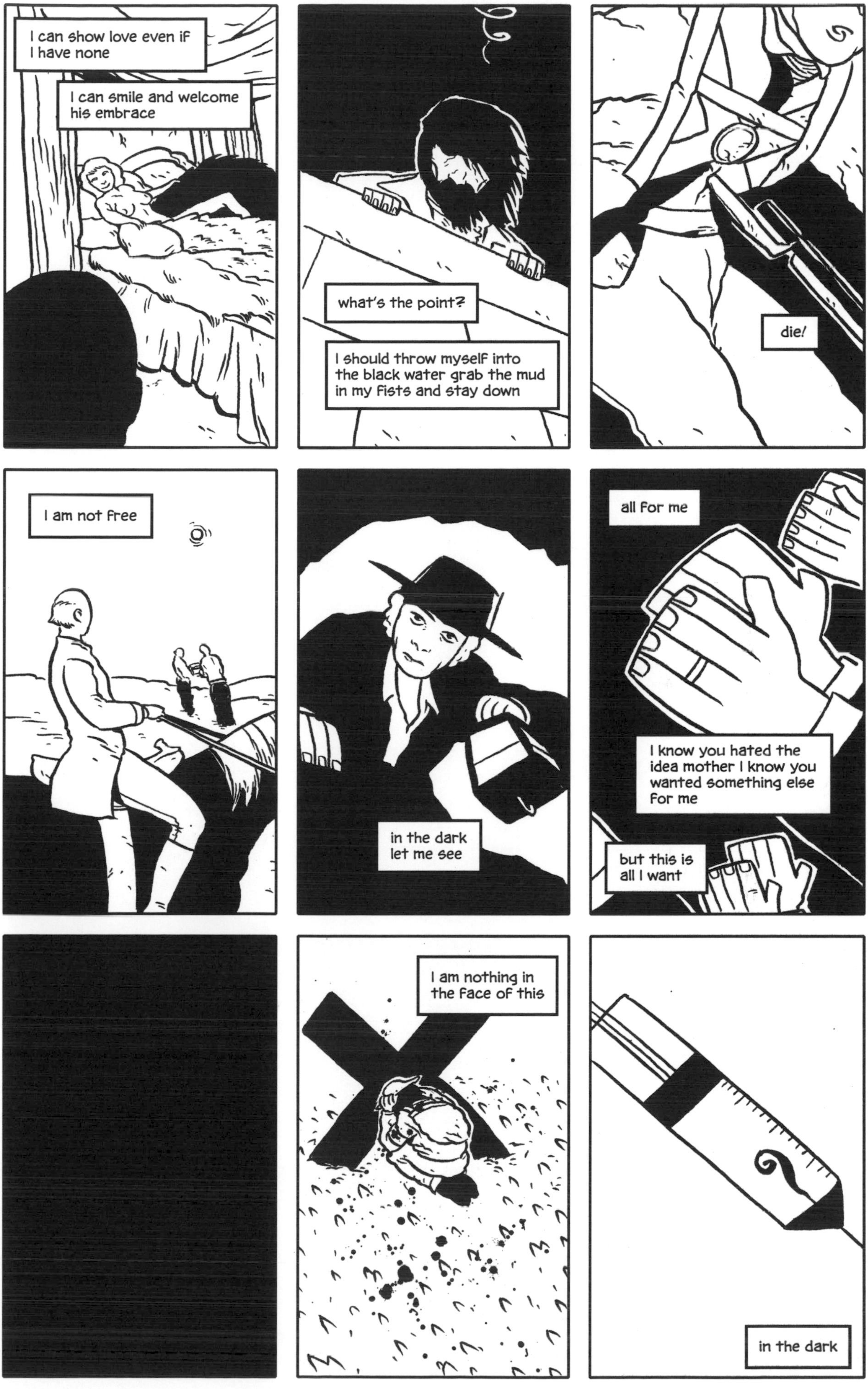
I can show love even if I have none
I can smile and welcome his embrace
what's the point?
I should throw myself into the black water grab the mud in my fists and stay down
die!
I am not free
in the dark let me see
all for me
I know you hated the idea mother I know you wanted something else for me
but this is all I want
I am nothing in the face of this
in the dark

my arrow flies in a storm

I give myself my life to this

to her

give it all to me

a boy I pray for a boy

I kiss his body warm hard skin heartbeat

a cry followed by sudden silence I stand they fall

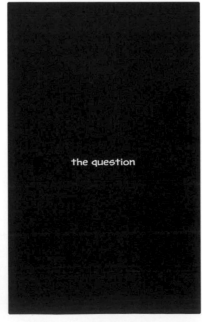

the question

and in the midst of this she wants me and we are wedded for what

for hope

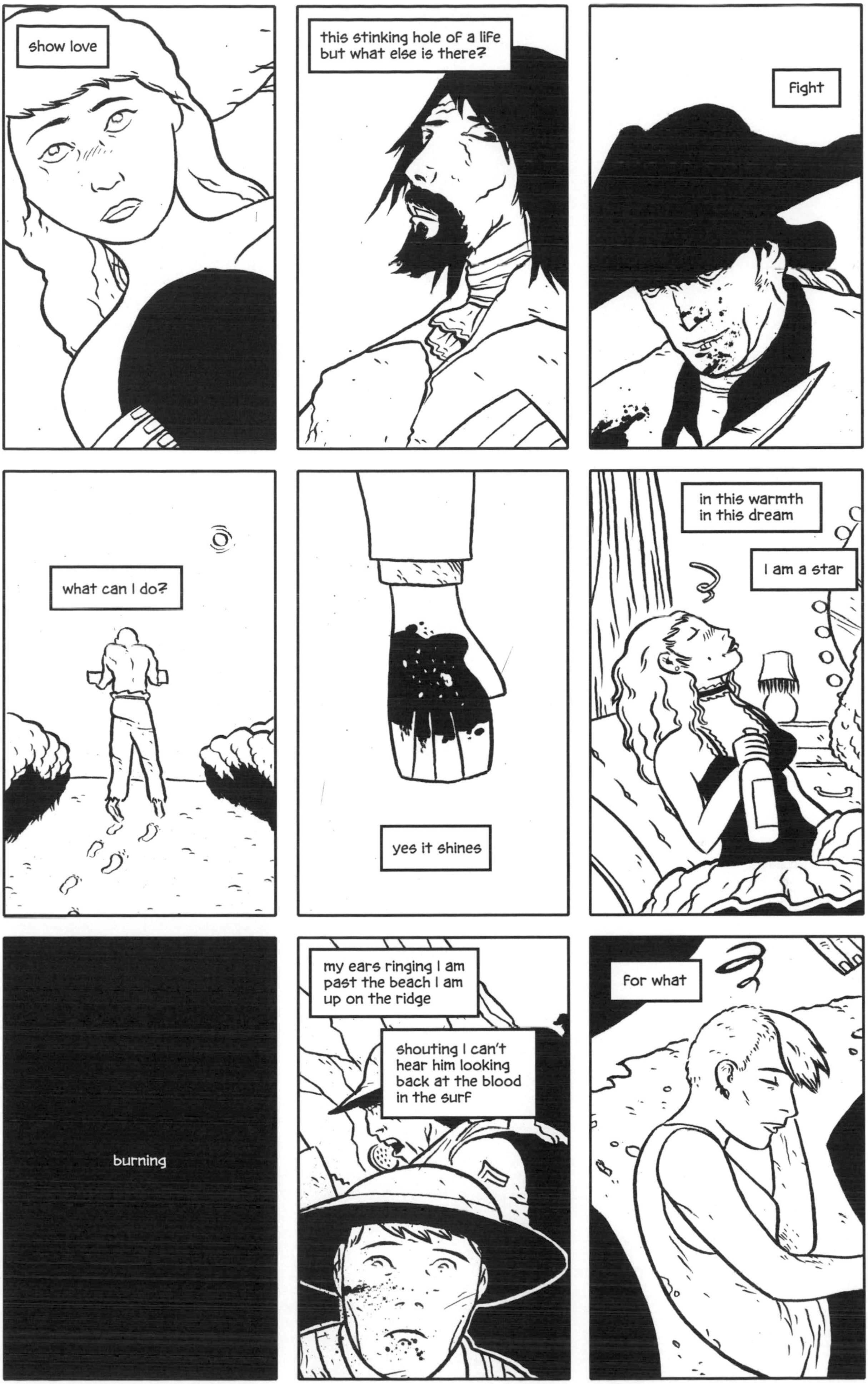
show love
this stinking hole of a life
but what else is there?
fight
what can I do?
yes it shines
in this warmth
in this dream
I am a star
burning
my ears ringing I am
past the beach I am
up on the ridge
shouting I can't
hear him looking
back at the blood
in the surf
for what

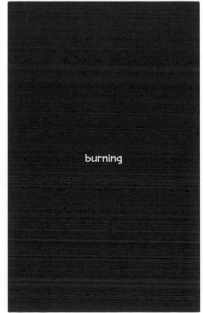

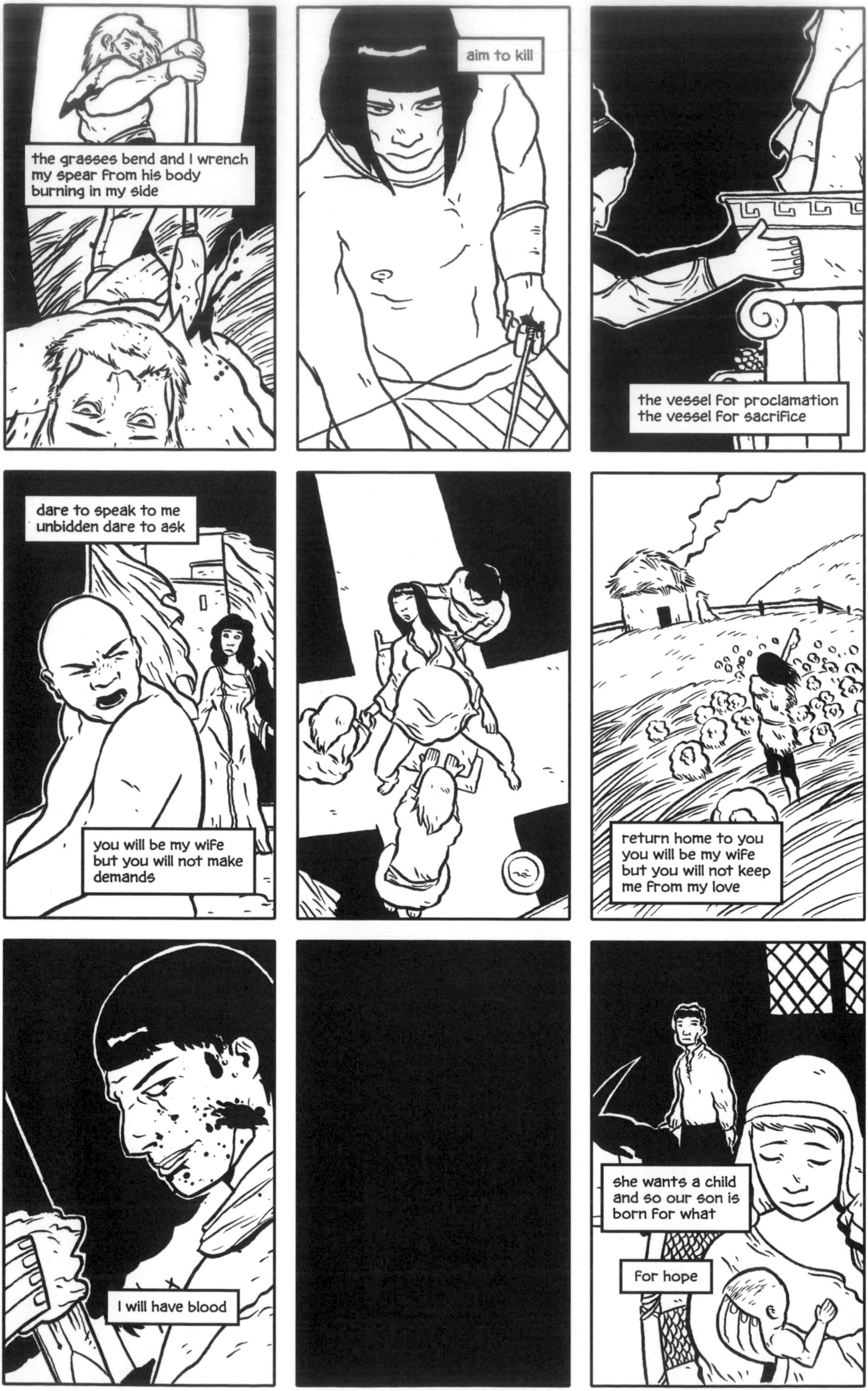
the grasses bend and I wrench my spear from his body burning in my side
aim to kill
the vessel for proclamation the vessel for sacrifice
dare to speak to me unbidden dare to ask
you will be my wife but you will not make demands
return home to you you will be my wife but you will not keep me from my love
I will have blood
she wants a child and so our son is born for what
for hope

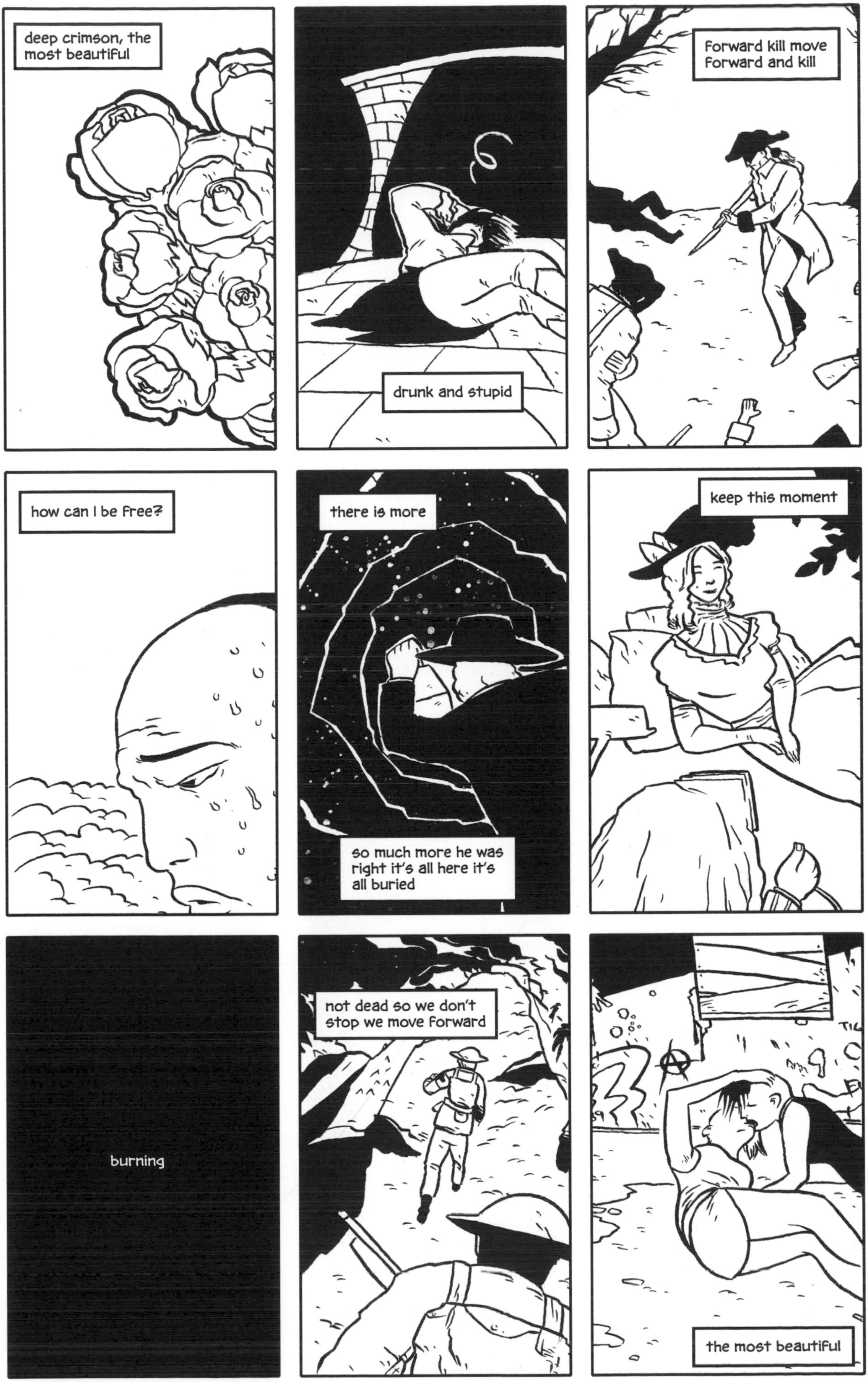
deep crimson, the most beautiful
drunk and stupid
Forward kill move forward and kill
how can I be free?
there is more
so much more he was right it's all here it's all buried
keep this moment
burning
not dead so we don't stop we move forward
the most beautiful

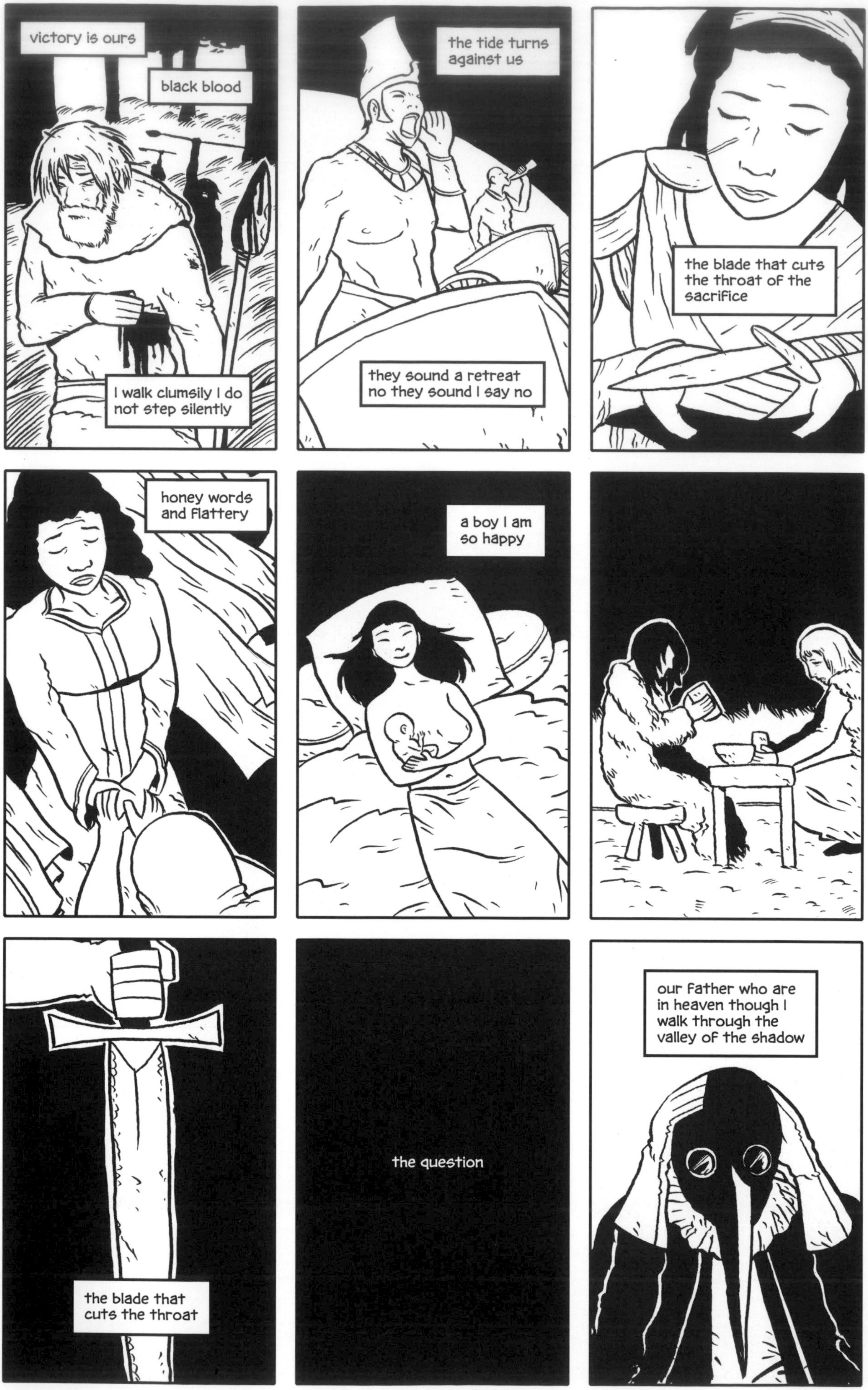
victory is ours
black blood
I walk clumsily I do not step silently
the tide turns against us
they sound a retreat no they sound I say no
the blade that cuts the throat of the sacrifice
honey words and flattery
a boy I am so happy
the blade that cuts the throat
the question
our father who are in heaven though I walk through the valley of the shadow

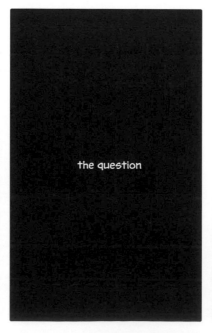

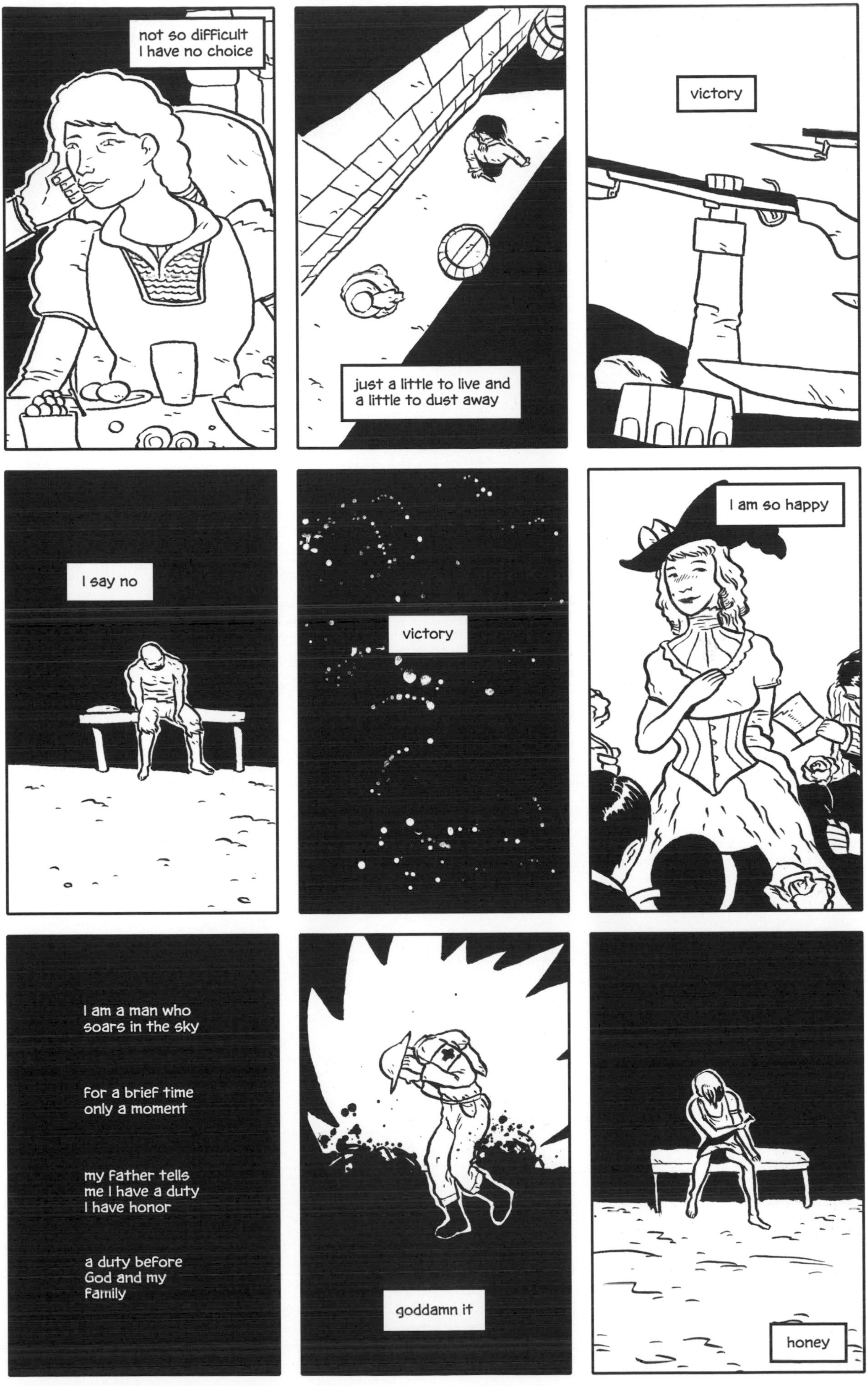
not so difficult
I have no choice
just a little to live and
a little to dust away
victory
I say no
victory
I am so happy
I am a man who
soars in the sky
for a brief time
only a moment
my father tells
me I have a duty
I have honor
a duty before
God and my
family
goddamn it
honey

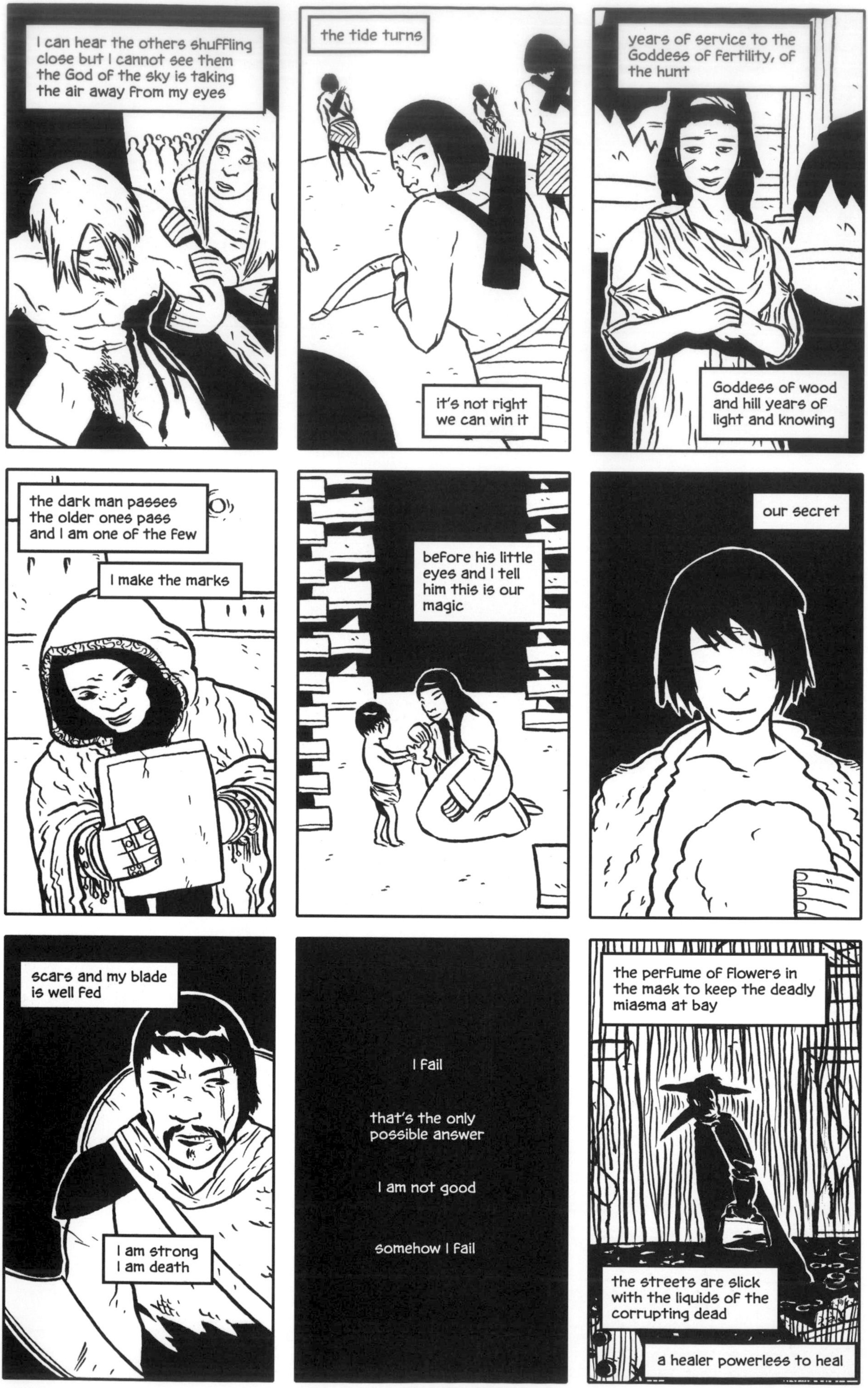
I can hear the others shuffling close but I cannot see them the God of the sky is taking the air away from my eyes
the tide turns
it's not right we can win it
years of service to the Goddess of fertility, of the hunt
Goddess of wood and hill years of light and knowing
the dark man passes the older ones pass and I am one of the few
I make the marks
before his little eyes and I tell him this is our magic
our secret
scars and my blade is well fed
I am strong I am death
I fail
that's the only possible answer
I am not good
somehow I fail
the perfume of flowers in the mask to keep the deadly miasma at bay
the streets are slick with the liquids of the corrupting dead
a healer powerless to heal

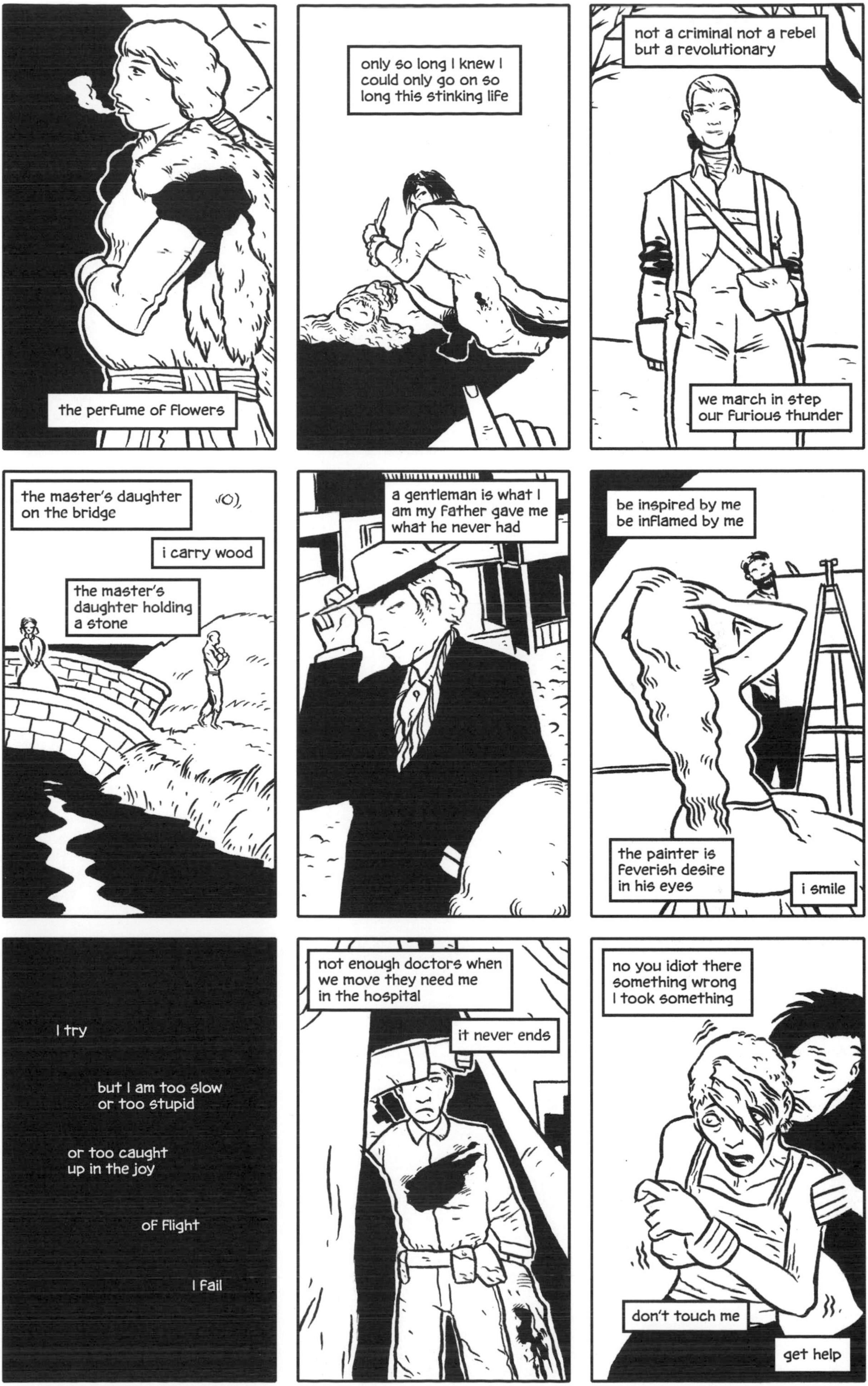
the perfume of flowers
only so long I knew I could only go on so long this stinking life
not a criminal not a rebel but a revolutionary
we march in step our furious thunder
the master's daughter on the bridge
i carry wood
the master's daughter holding a stone
a gentleman is what I am my father gave me what he never had
be inspired by me be inflamed by me
the painter is feverish desire in his eyes
i smile
I try
but I am too slow or too stupid
or too caught up in the joy
of flight
I fail
not enough doctors when we move they need me in the hospital
it never ends
no you idiot there something wrong I took something
don't touch me
get help

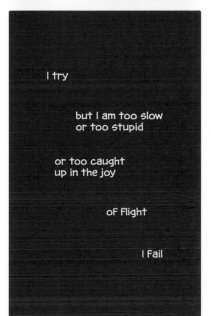

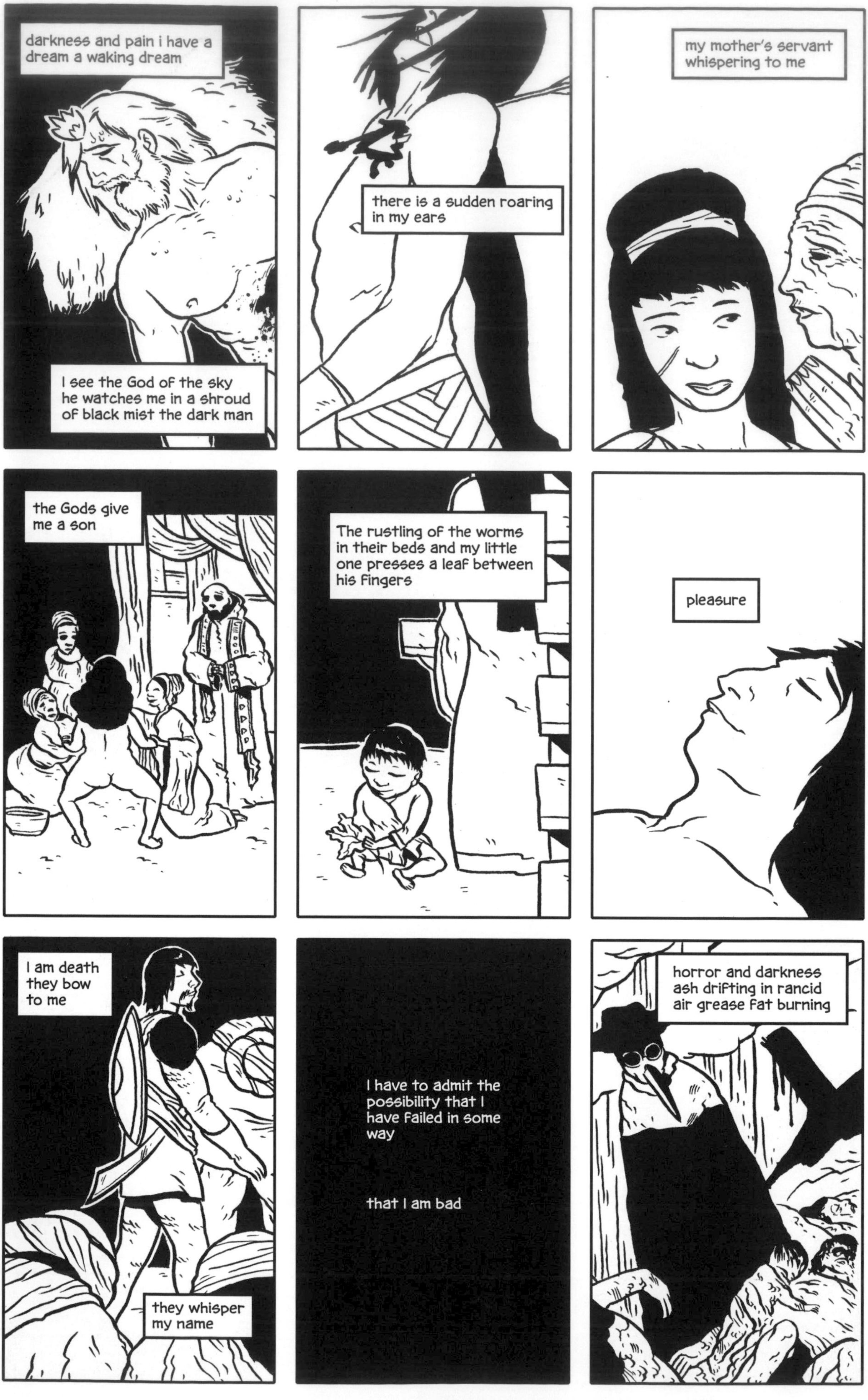
darkness and pain i have a dream a waking dream
I see the God of the sky he watches me in a shroud of black mist the dark man
there is a sudden roaring in my ears
my mother's servant whispering to me
the Gods give me a son
The rustling of the worms in their beds and my little one presses a leaf between his fingers
pleasure
I am death they bow to me
they whisper my name
I have to admit the possibility that I have failed in some way
that I am bad
horror and darkness ash drifting in rancid air grease fat burning

whispering in my ear and I am smiling but

so this is it this is how it will end gripped by fear what a waste what a filthy waste

we do what we must do

I will have everything

I walk with a gentleman

I will have him if I want

if I don't admit that possibility

then I am too small to see the meaning

what a waste

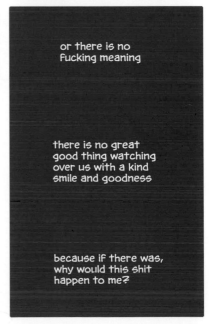

or there is no fucking meaning

there is no great good thing watching over us with a kind smile and goodness

because if there was, why would this shit happen to me?

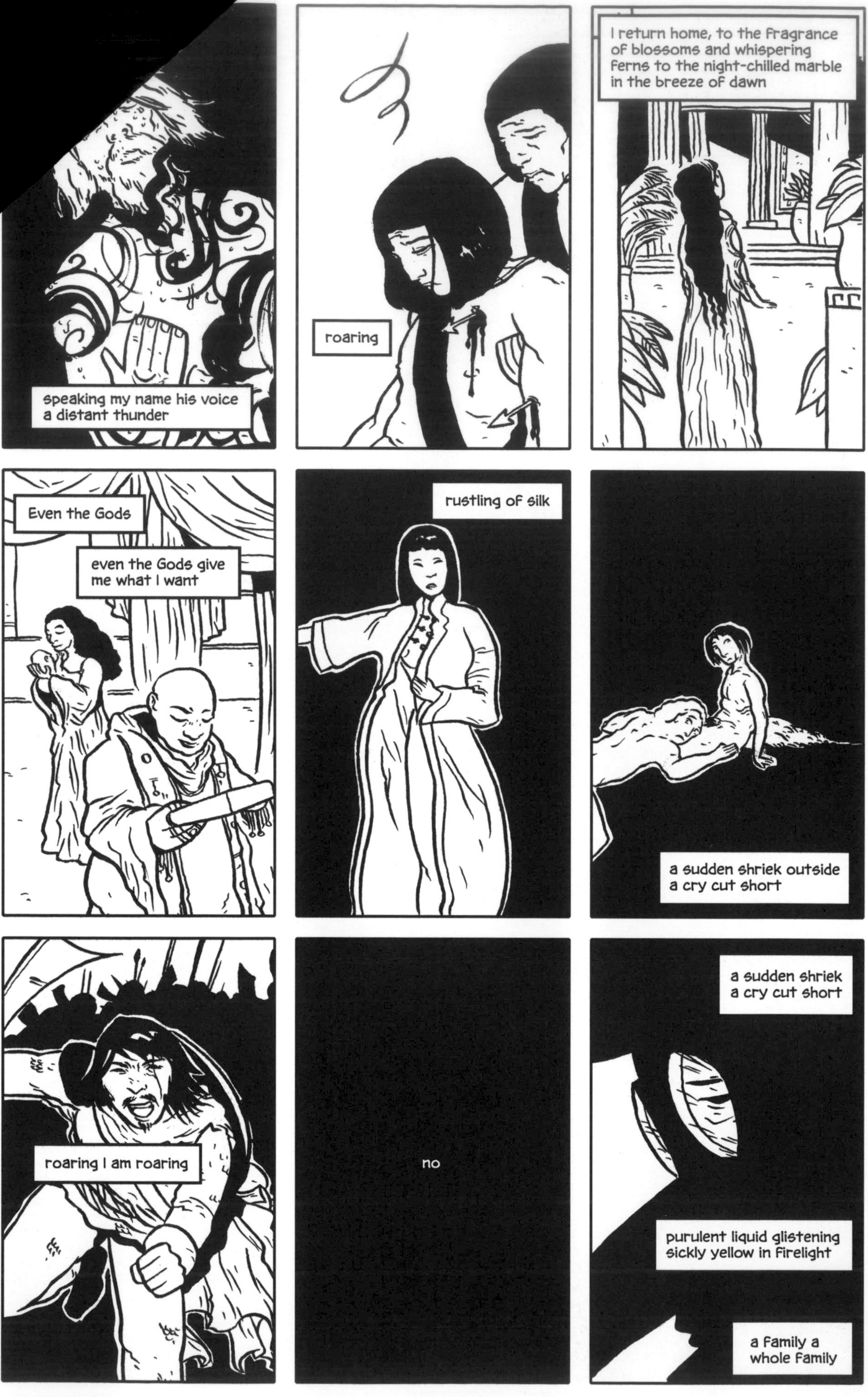
speaking my name his voice a distant thunder
roaring
I return home, to the fragrance of blossoms and whispering ferns to the night-chilled marble in the breeze of dawn
Even the Gods
even the Gods give me what I want
rustling of silk
a sudden shriek outside a cry cut short
roaring I am roaring
no
a sudden shriek a cry cut short
purulent liquid glistening sickly yellow in firelight
a family a whole family

humming a sweet tune I am heavy with child

all for nothing all to end up on the gallows twisting and rotten

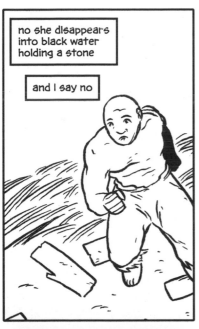

no she disappears into black water holding a stone

and I say no

a man so high his paper white his pen gilded with gold

someone shouts

a crude name

Jesus this one doesn't have a chance in Hell what am I even doing out here

what's the point

I'm supposed to accept that there's a meaning I can't see or understand?

I'm a girl who can't fit herself in with the world around me

I feel inverted and distorted

and I am abandoned and all I need to do is be good? And "he" will make everthing okay?

sorry, but I don't think so

brace yourself he says
in among the roaring
brace yourself

oh mother

don't tell me what
you need. I know what
you need. I'm the one.

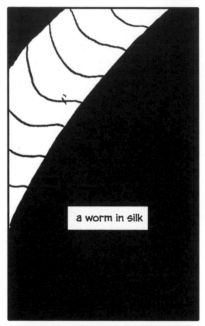

a worm in silk

blood and screaming
wolves there are wolves

bear the cross and die
before me

bear the cross and give
me your blood give me
your fear

doubt is poison

but yes

the sickly yellow valley
of the running dripping
shadow of greasy
black death

help me to my chamber

yes I can read it you scrubbed shits I learned it in the monastery

I learned it under the hands of the stinking bastard monk his weight on my back my ass this will spare me I almost laugh

come what may

disappearing into black water

signed and sealed

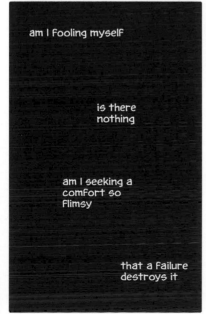

am I fooling myself

is there nothing

am I seeking a comfort so Flimsy

that a Failure destroys it

blood and bone

prove me wrong

99

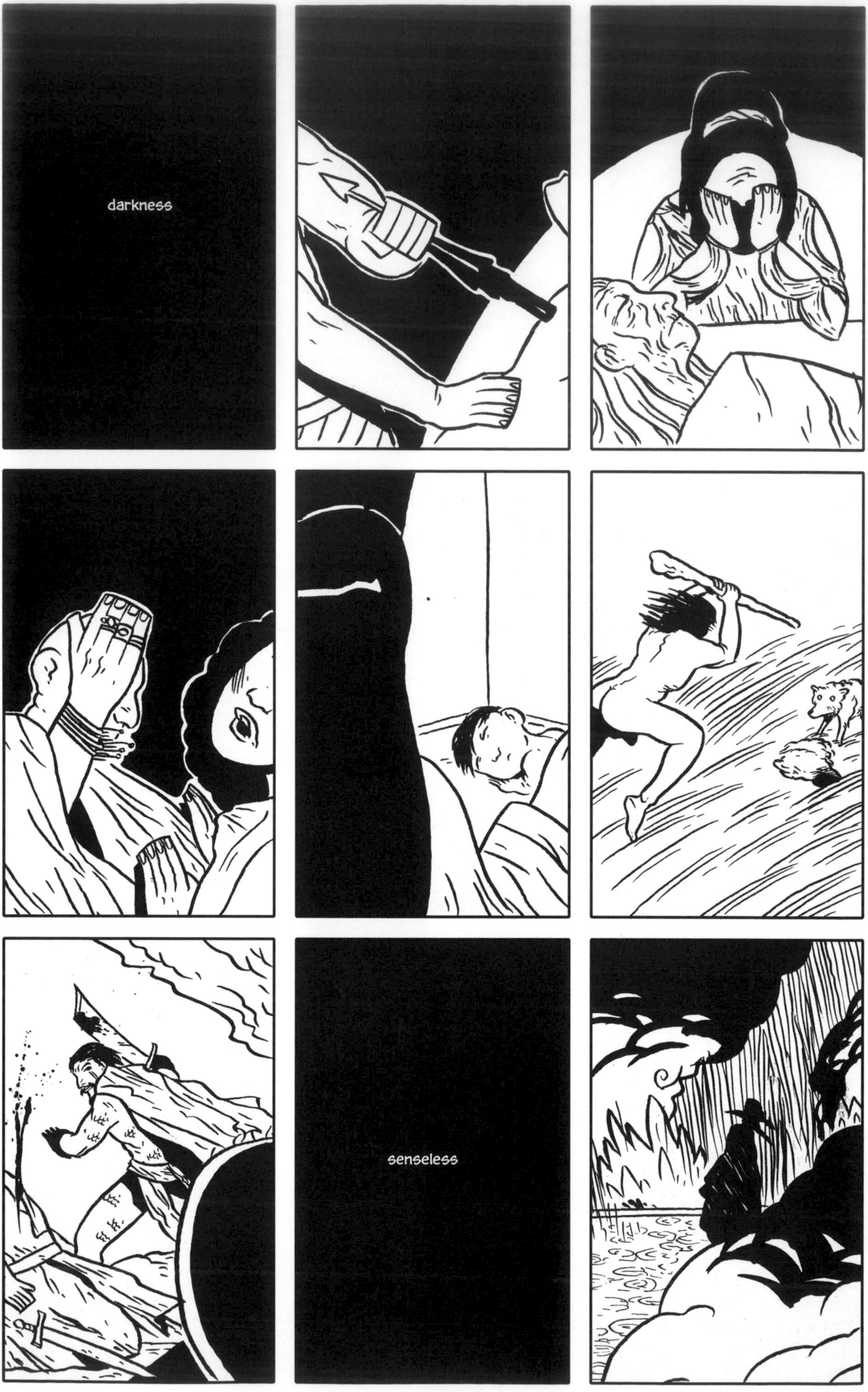
darkness
senseless

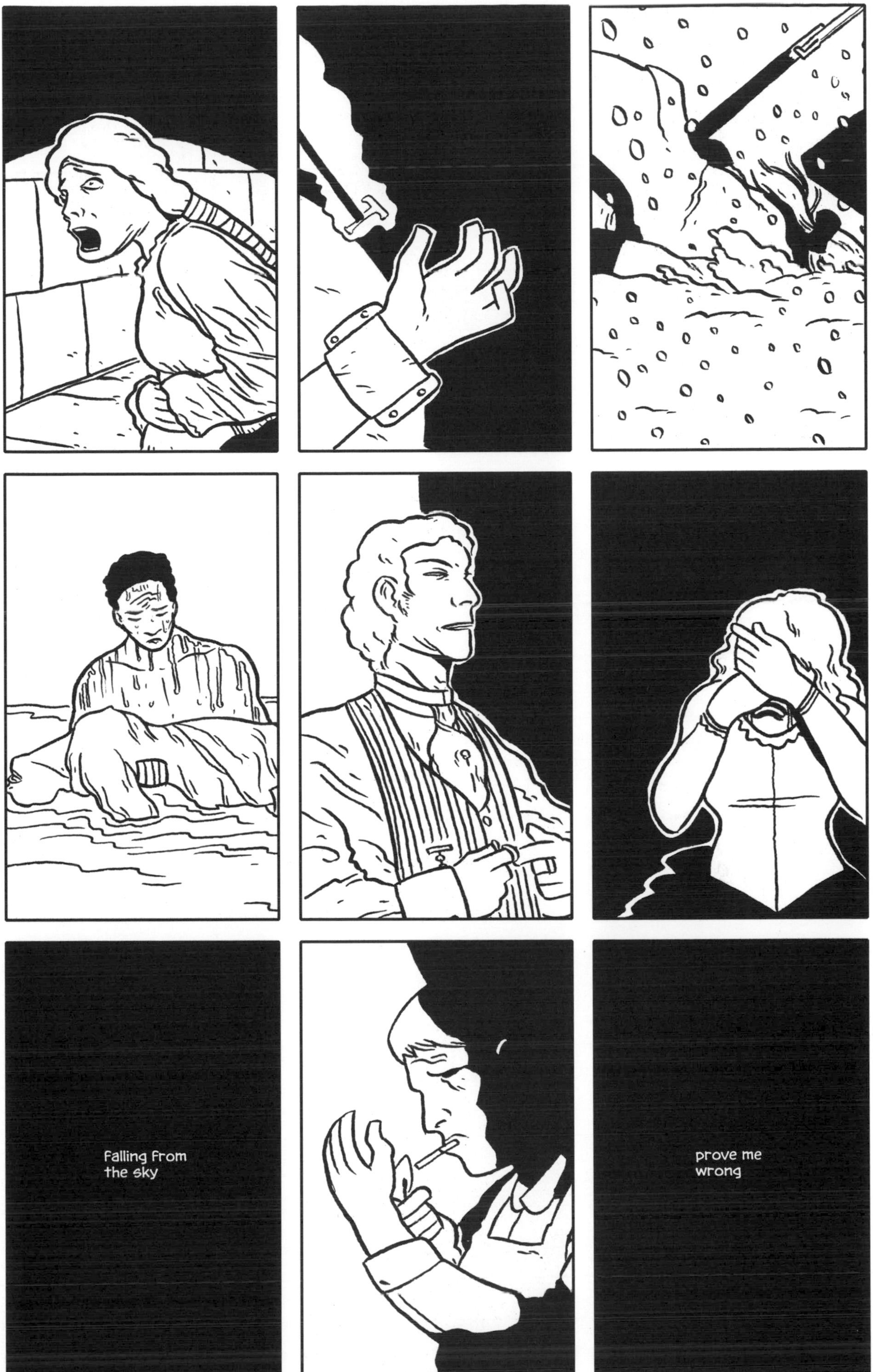
Falling from
the sky
prove me
wrong

in this world of darkness
we are very small

in this world of water
and wind, fire and stone

and whispering wood

and the world knows
things we can never
know

not dead I am not dead

my steps heavy and sure
I vow never to return

my mother lived and
died in this house
never learned never
knew the world

angry so angry

your fault this

you did this to me

I want to hold my son

but you take him
and I am heavy again

a wolf

I tear my enemy from his
mount with my bare hands

my bare hands my teeth
showing I am a lion
I am a wolf

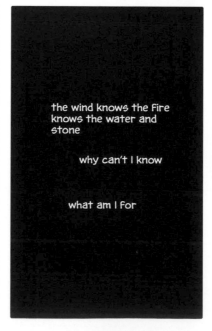

the wind knows the fire
knows the water and
stone

why can't I know

what am I for

heavy smoke of burning
bodies rolls over the
cobblestone and if this
is it if this is the end

then end it now

blow your trumpets and
render your judgement
because I am tired and

a sudden pain and hot damp

you bastards, you bastards is this a joke? you shits my hand burns my hand

is this mercy?

where am I

with my hands I lift her out of black water and she is light as a bundle of twigs

I am light as a feather

He will not be seen with me

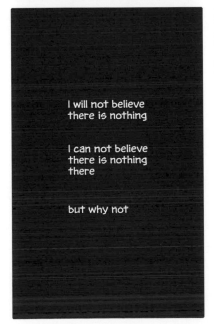

I will not believe there is nothing

I can not believe there is nothing there

but why not

smoke and thunder

the earth heaves and metal screams the noise it never stops

because I am afraid

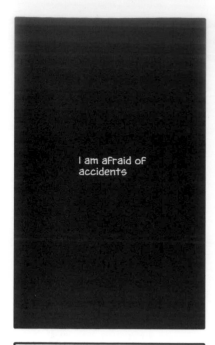

I am afraid of accidents

though I am struck down I rise again

I gaze out into the night and I know who I am and where I will go

you see I do need you

I gave the secret away

bleating and screaming terrified I left them and the wolves

dealing death

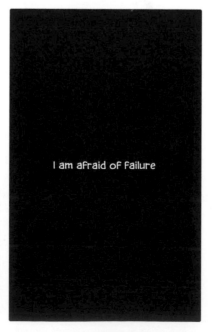

I am afraid of failure

God all this noise all the wailing and coughing God I can't hear I can't hear you and I don't

God!

a little to live on, a little to dust away am I supposed to say thank you? For this?

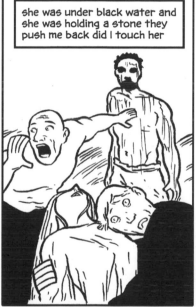

she was under black water and she was holding a stone they push me back did I touch her

though I am not from this place though I am not born wealthy but made

who wants to be seen with me I sing who wants

I am afraid of abandonment

a gust of wind and I am alive even in madness the smoke is sweet the wind is cool

I am afraid of darkness

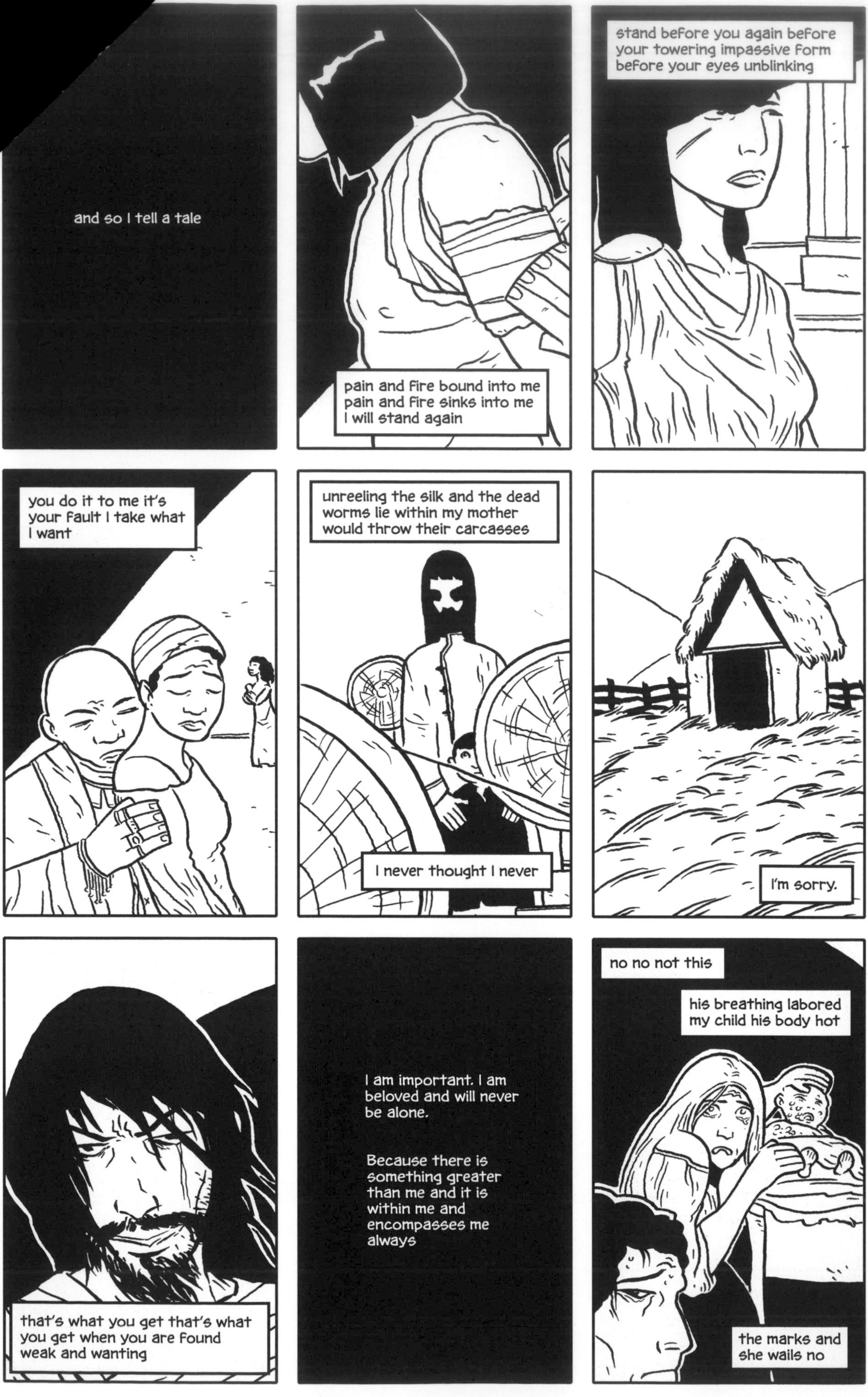
and so I tell a tale
pain and fire bound into me
pain and fire sinks into me
I will stand again
stand before you again before
your towering impassive form
before your eyes unblinking
you do it to me it's
your fault I take what
I want
unreeling the silk and the dead
worms lie within my mother
would throw their carcasses
I never thought I never
I'm sorry.
that's what you get that's what
you get when you are found
weak and wanting
I am important. I am
beloved and will never
be alone.
Because there is
something greater
than me and it is
within me and
encompasses me
always
no no not this
his breathing labored
my child his body hot
the marks and
she wails no

my Lord presses a cool hand to my burning flesh I am shivering into pieces

he loves me

this is the evil time of night I am a mill

I am a mill of filth and evil

so many of us chopped to bits men chopped

she sent herself into black water I only wanted to bring her out

perfume and kerosene and no matter what they say I sing and when I sing

they love me

but more than that

when I sing I am in love

that it knows me and loves me

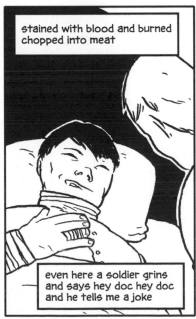

stained with blood and burned chopped into meat

even here a soldier grins and says hey doc hey doc and he tells me a joke

even though it knows me it loves me

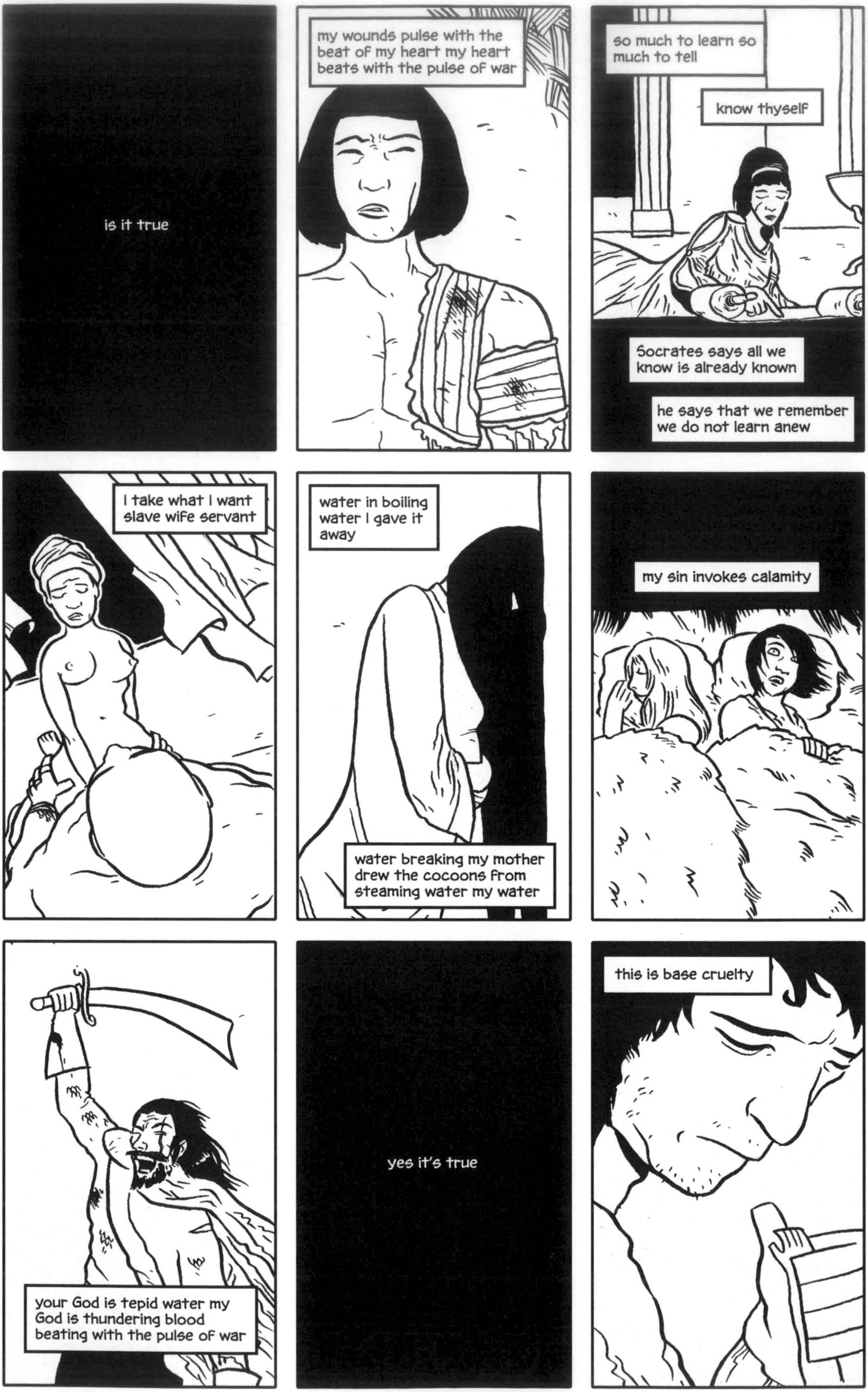
is it true
my wounds pulse with the beat of my heart my heart beats with the pulse of war
so much to learn so much to tell
know thyself
Socrates says all we know is already known
he says that we remember we do not learn anew
I take what I want slave wife servant
water in boiling water I gave it away
water breaking my mother drew the cocoons from steaming water my water
my sin invokes calamity
your God is tepid water my God is thundering blood beating with the pulse of war
yes it's true
this is base cruelty

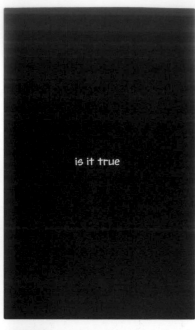

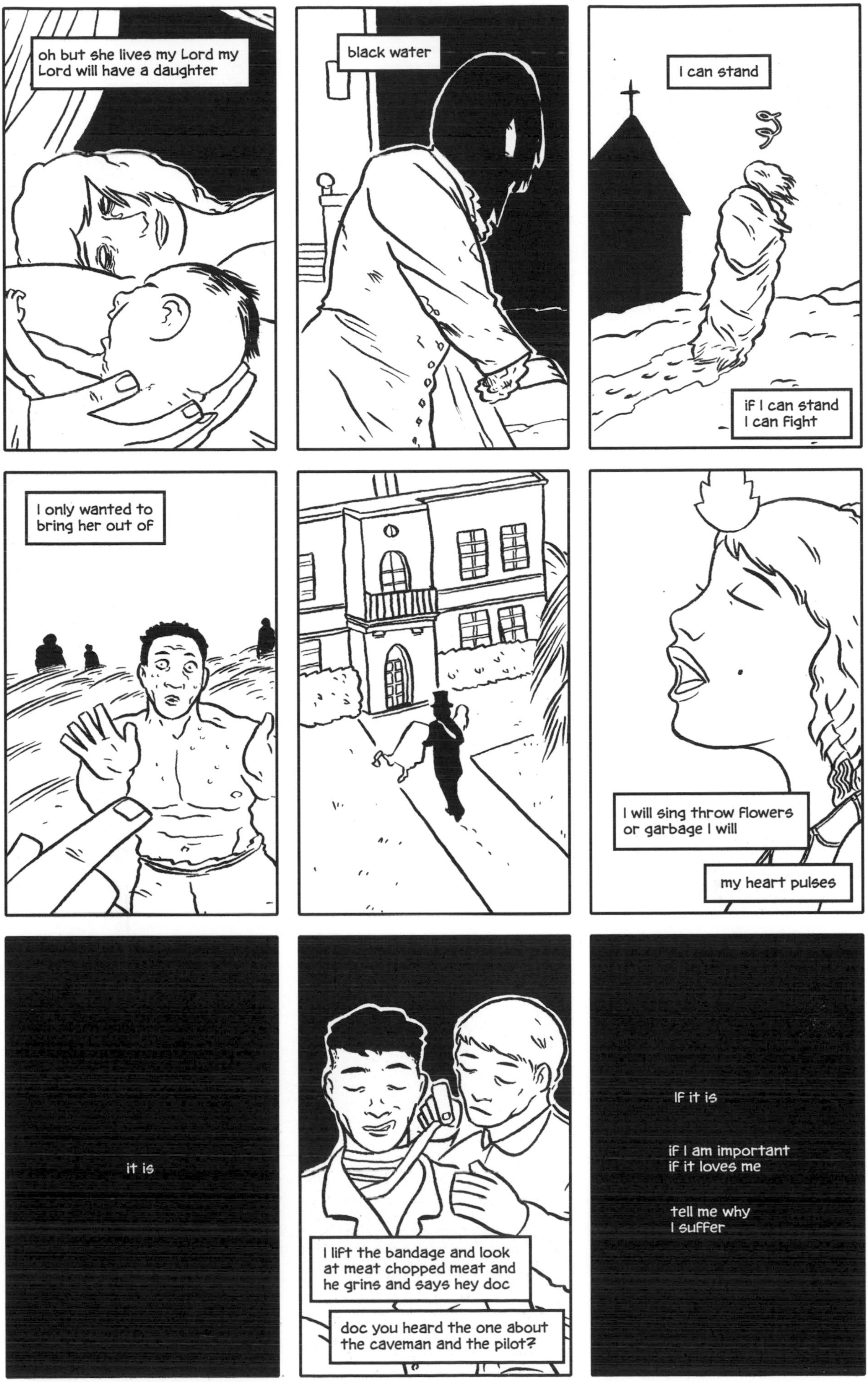
oh but she lives my Lord my Lord will have a daughter
black water
I can stand
if I can stand I can fight
I only wanted to bring her out of
I will sing throw flowers or garbage I will
my heart pulses
it is
I lift the bandage and look at meat chopped meat and he grins and says hey doc
doc you heard the one about the caveman and the pilot?
If it is
if I am important if it loves me
tell me why I suffer

take me back to the line
I tell them take me back

let me show that I am
unbroken let me look
at the enemy and know

all we are is memory
my mother is gone

don't look at me like
that don't make me
tell you again

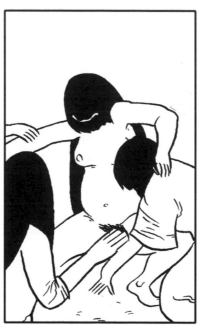

Forgive me how will we
live? Forgive me

nobody deserves my
pain but me if I lie
if I am evil

send it to me

whatever you
have send it

what possible gain
what possible purpose

I would give myself
you take him instead

are you perverse

110

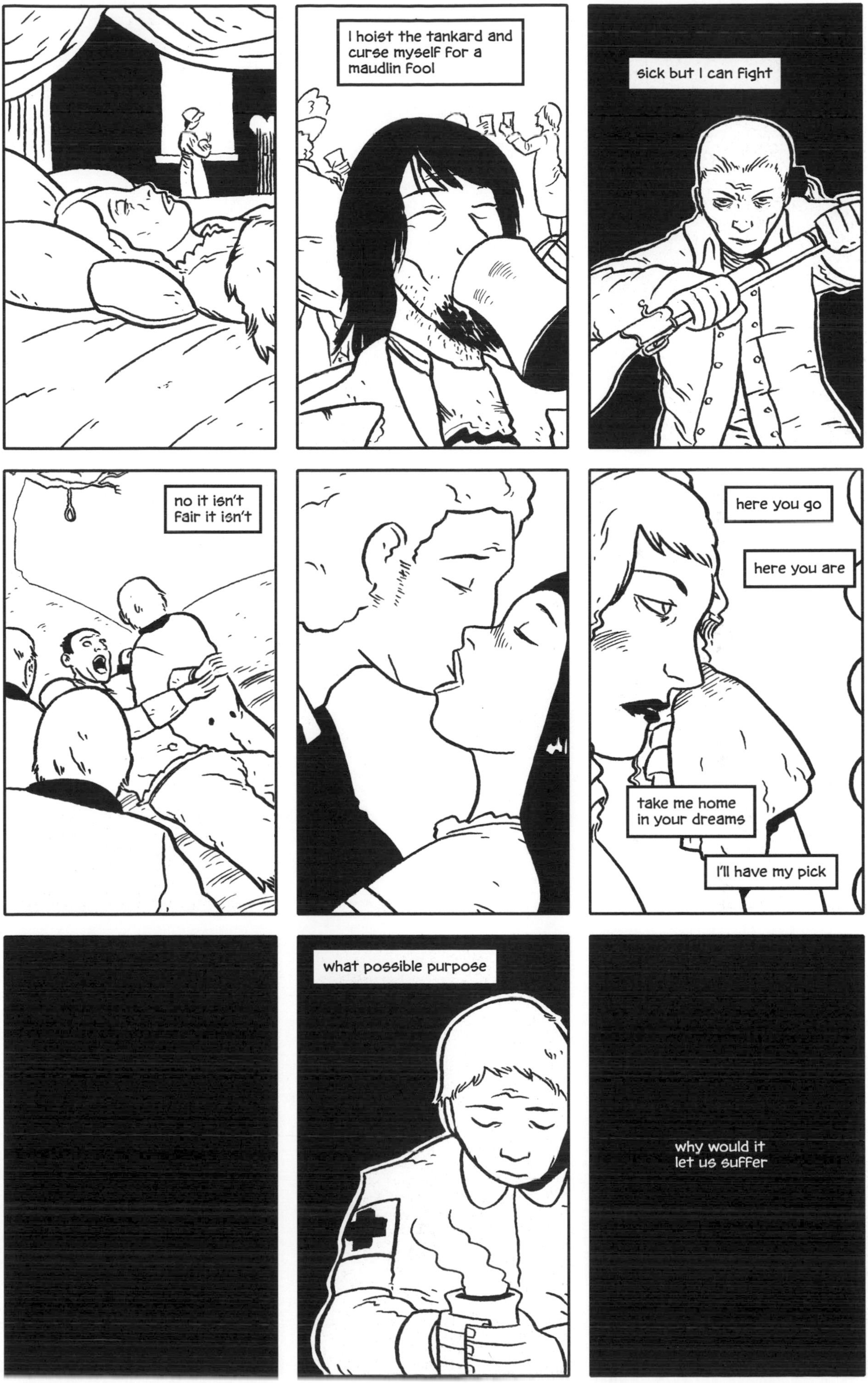
I hoist the tankard and curse myself for a maudlin fool
sick but I can fight
no it isn't fair it isn't
here you go
here you are
take me home in your dreams
I'll have my pick
what possible purpose
why would it let us suffer

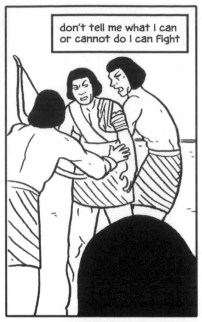

don't tell me what I can or cannot do I can fight

offer up your gold for what beg the Goddess on your knees for what

blessed boy

what little remains

comes to me

what possible reason madness and cruelty

murderer

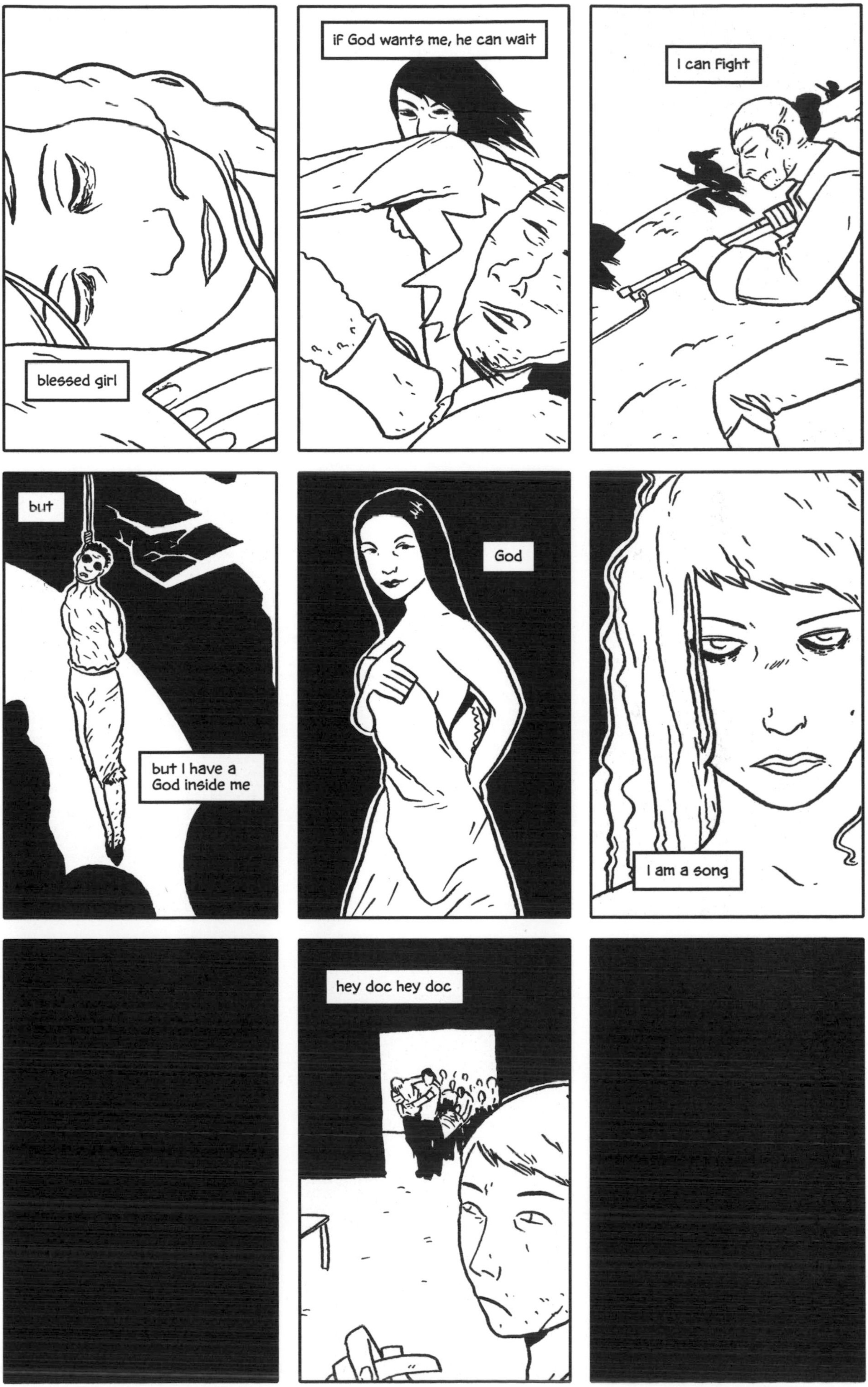
blessed girl
if God wants me, he can wait
I can fight
but
but I have a God inside me
God
I am a song
hey doc hey doc

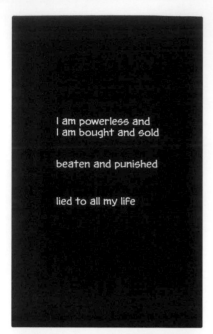

I am powerless and
I am bought and sold

beaten and punished

lied to all my life

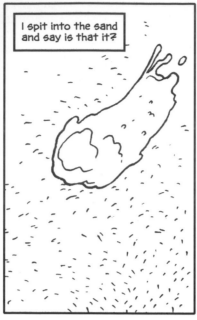

I spit into the sand
and say is that it?

give what you have
and for what? to bear your
marks with greater pride?

I bear a mark

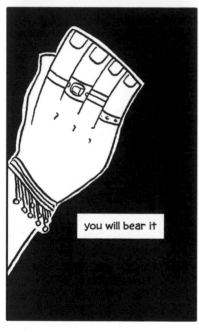

you will bear it

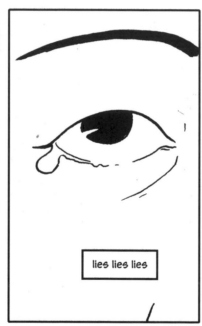

lies lies lies

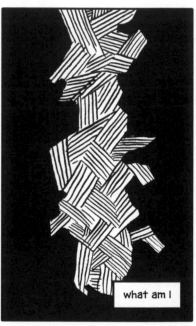

what am I

just another animal under
the blade the wounds I
bear the little marks

nothing

no

I live in Hell

in corruption

the streets seethe
with worms and rot

must I sleep now?
I want to see my daughter
we laugh in sooty heat and I call for another
dear Lord, while we stand we can fight
though we cough and stumble we can fight
choking
heaven I am in heaven
I will live forever
what am I not seeing?
what is this?
what am I?
what am I?

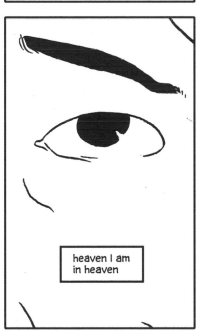

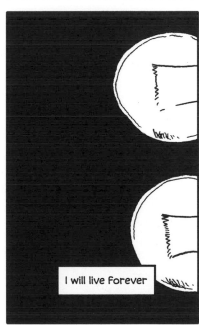

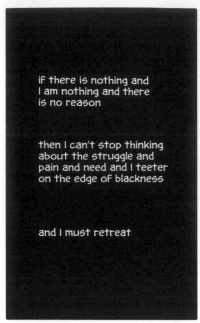

if there is nothing and I am nothing and there is no reason

then I can't stop thinking about the struggle and pain and need and I teeter on the edge of blackness

and I must retreat

the wound is deep and in time the arm collapses to my side weak and withered

I learn to live such as I may but I can no longer draw a bow

in time

come with me son

in time you will learn

the worms are a multitude now a forest rustling in the shelves servants flow in and out of the nursery and they tend the worms they ply the secret

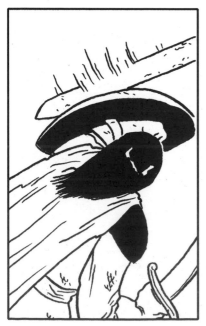

with open eyes I know I choose to step back

he wasn't enough in the passage of the plague my wife falls my last love and hope you took

everyone

I teeter in the garden

did I dream the years

years look at me you bastard I am a mill

I grind people and spit out gold you saved me for this

victory is ours we are free

with open eyes I say yes I am enfolded and infused with something

I am small and it is huge

I keep it within me

we all do

I walk in the street with my love father I own this street

a warm spring day and a perfect cup of coffee

I hear someone whisper my name in wonder and I smile

every night I sing every season I take a lover

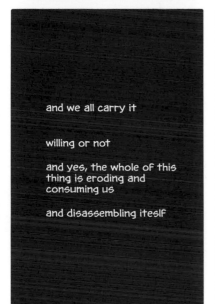

and we all carry it

willing or not

and yes, the whole of this thing is eroding and consuming us

and disassembling iteslf

victory

I mumble around my smoke

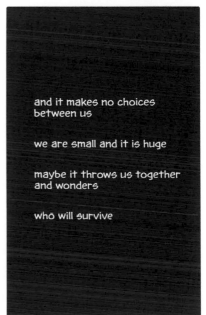

and it makes no choices between us

we are small and it is huge

maybe it throws us together and wonders

who will survive

but why?

listen to me I am what I am because the clash never ends

the clash claims us all some die in glory and some are shamed to live on

time comes and we rise in their estimation fertility and strength are in demand

listen to me it's simple

yes I will sully my hands with work

don't forget that my mother built this I built this not you

listen to me

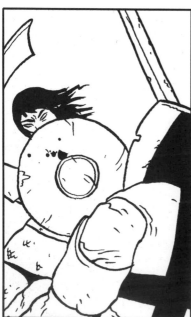

and to serve what?

the lucky few they say we are the lucky few the survivors

in my garden I fall

dreaming I fall

teetering on the crooked path

we tore it down and we pledge to build it up again

if I choose to believe what I have chosen to believe

I will provide for my children the way you provided for me I laugh among the big men but I know what I am and what you did for me

the new season

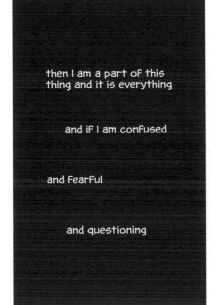

then I am a part of this thing and it is everything

and if I am confused

and fearful

and questioning

and I mumble as they hand me my paper they say I am a doctor

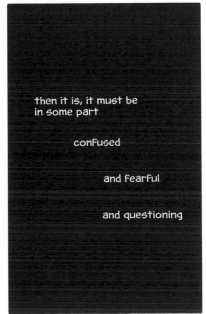

then it is, it must be in some part

confused

and fearful

and questioning

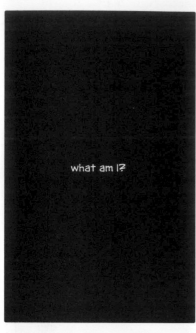

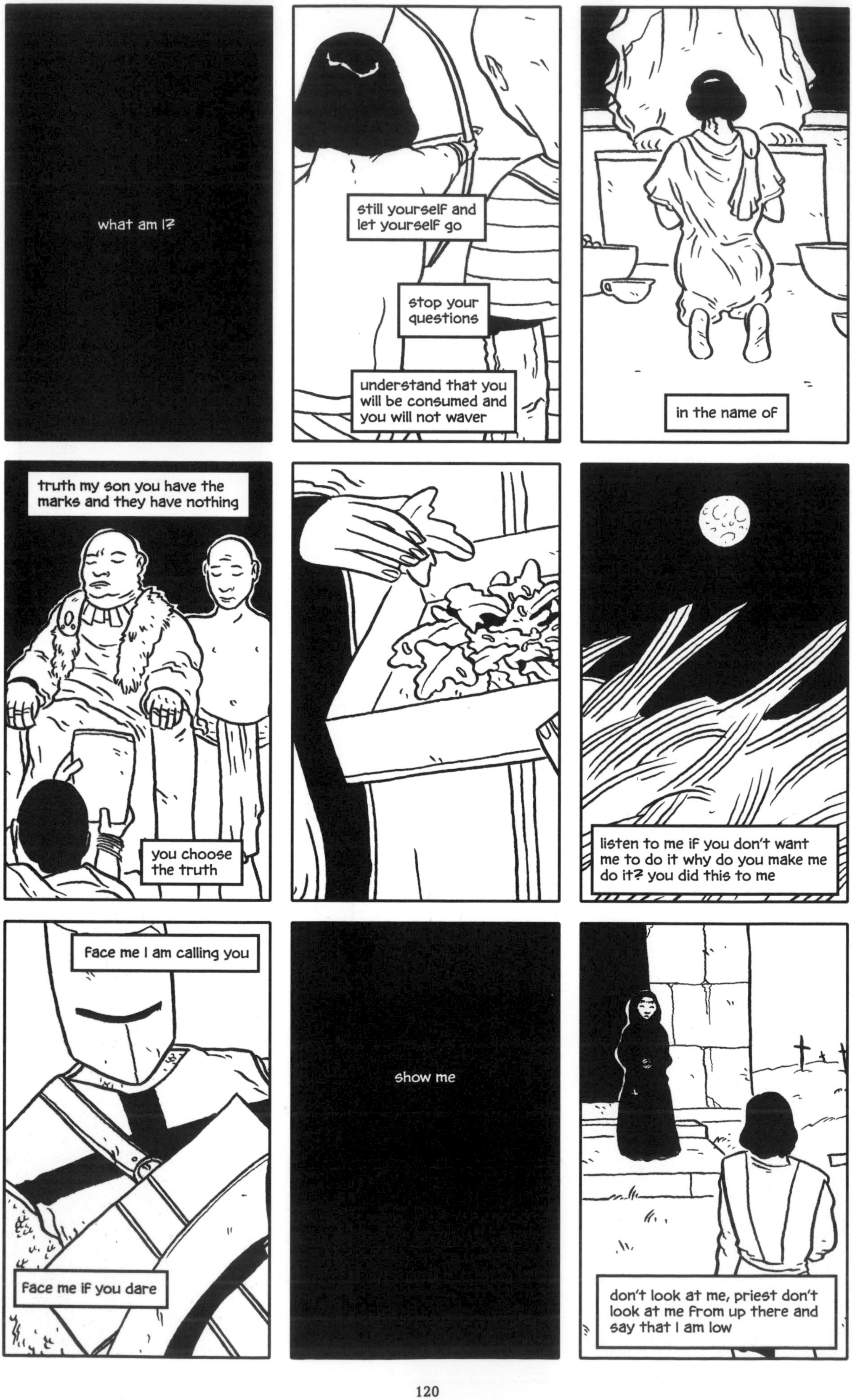
what am I?
still yourself and let yourself go
stop your questions
understand that you will be consumed and you will not waver
in the name of
truth my son you have the marks and they have nothing
you choose the truth
listen to me if you don't want me to do it why do you make me do it? you did this to me
face me I am calling you
face me if you dare
show me
don't look at me, priest don't look at me from up there and say that I am low

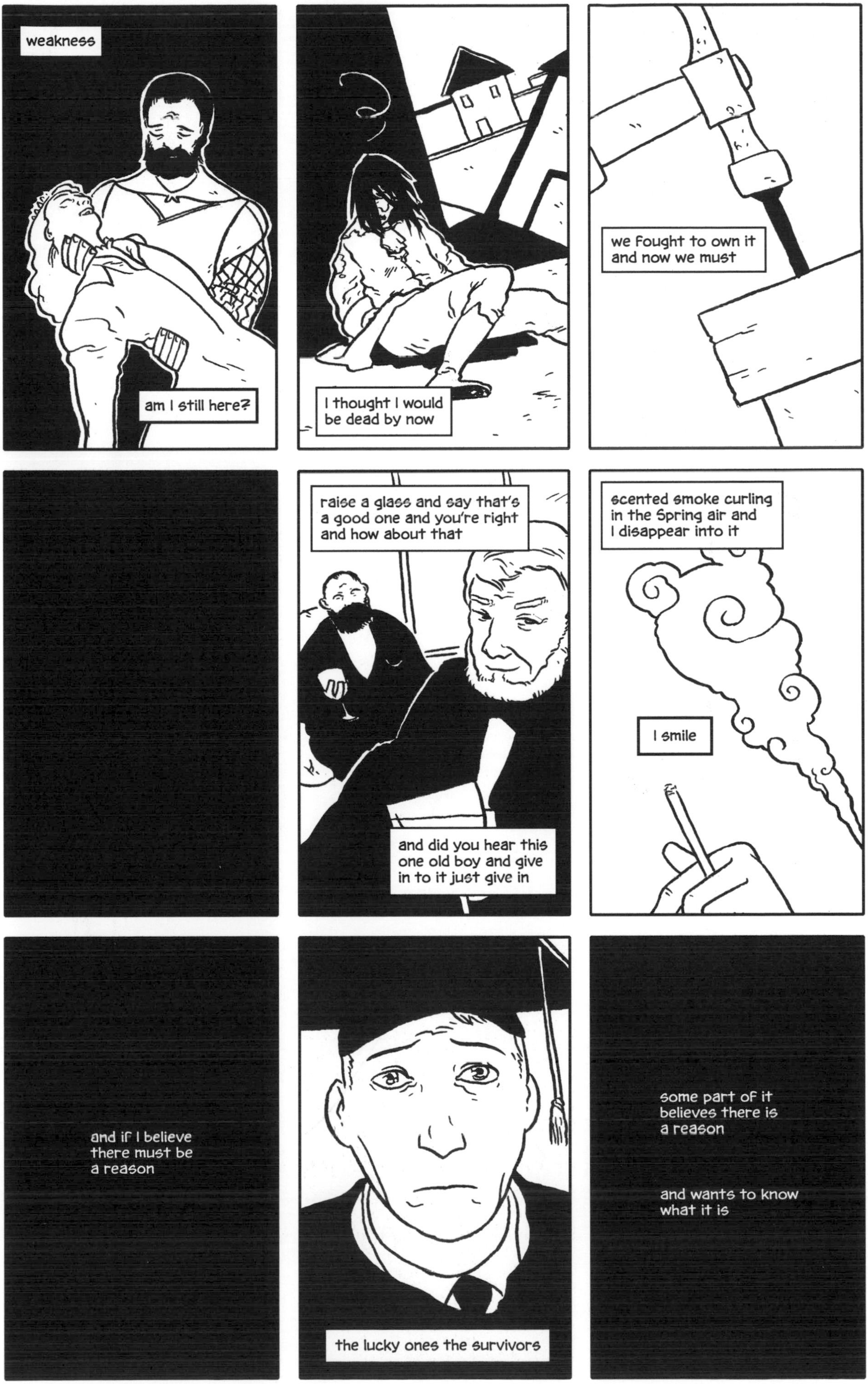
weakness
am I still here?
I thought I would be dead by now
we fought to own it and now we must
raise a glass and say that's a good one and you're right and how about that
and did you hear this one old boy and give in to it just give in
scented smoke curling in the Spring air and I disappear into it
I smile
and if I believe there must be a reason
the lucky ones the survivors
some part of it believes there is a reason
and wants to know what it is

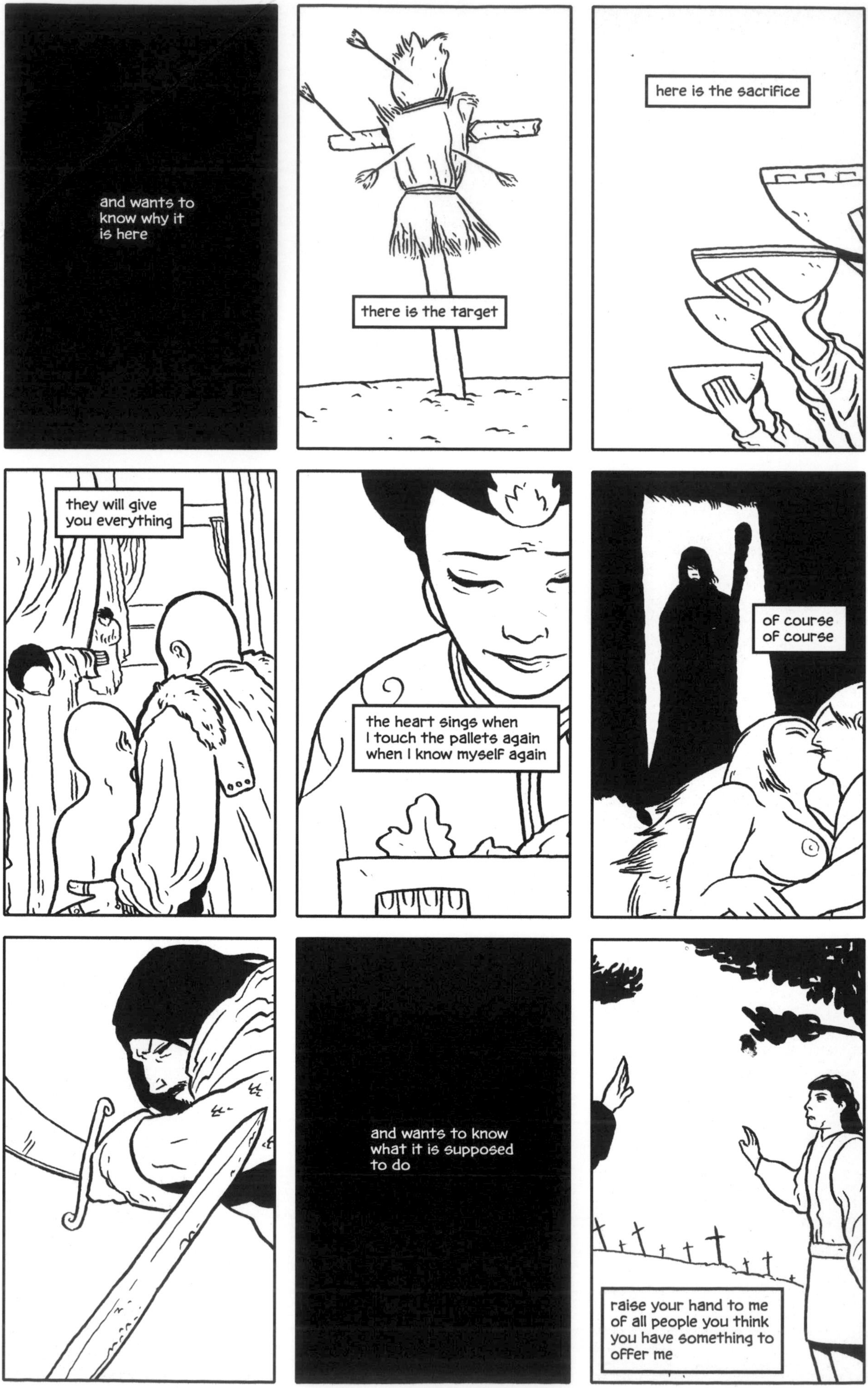
and wants to
know why it
is here
there is the target
here is the sacrifice
they will give
you everything
the heart sings when
I touch the pallets again
when I know myself again
of course
of course
and wants to know
what it is supposed
to do
raise your hand to me
of all people you think
you have something to
offer me

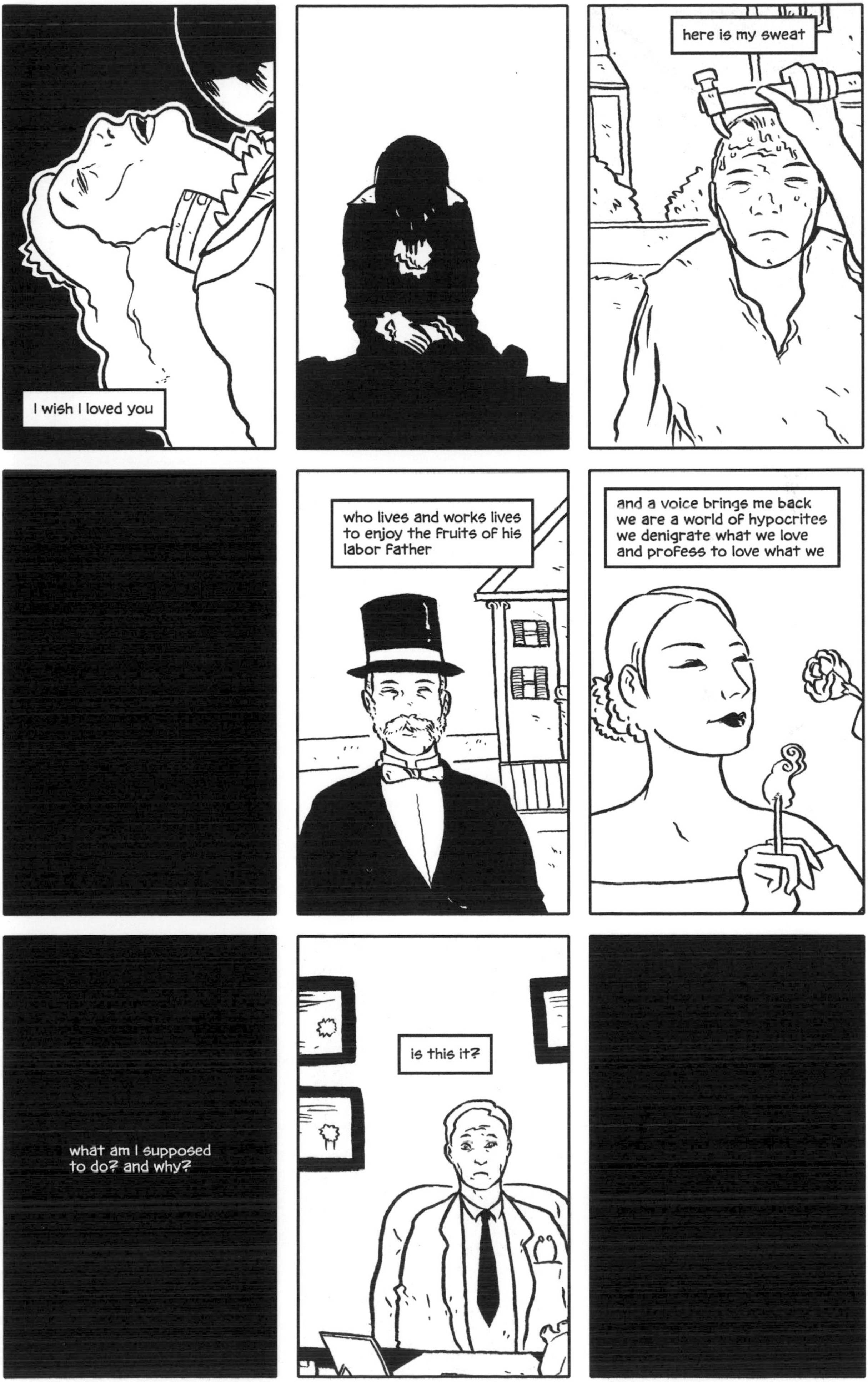
I wish I loved you
here is my sweat
who lives and works lives to enjoy the fruits of his labor Father
and a voice brings me back we are a world of hypocrites we denigrate what we love and profess to love what we
what am I supposed to do? and why?
is this it?

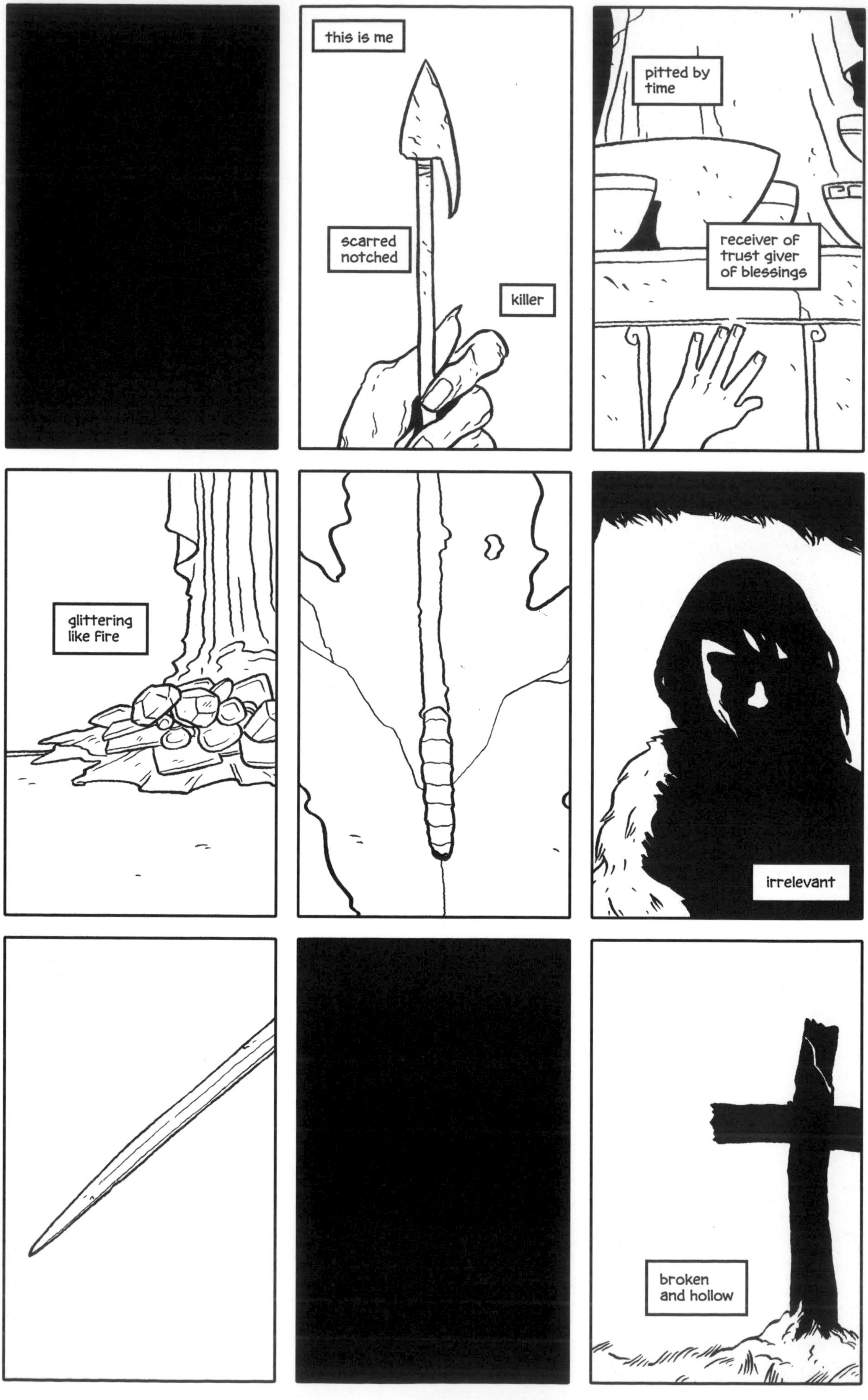
this is me
scarred notched
killer
pitted by time
receiver of trust giver of blessings
glittering like fire
irrelevant
broken and hollow

this is me
faint and failing
searching
treading the ground
I swore I would never
standing proud
eyes turned
to the moon
this is me
the lucky one

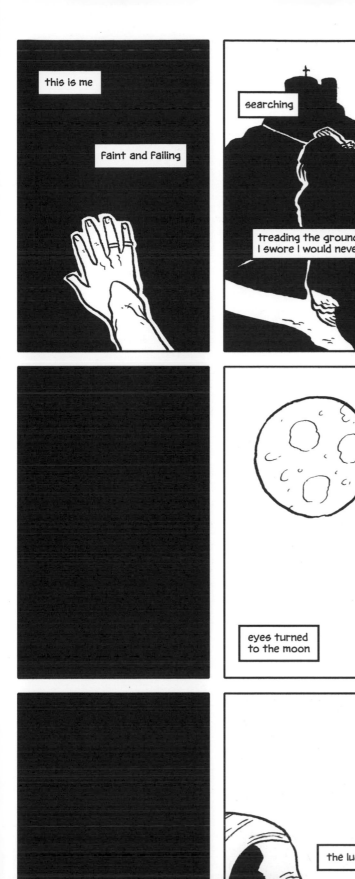

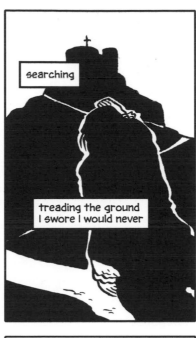

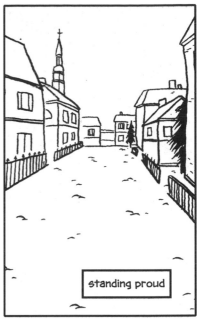

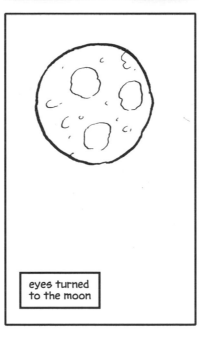

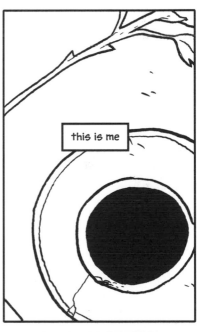

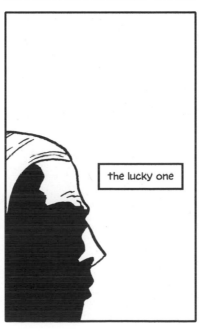

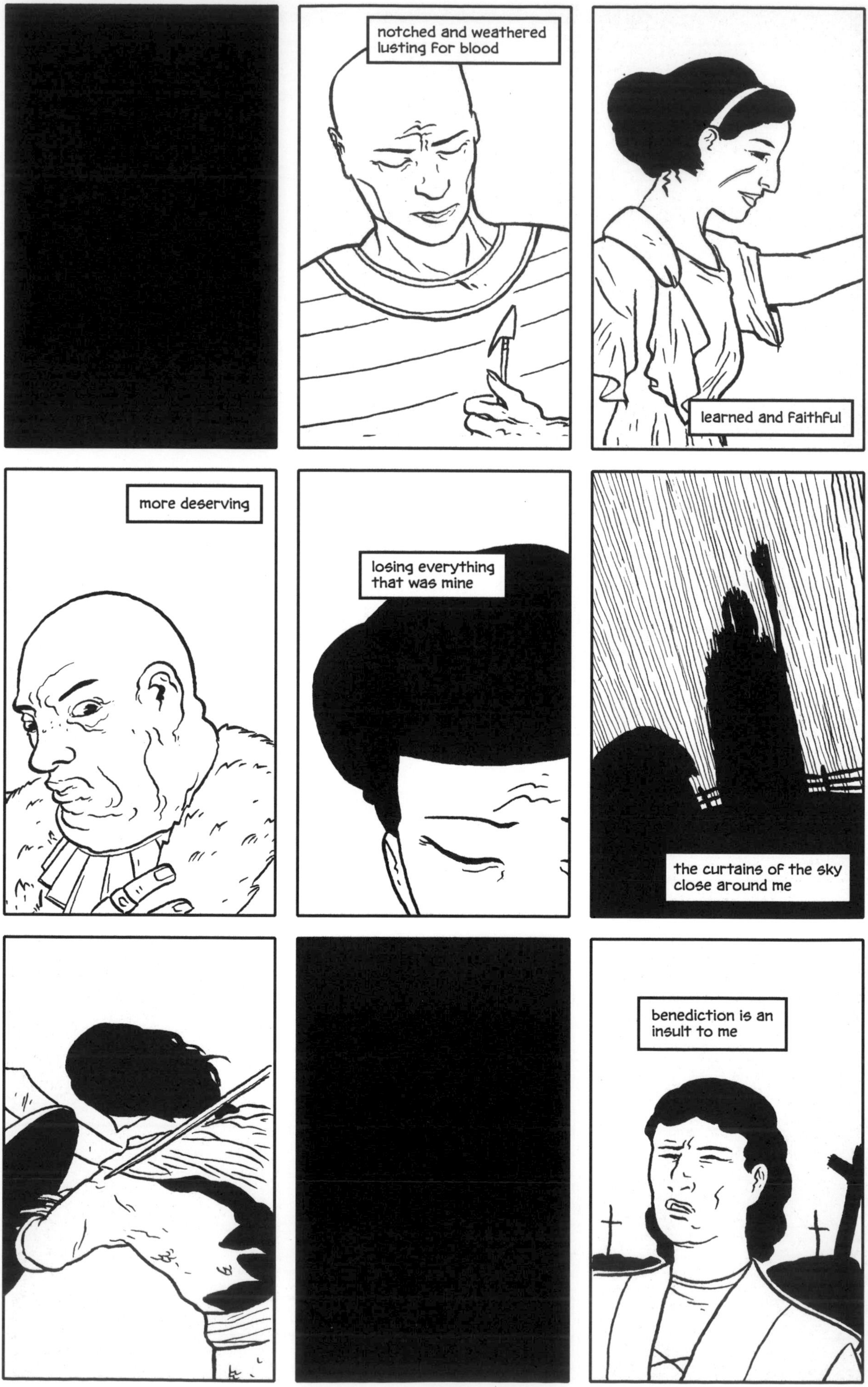
notched and weathered
lusting for blood
learned and faithful
more deserving
losing everything
that was mine
the curtains of the sky
close around me
benediction is an
insult to me

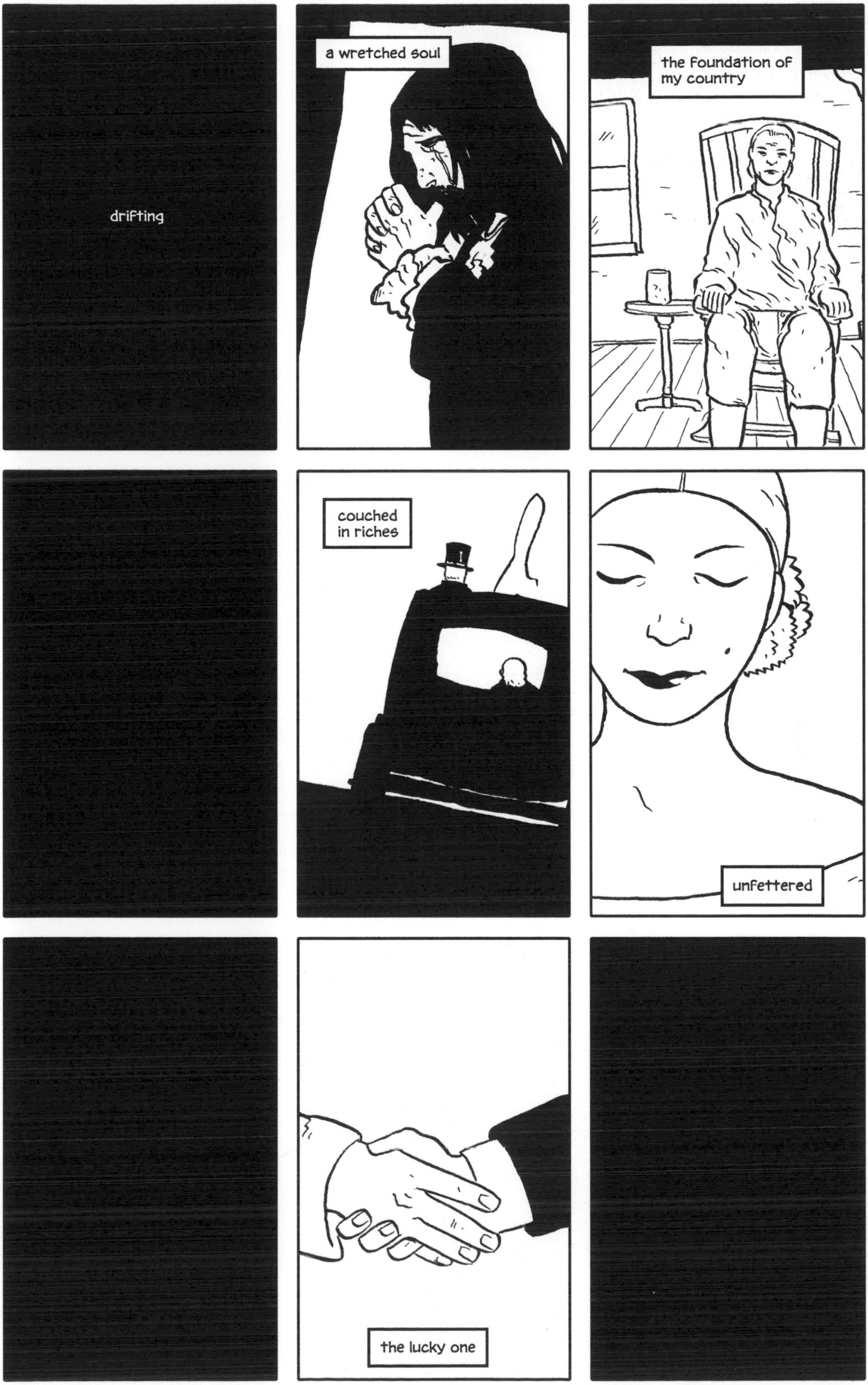
drifting
a wretched soul
the foundation of my country
couched in riches
unfettered
the lucky one

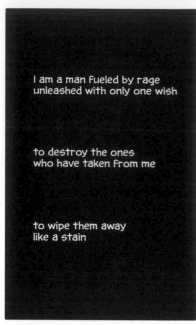

I am a man fueled by rage unleashed with only one wish

to destroy the ones who have taken from me

to wipe them away like a stain

when war breaks once more I ride with the chariot a thousand men march chanting my name

changes are wrought within me within us all

where is my reward?

I have been pushed aside the silk is made and traded my magic is sold

my sons are raised by servants

if you didn't want me to do it why did you make me want it?

cleaved

no more questions

no more worry no more regret I have a small fire and it warms me I have an apple to eat and a knife to cut it with

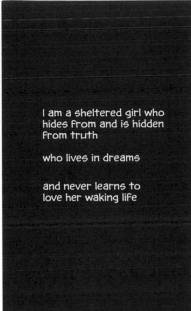

I am a sheltered girl who hides from and is hidden from truth

who lives in dreams

and never learns to love her waking life

it took me a long time to come back to this they ruined it he ruined it

look at me now and tell me if I was meant to live this way

I bled for this

a good cigar and a great house

the hushed whispers of an expectant audience

waiting listening

a Friday afternoon the motor purrs the sun in the sky

changes are wrought within me

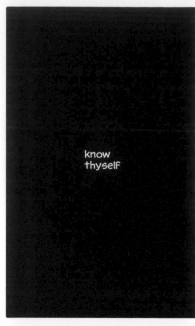

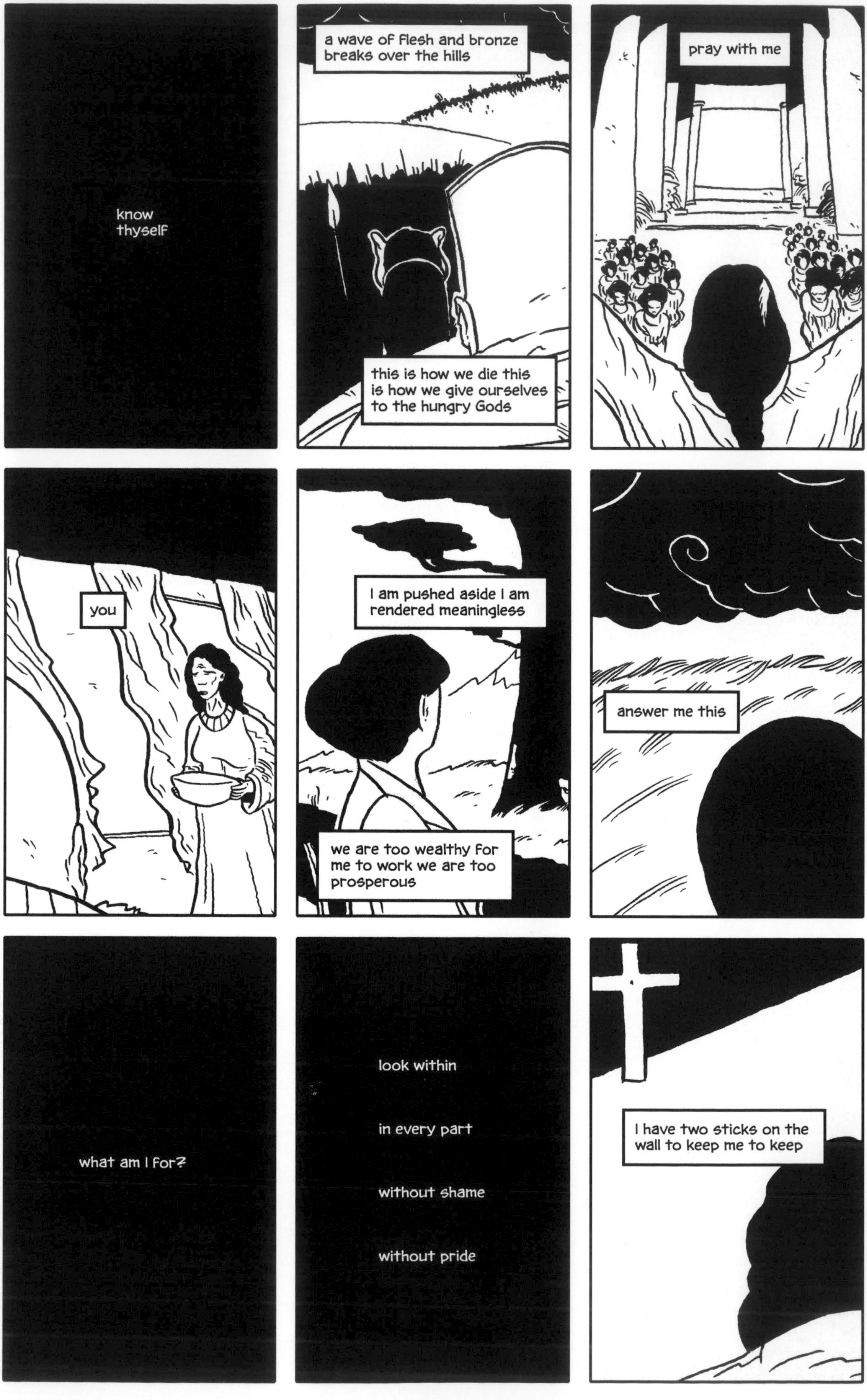
know thyself
a wave of flesh and bronze breaks over the hills
this is how we die this is how we give ourselves to the hungry Gods
pray with me
you
I am pushed aside I am rendered meaningless
we are too wealthy for me to work we are too prosperous
answer me this
what am I for?
look within
in every part
without shame
without pride
I have two sticks on the wall to keep me to keep

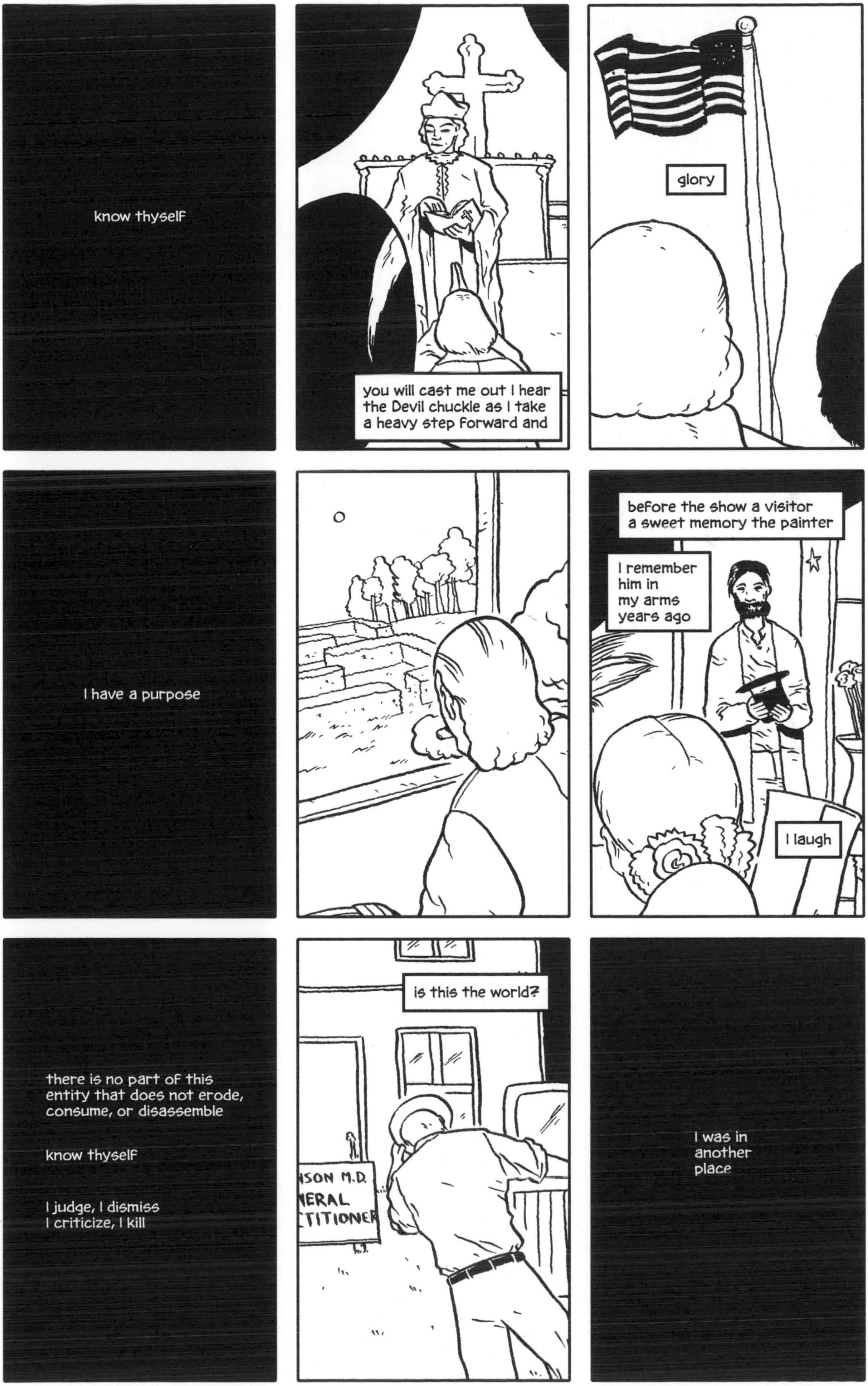
know thyself
you will cast me out I hear the Devil chuckle as I take a heavy step forward and
glory
I have a purpose
before the show a visitor a sweet memory the painter
I remember him in my arms years ago
I laugh
there is no part of this entity that does not erode, consume, or disassemble
know thyself
I judge, I dismiss I criticize, I kill
is this the world?
NSON M.D.
NERAL
CTITIONER
I was in another place

there is no feeling part of this entity that does not feel a need

we all feel a need

at my word a thousand arrows are nocked

at my word a thousand bows are raised

dance with me

I'm sick of you!

I'm sick of your need, of your demands

I'm sick

without my work

Answer me!

know thyself

duty

need

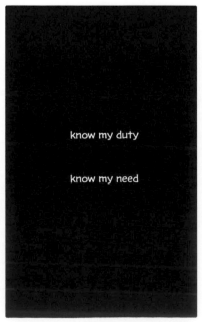

know my duty

know my need

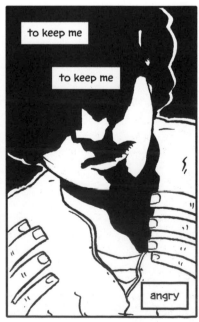

to keep me

to keep me

angry

I need to ask
questions

I need to
call out

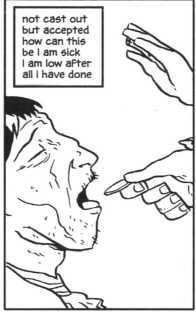

not cast out
but accepted
how can this
be I am sick
I am low after
all I have done

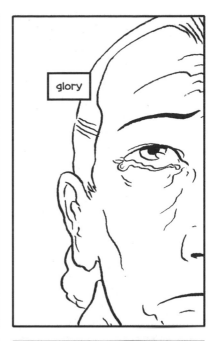

glory

to respond

a game on
the summer
lawn

the laughter of
children trills
and they call
out to me

and he sours it
with a sordid
demand

I do not brook
the demands
of men

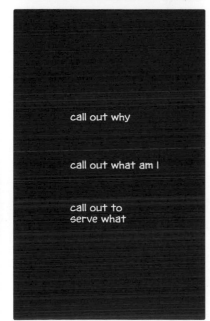

call out why

call out what am I

call out to
serve what

how can I be here when
I was over there?

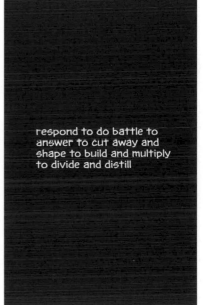

respond to do battle to
answer to cut away and
shape to build and multiply
to divide and distill

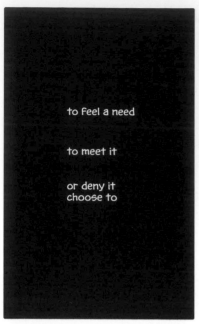

to feel a need

to meet it

or deny it
choose to

blacken the sky and rain down
in a whistling horde to winnow

raise the voices
of the chorus
change the pitch

she looks up
eyes glowing
in Firelight and
I see something
snap into place

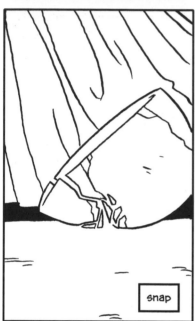

snap

servants to feed me

servants to dress me

servants to clear
the path before me

ANSWER ME!

WHY?

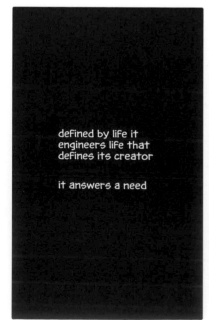

defined by life it
engineers life that
defines its creator

it answers a need

its needs provoke
our needs

our needs define
its needs

hundreds died in Fever and
pain before my eyes and
these sticks on every wall

what did they stave off?
who did they protect?

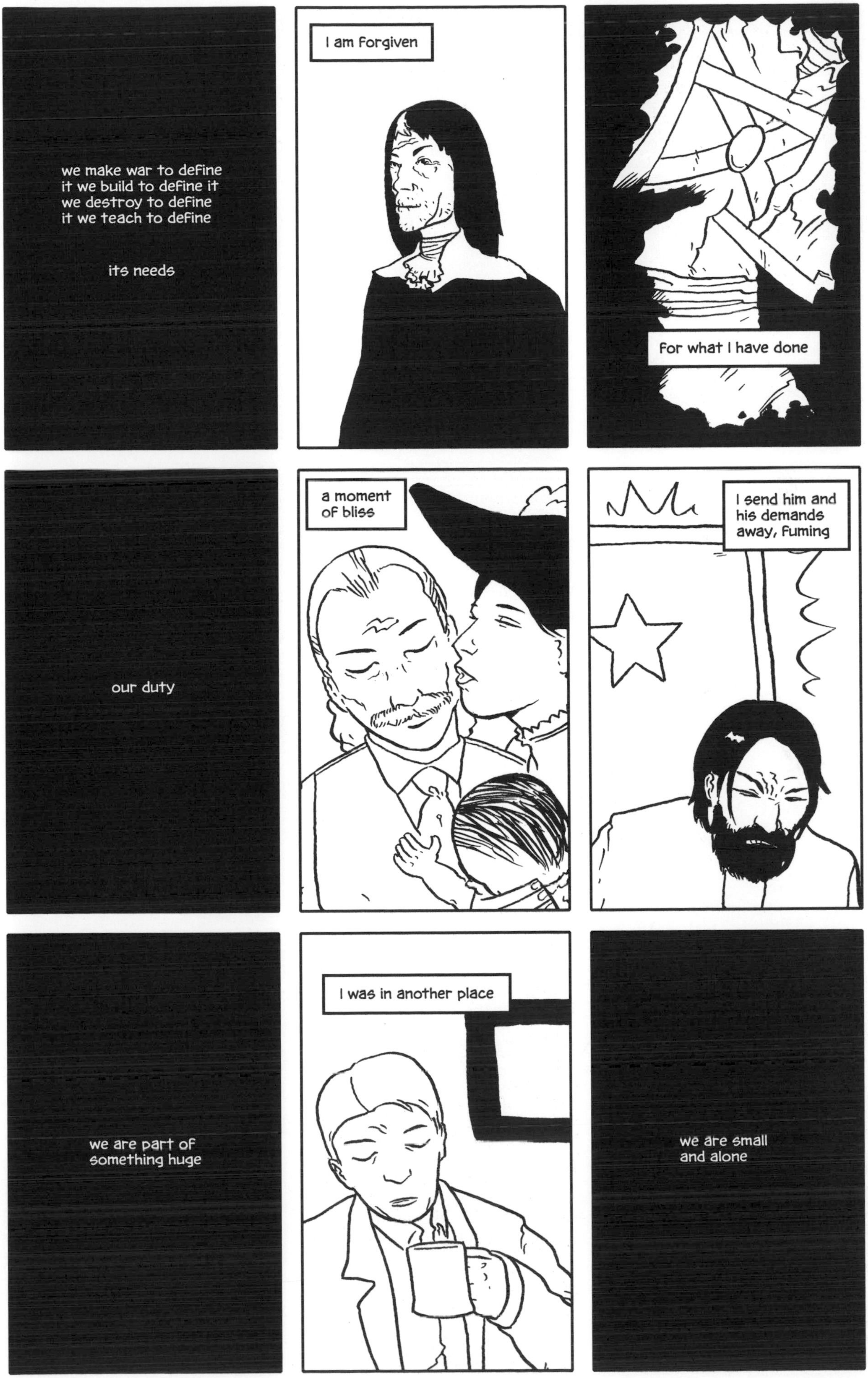
we make war to define
it we build to define it
we destroy to define
it we teach to define
its needs
I am forgiven
for what I have done
our duty
a moment
of bliss
I send him and
his demands
away, fuming
we are part of
something huge
I was in another place
we are small
and alone

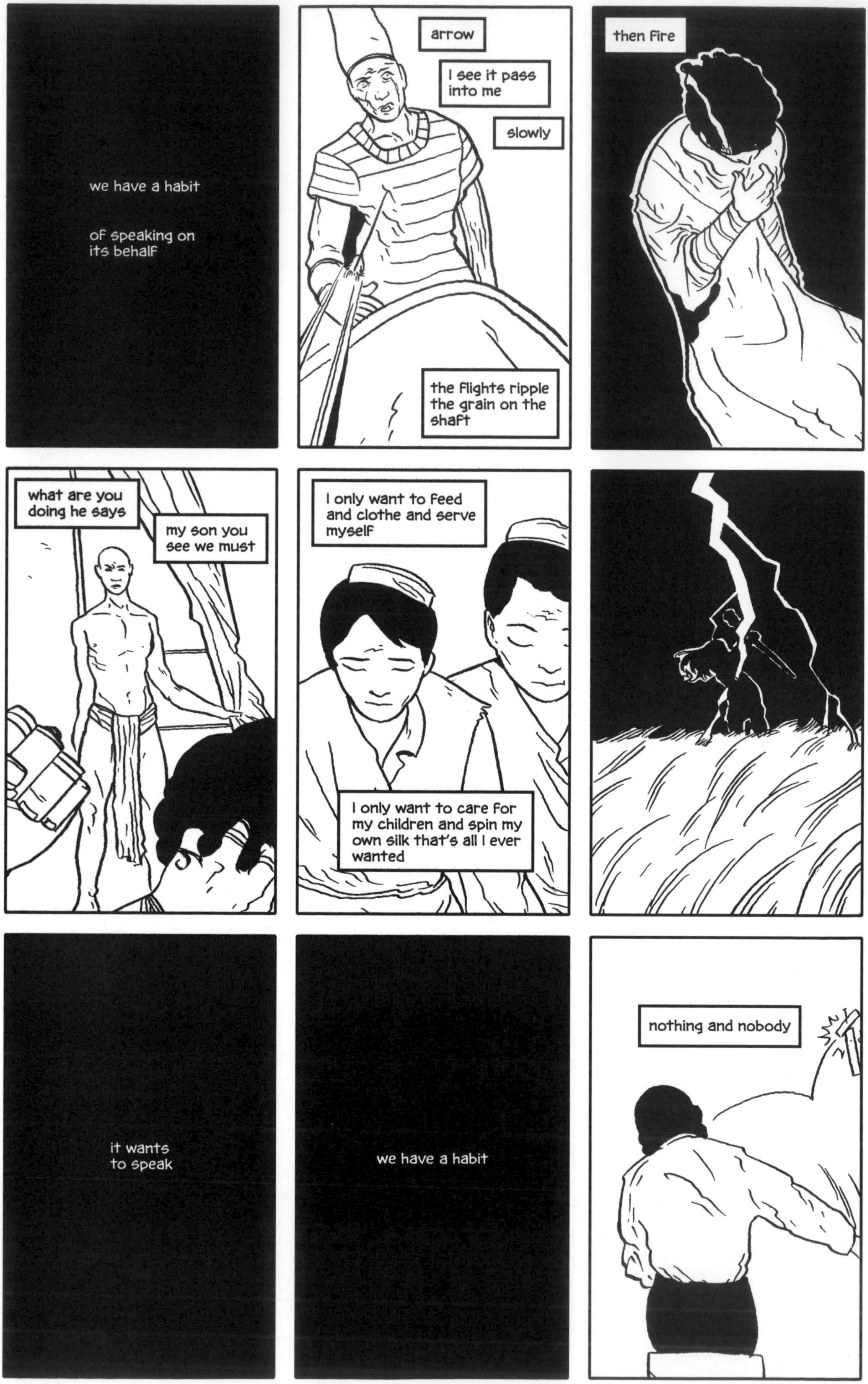
we have a habit
of speaking on its behalf
arrow
I see it pass into me
slowly
the flights ripple the grain on the shaft
then fire
what are you doing he says
my son you see we must
I only want to feed and clothe and serve myself
I only want to care for my children and spin my own silk that's all I ever wanted
it wants to speak
we have a habit
nothing and nobody

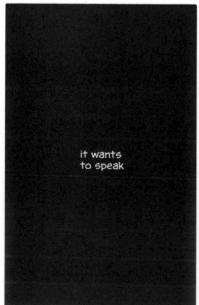

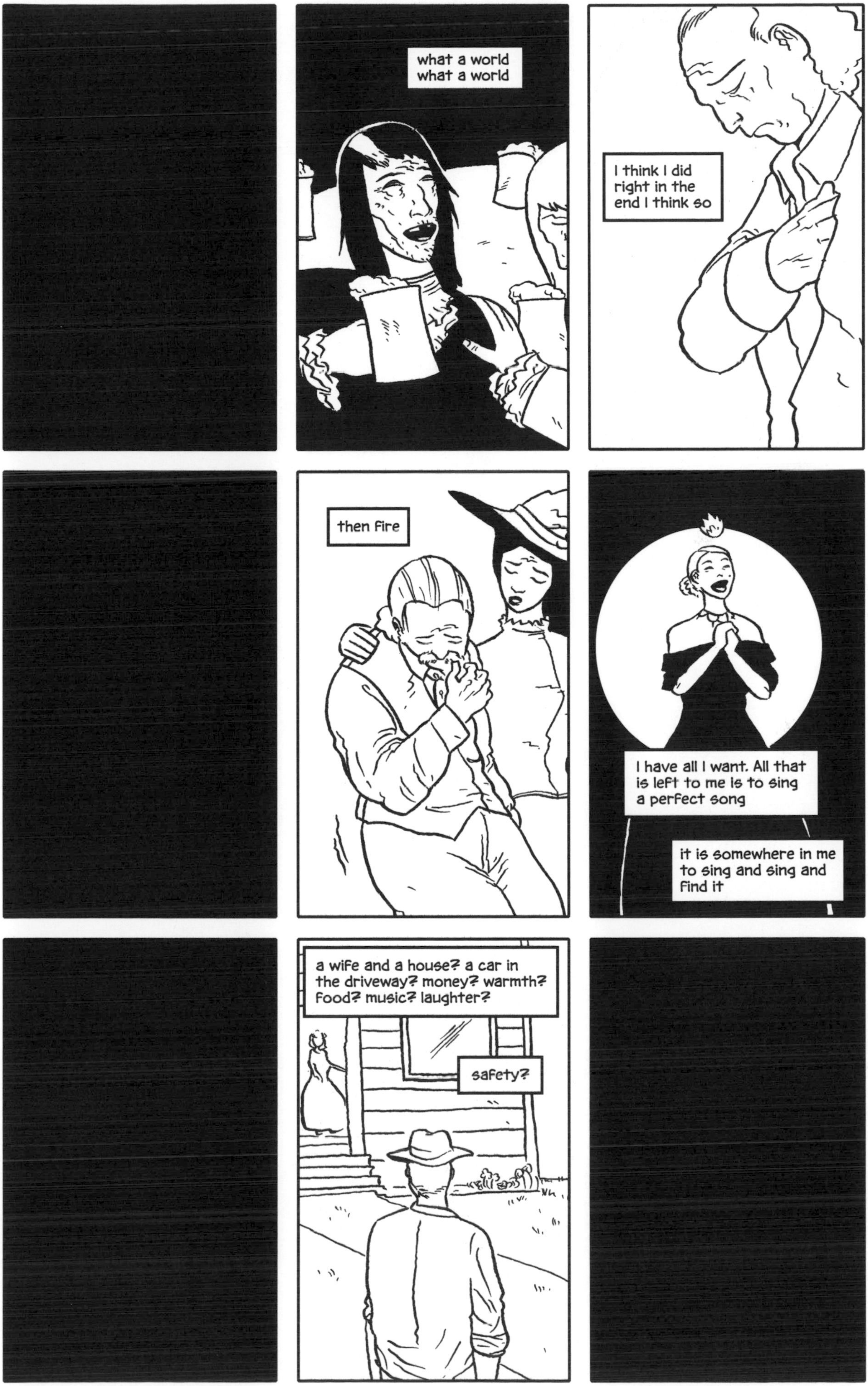
what a world
what a world
I think I did right in the end I think so
then fire
I have all I want. All that is left to me is to sing a perfect song
it is somewhere in me to sing and sing and find it
a wife and a house? a car in the driveway? money? warmth? food? music? laughter?
safety?

dear God

I do believe in you

but I have no idea
what you are

or what you represent
or what purpose you
serve

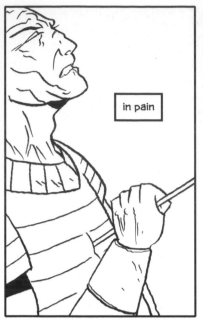

in pain

but a small
pain and already
it begins to fade

all these
concerned
faces

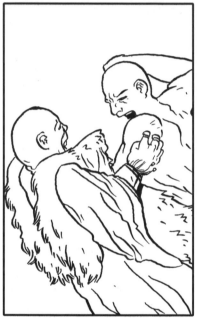

you never
understood

burning

or what we have
to do with it

or what effect
we have on you

or what effect
you have on us

I am a man who is
fired by desire by
need though he is
taught it is
perverse

I know there is no mercy
and there is no justice

and no protection

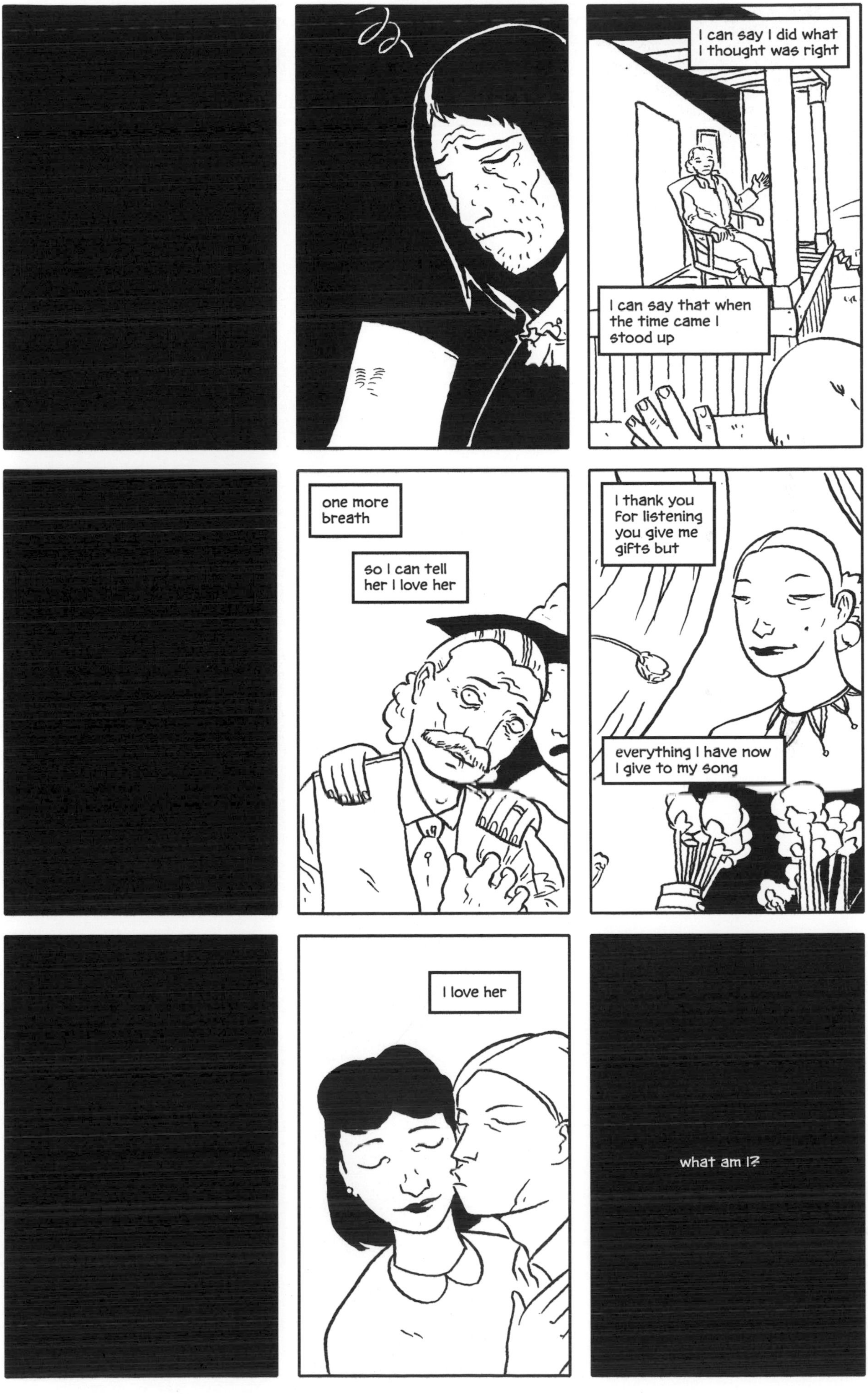
I can say I did what I thought was right
I can say that when the time came I stood up
one more breath
so I can tell her I love her
I thank you for listening you give me gifts but
everything I have now I give to my song
I love her
what am I?

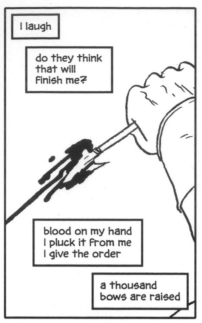
I laugh

do they think that will finish me?

blood on my hand
I pluck it from me
I give the order

a thousand bows are raised

when my time comes

our Goddess will take me up

my son did I not teach you

my sons

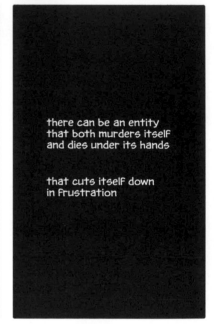
there can be an entity that both murders itself and dies under its hands

that cuts itself down in frustration

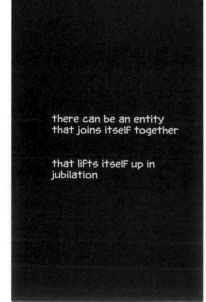
there can be an entity that joins itself together

that lifts itself up in jubilation

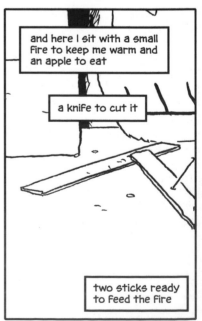
and here I sit with a small fire to keep me warm and an apple to eat

a knife to cut it

two sticks ready to feed the fire

sooner or later I am left with myself again

staggering at the edge of black water

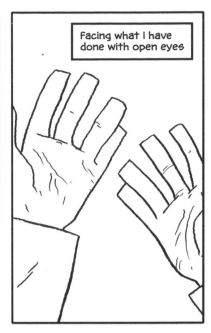

facing what I have done with open eyes

insofar as there is something beyond comprehending

it is beyond comprehending

God

a sudden shout

why

a soft bed and clean sheets? a calm and quiet night?

why?

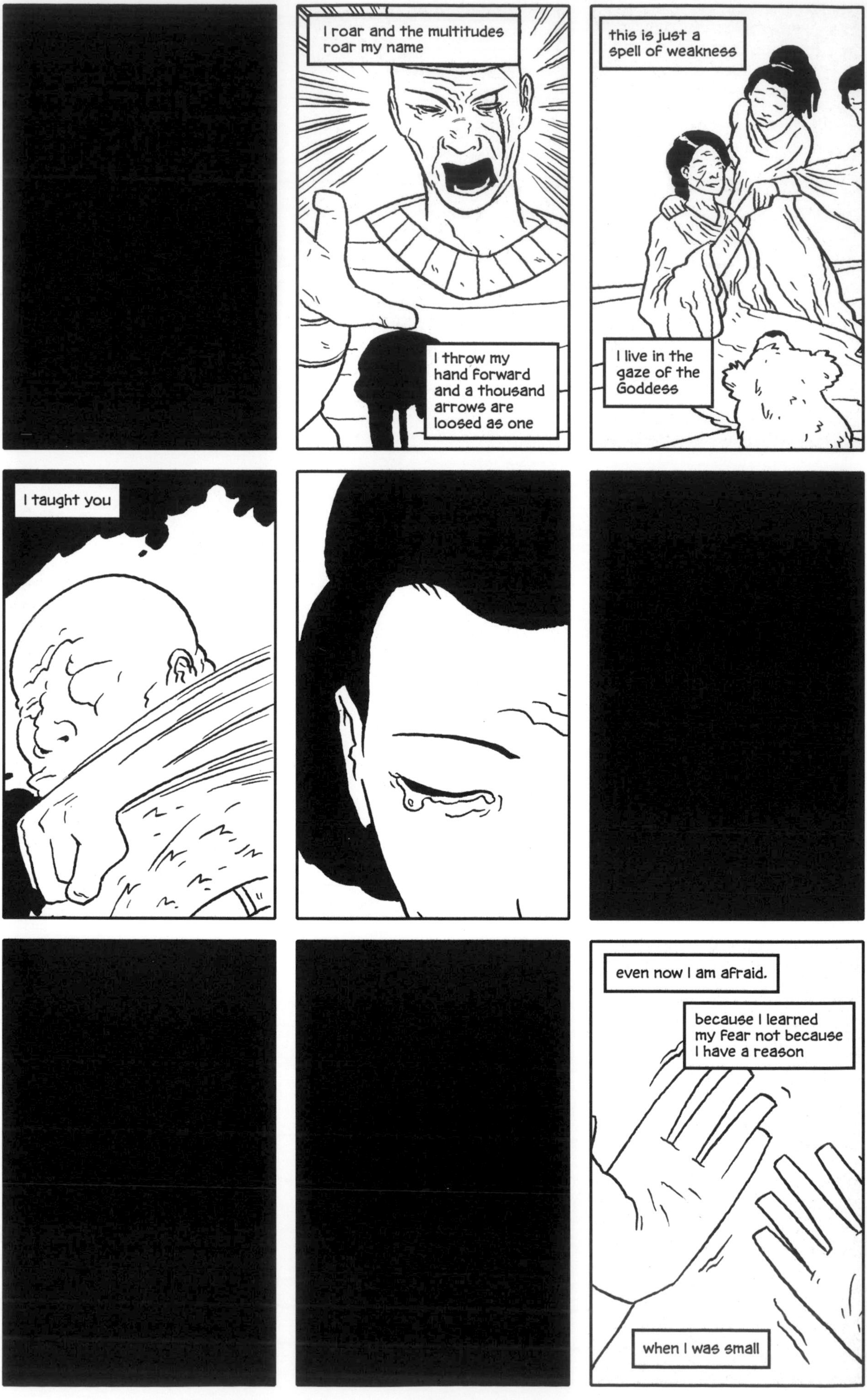
I roar and the multitudes roar my name
I throw my hand forward and a thousand arrows are loosed as one
this is just a spell of weakness
I live in the gaze of the Goddess
I taught you
even now I am afraid.
because I learned my fear not because I have a reason
when I was small

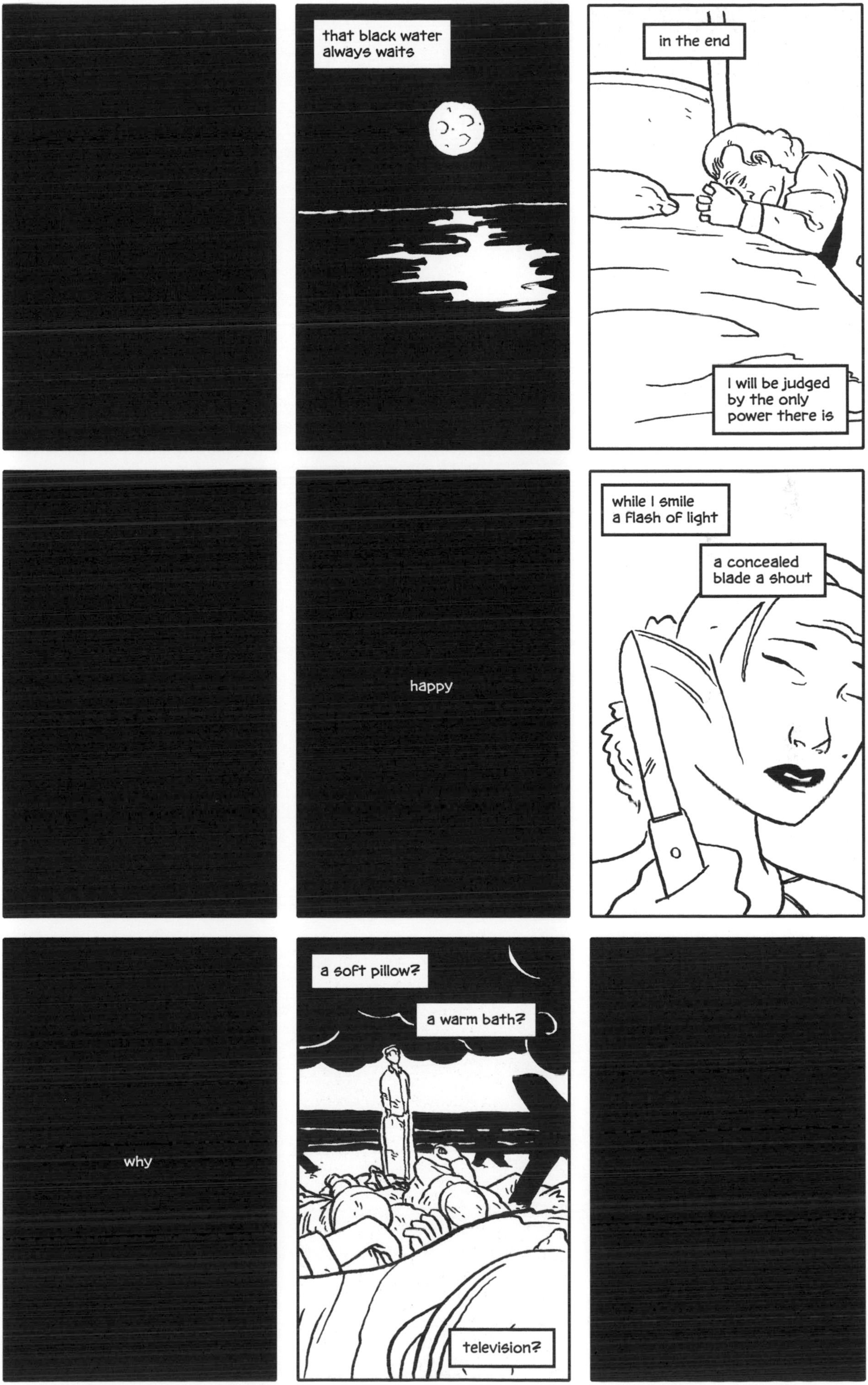
that black water
always waits
in the end
I will be judged
by the only
power there is
happy
while I smile
a flash of light
a concealed
blade a shout
why
a soft pillow?
a warm bath?
television?

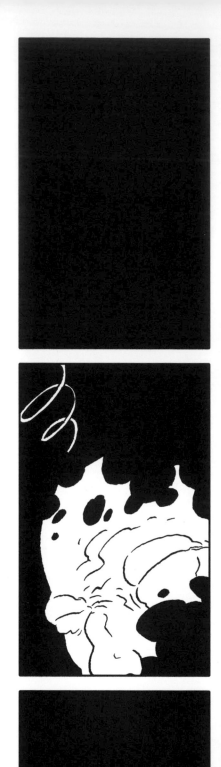

I cannot die

I am not a man
I am a weapon

you stare
amazed

don't stop
dancing

a hush in Autumn twilight
I stand amazed

black water
ripples

why

I wait I admit I wait for
something to happen

now I have transgressed
now I will be punished

if you
exist

144

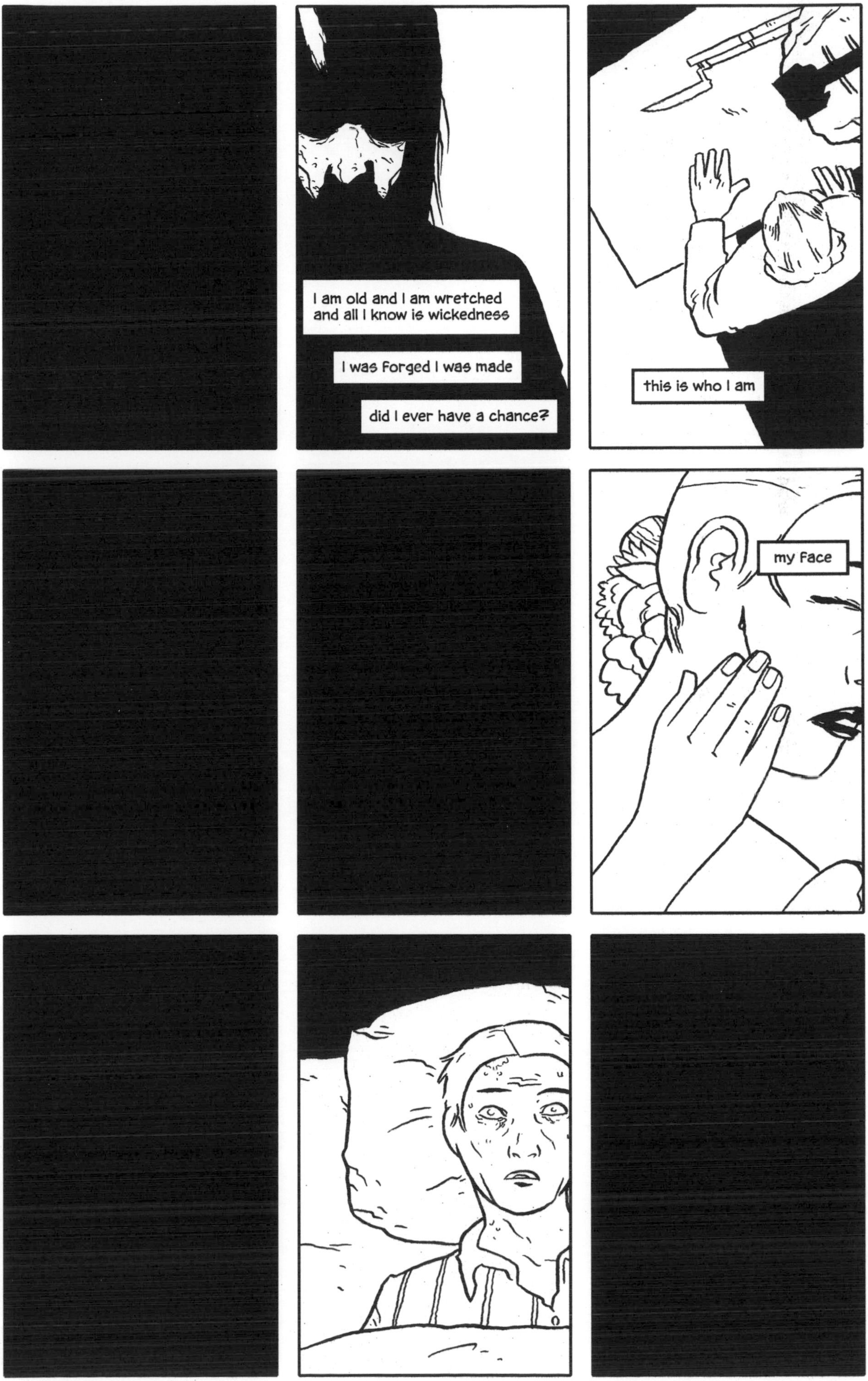
I am old and I am wretched and all I know is wickedness
I was forged I was made
did I ever have a chance?
this is who I am
my face

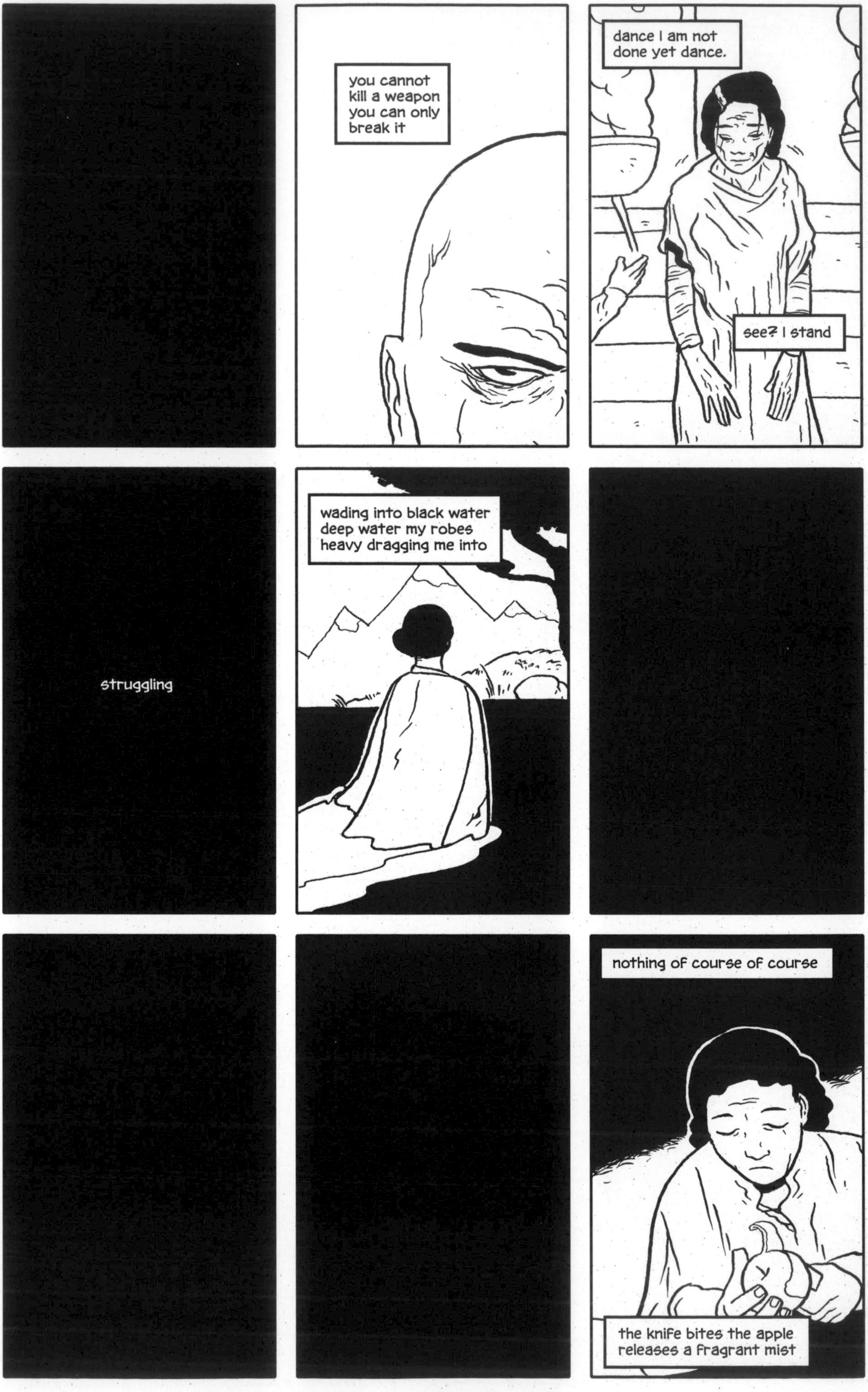
you cannot kill a weapon you can only break it
dance I am not done yet dance.
see? I stand
struggling
wading into black water deep water my robes heavy dragging me into
nothing of course of course
the knife bites the apple releases a fragrant mist

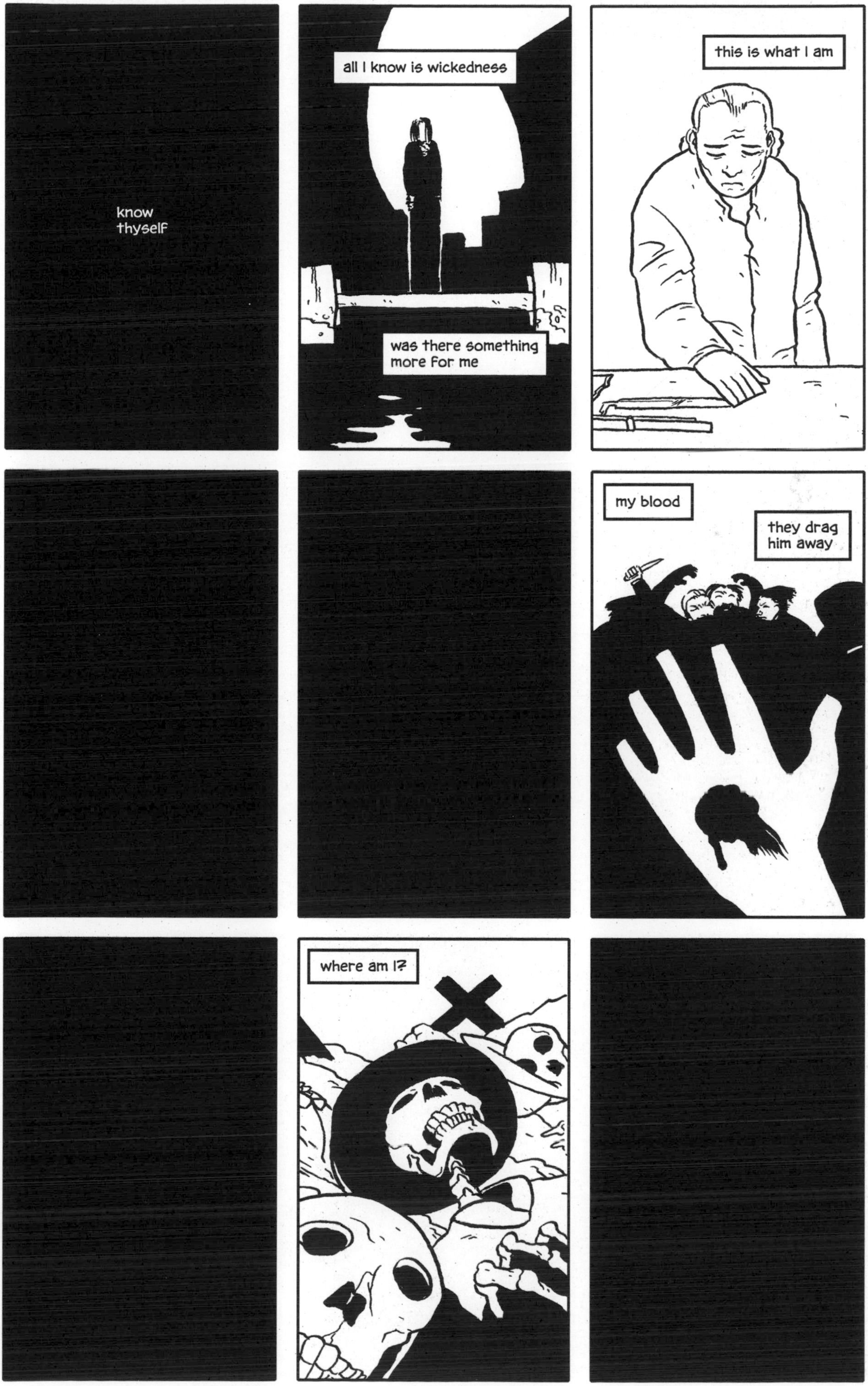

know
thyself

all I know is wickedness

was there something
more for me

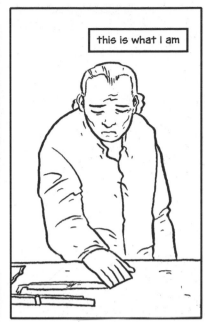

this is what I am

my blood

they drag
him away

where am I?

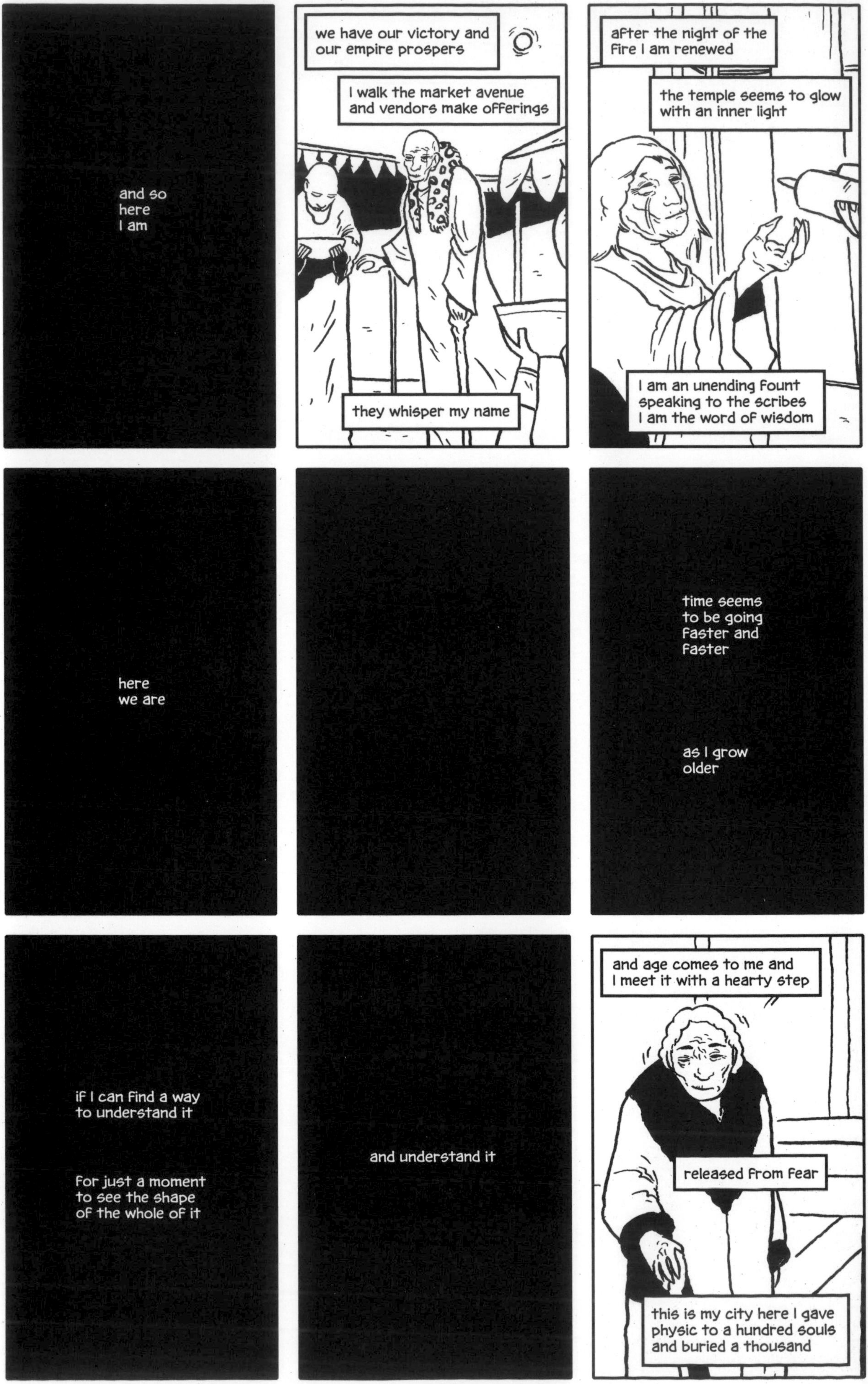
and so here I am
we have our victory and our empire prospers
I walk the market avenue and vendors make offerings
they whisper my name
after the night of the fire I am renewed
the temple seems to glow with an inner light
I am an unending fount speaking to the scribes I am the word of wisdom
here we are
time seems to be going faster and faster
as I grow older
if I can find a way to understand it
for just a moment to see the shape of the whole of it
and understand it
and age comes to me and I meet it with a hearty step
released from fear
this is my city here I gave physic to a hundred souls and buried a thousand

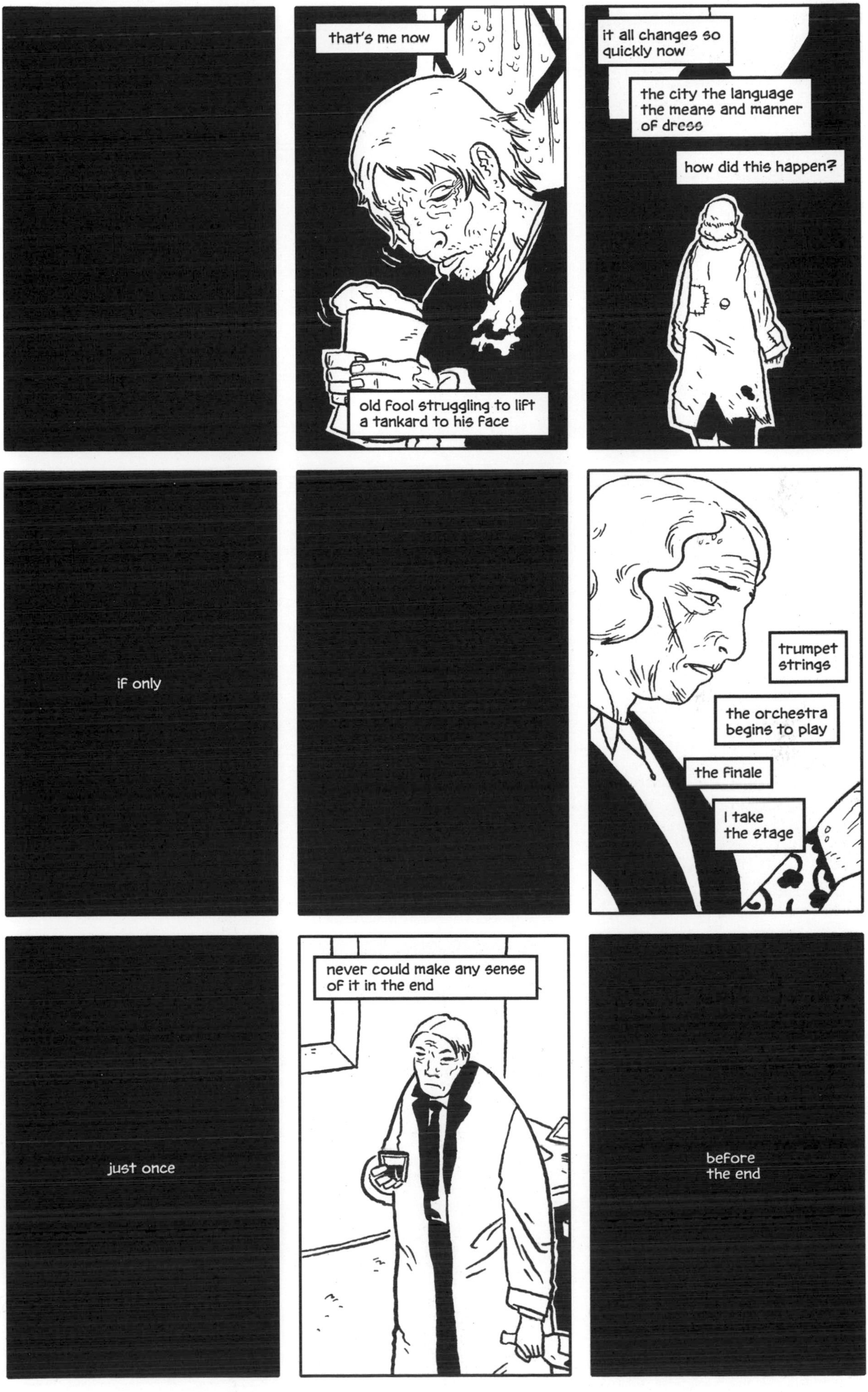
that's me now
old fool struggling to lift a tankard to his face
it all changes so quickly now
the city the language the means and manner of dress
how did this happen?
if only
trumpet strings
the orchestra begins to play
the finale
I take the stage
just once
never could make any sense of it in the end
before the end

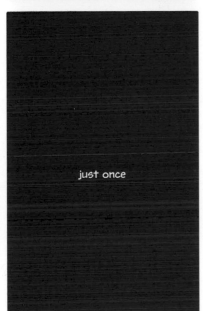

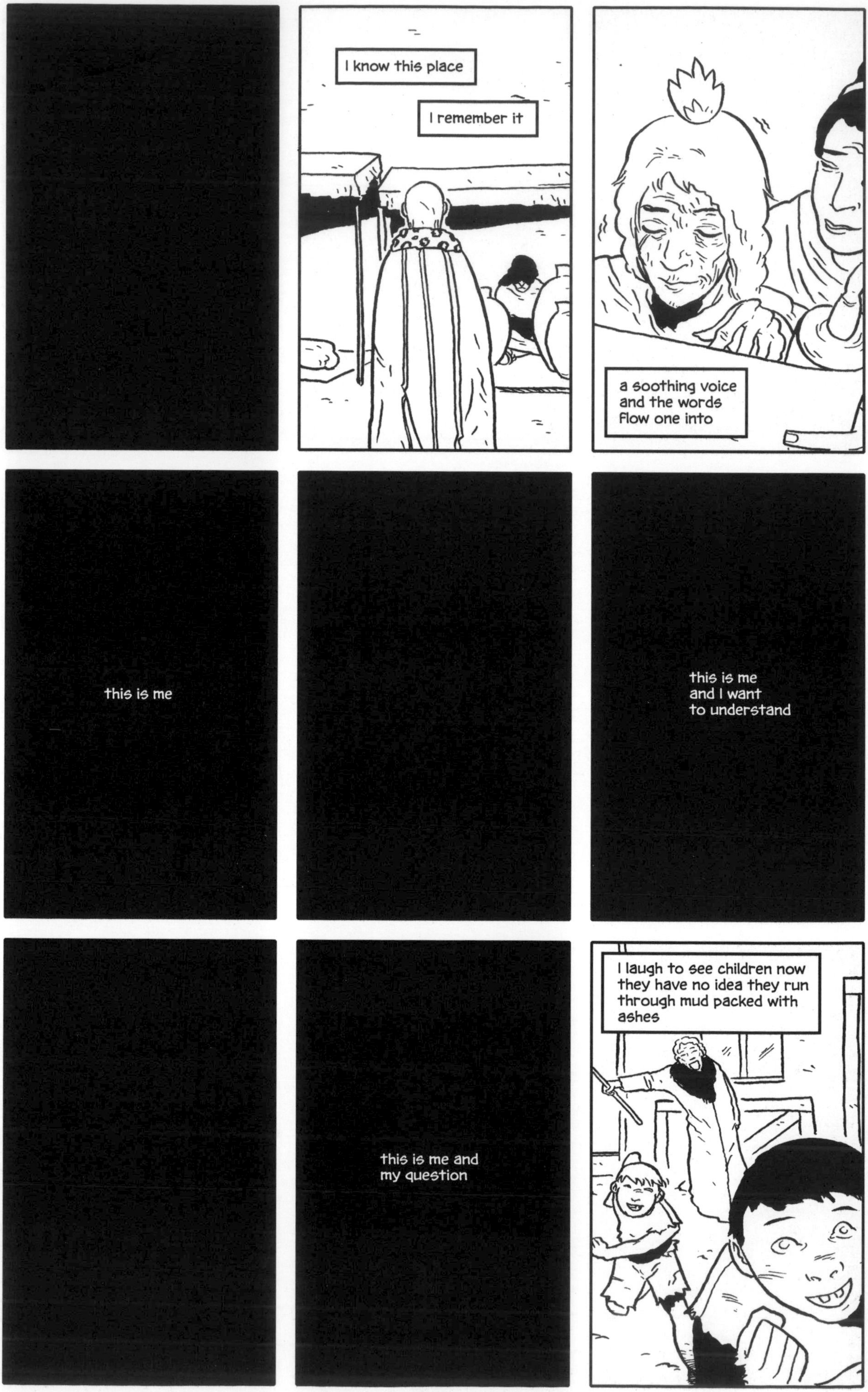
I know this place
I remember it
a soothing voice and the words flow one into
this is me
this is me and I want to understand
this is me and my question
I laugh to see children now they have no idea they run through mud packed with ashes

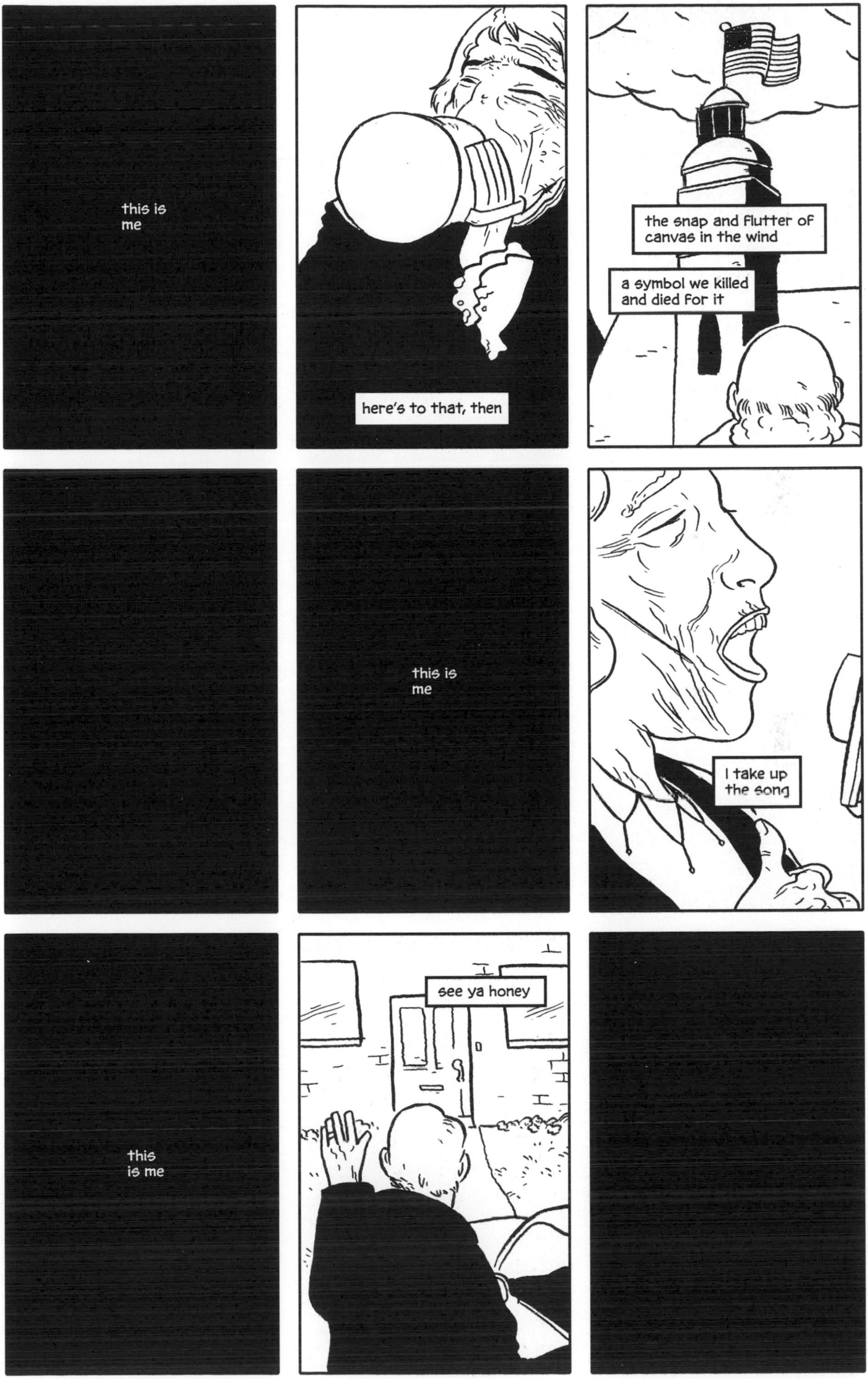
this is
me
here's to that, then
the snap and flutter of
canvas in the wind
a symbol we killed
and died for it
this is
me
I take up
the song
this
is me
see ya honey

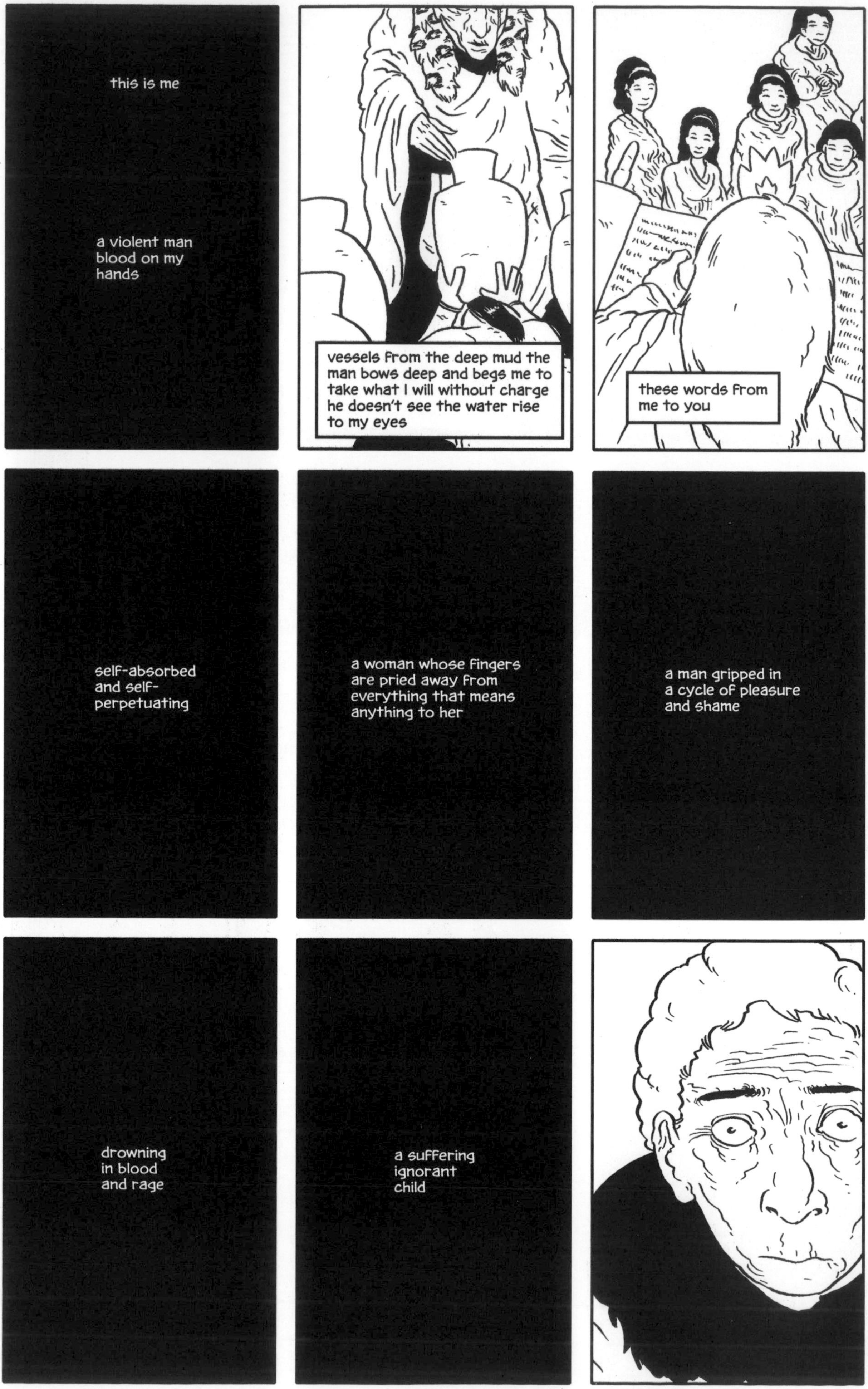
this is me
a violent man
blood on my
hands
vessels from the deep mud the
man bows deep and begs me to
take what I will without charge
he doesn't see the water rise
to my eyes
these words from
me to you
self-absorbed
and self-
perpetuating
a woman whose fingers
are pried away from
everything that means
anything to her
a man gripped in
a cycle of pleasure
and shame
drowning
in blood
and rage
a suffering
ignorant
child

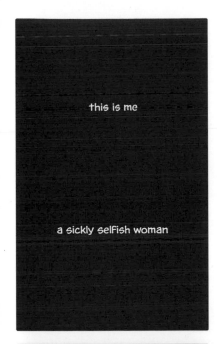

this is me

a sickly selfish woman

here's to me then the great soul!

to the great works I've wrought!

a carriage a rude shout

because I am an obstruction

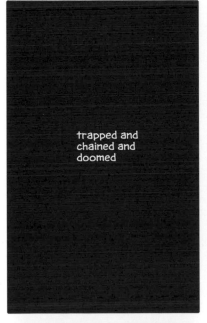

trapped and chained and doomed

benefiting from good fortune

it swells in me and I let it out I let it all out

this is me and all I am all my love and pleasure and

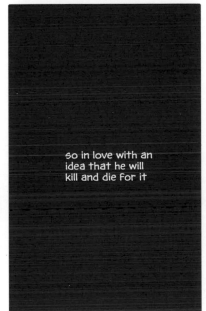

so in love with an idea that he will kill and die for it

seeya buddy!

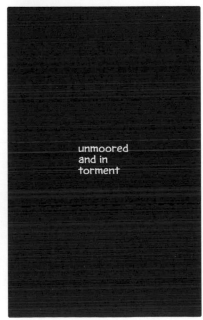

unmoored and in torment

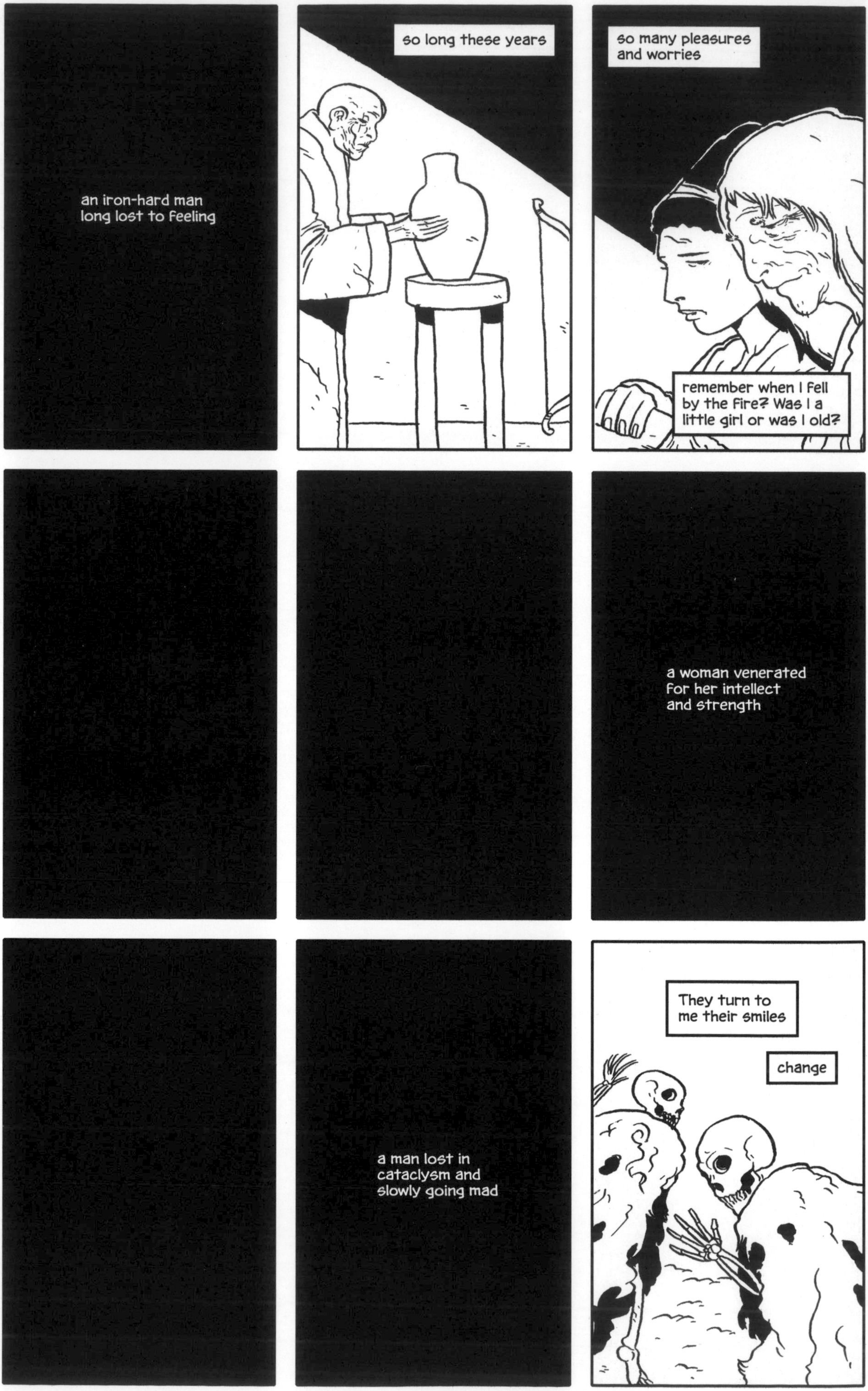
an iron-hard man
long lost to feeling
so long these years
so many pleasures
and worries
remember when I fell
by the fire? Was I a
little girl or was I old?
a woman venerated
for her intellect
and strength
a man lost in
cataclysm and
slowly going mad
They turn to
me their smiles
change

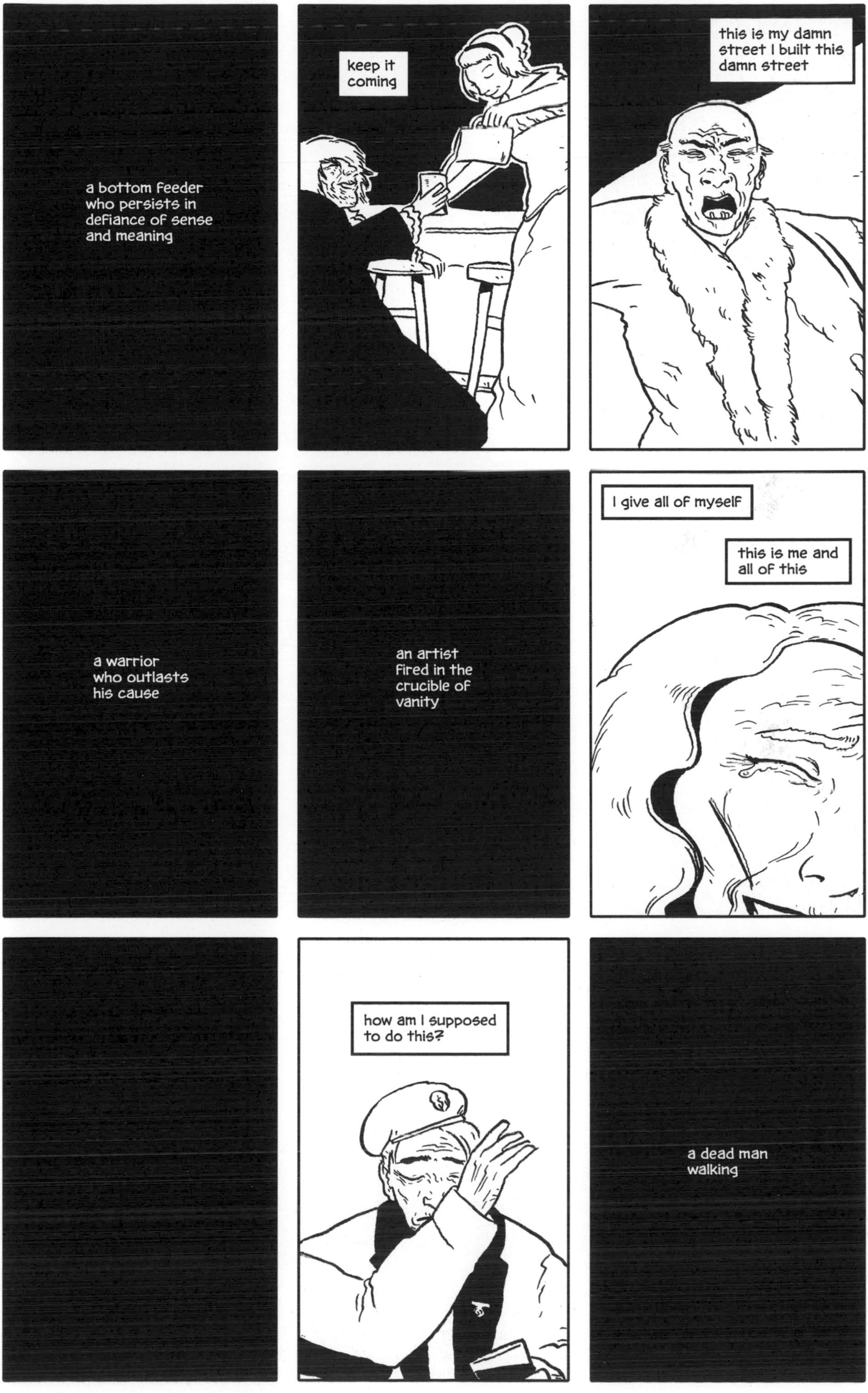
a bottom feeder who persists in defiance of sense and meaning
keep it coming
this is my damn street I built this damn street
a warrior who outlasts his cause
an artist fired in the crucible of vanity
I give all of myself
this is me and all of this
how am I supposed to do this?
a dead man walking

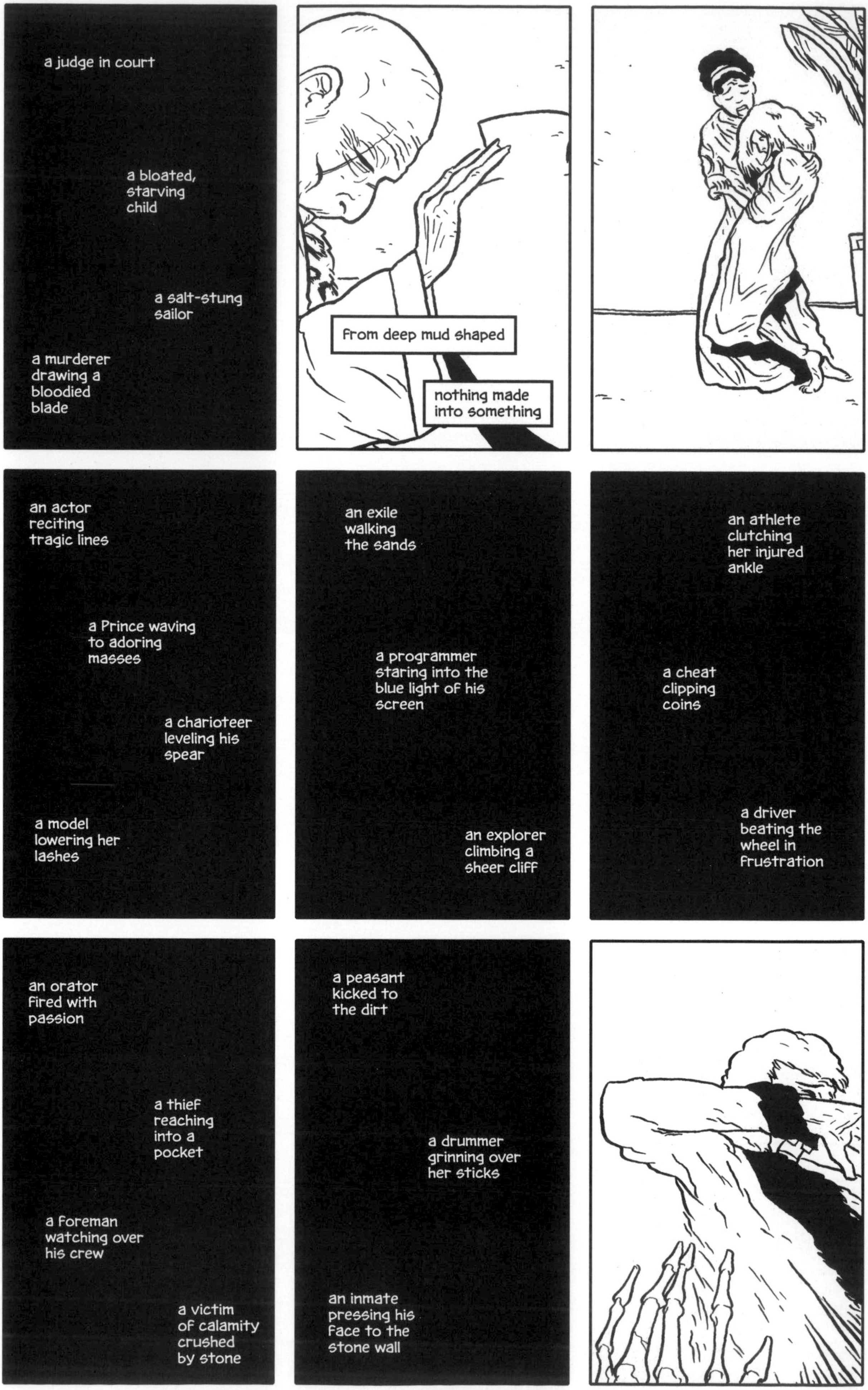

a judge in court

a bloated,
starving
child

a salt-stung
sailor

a murderer
drawing a
bloodied
blade

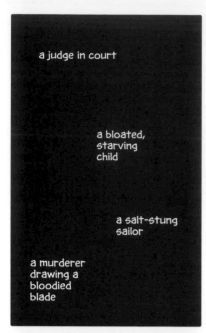

From deep mud shaped

nothing made
into something

an actor
reciting
tragic lines

a Prince waving
to adoring
masses

a charioteer
leveling his
spear

a model
lowering her
lashes

an exile
walking
the sands

a programmer
staring into the
blue light of his
screen

an explorer
climbing a
sheer cliff

an athlete
clutching
her injured
ankle

a cheat
clipping
coins

a driver
beating the
wheel in
frustration

an orator
fired with
passion

a thief
reaching
into a
pocket

a foreman
watching over
his crew

a victim
of calamity
crushed
by stone

a peasant
kicked to
the dirt

a drummer
grinning over
her sticks

an inmate
pressing his
face to the
stone wall

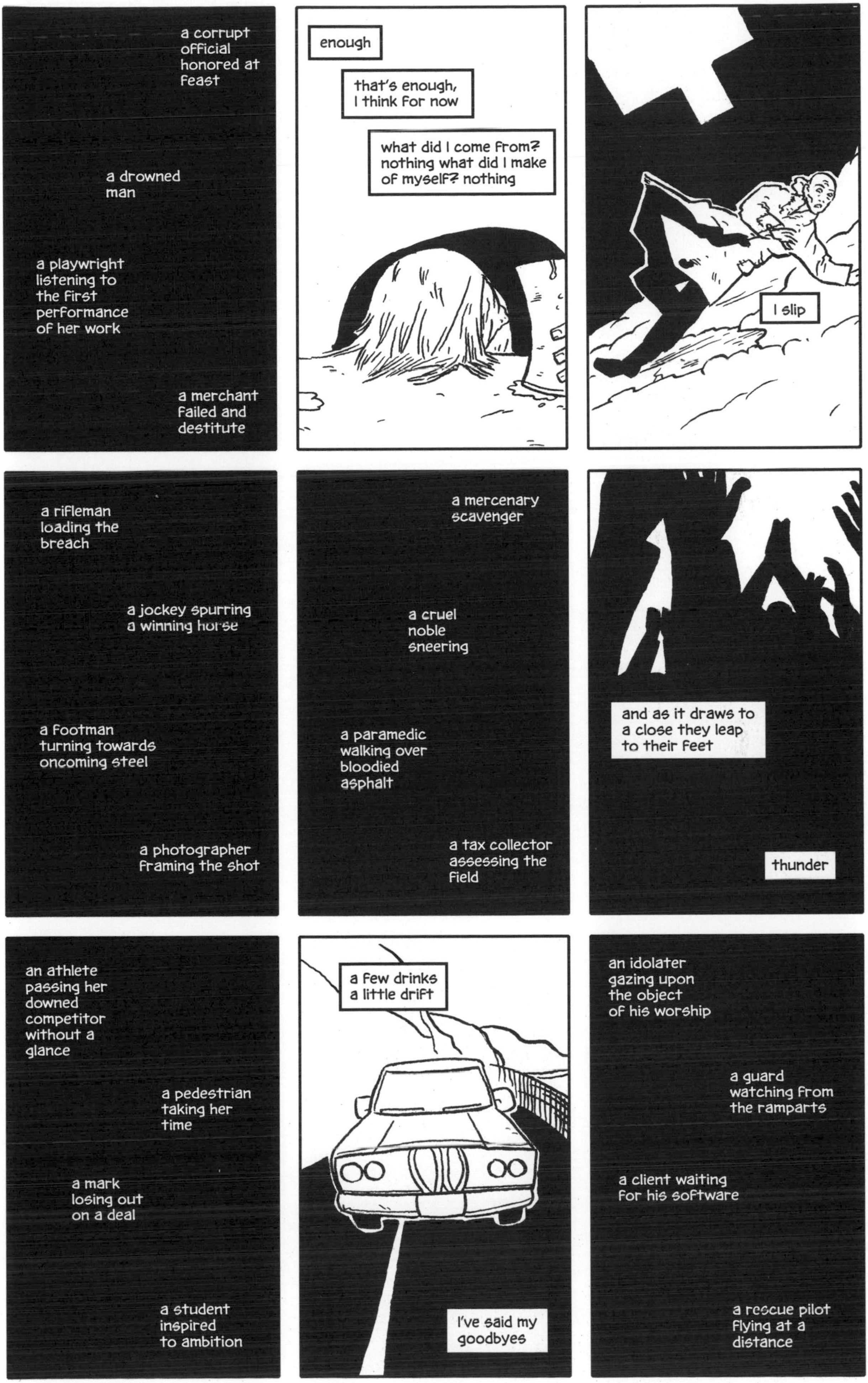
a corrupt official honored at feast
a drowned man
a playwright listening to the first performance of her work
a merchant failed and destitute
enough
that's enough, I think for now
what did I come from? nothing what did I make of myself? nothing
I slip
a rifleman loading the breach
a jockey spurring a winning horse
a footman turning towards oncoming steel
a photographer framing the shot
a mercenary scavenger
a cruel noble sneering
a paramedic walking over bloodied asphalt
a tax collector assessing the field
and as it draws to a close they leap to their feet
thunder
an athlete passing her downed competitor without a glance
a pedestrian taking her time
a mark losing out on a deal
a student inspired to ambition
a few drinks a little drift
I've said my goodbyes
an idolater gazing upon the object of his worship
a guard watching from the ramparts
a client waiting for his software
a rescue pilot flying at a distance

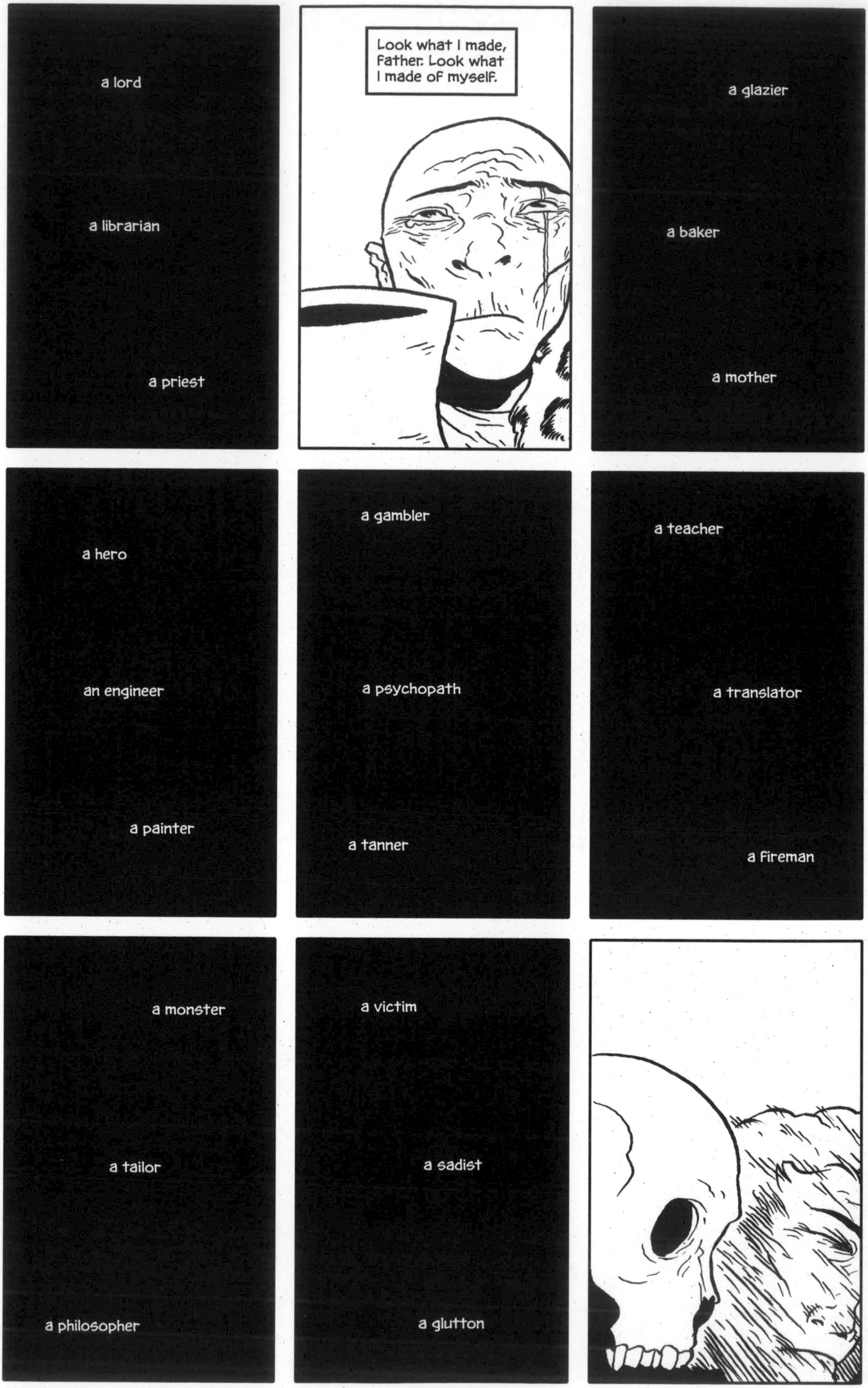
a lord
a librarian
a priest
Look what I made, father. Look what I made of myself.
a glazier
a baker
a mother
a hero
an engineer
a painter
a gambler
a psychopath
a tanner
a teacher
a translator
a fireman
a monster
a tailor
a philosopher
a victim
a sadist
a glutton

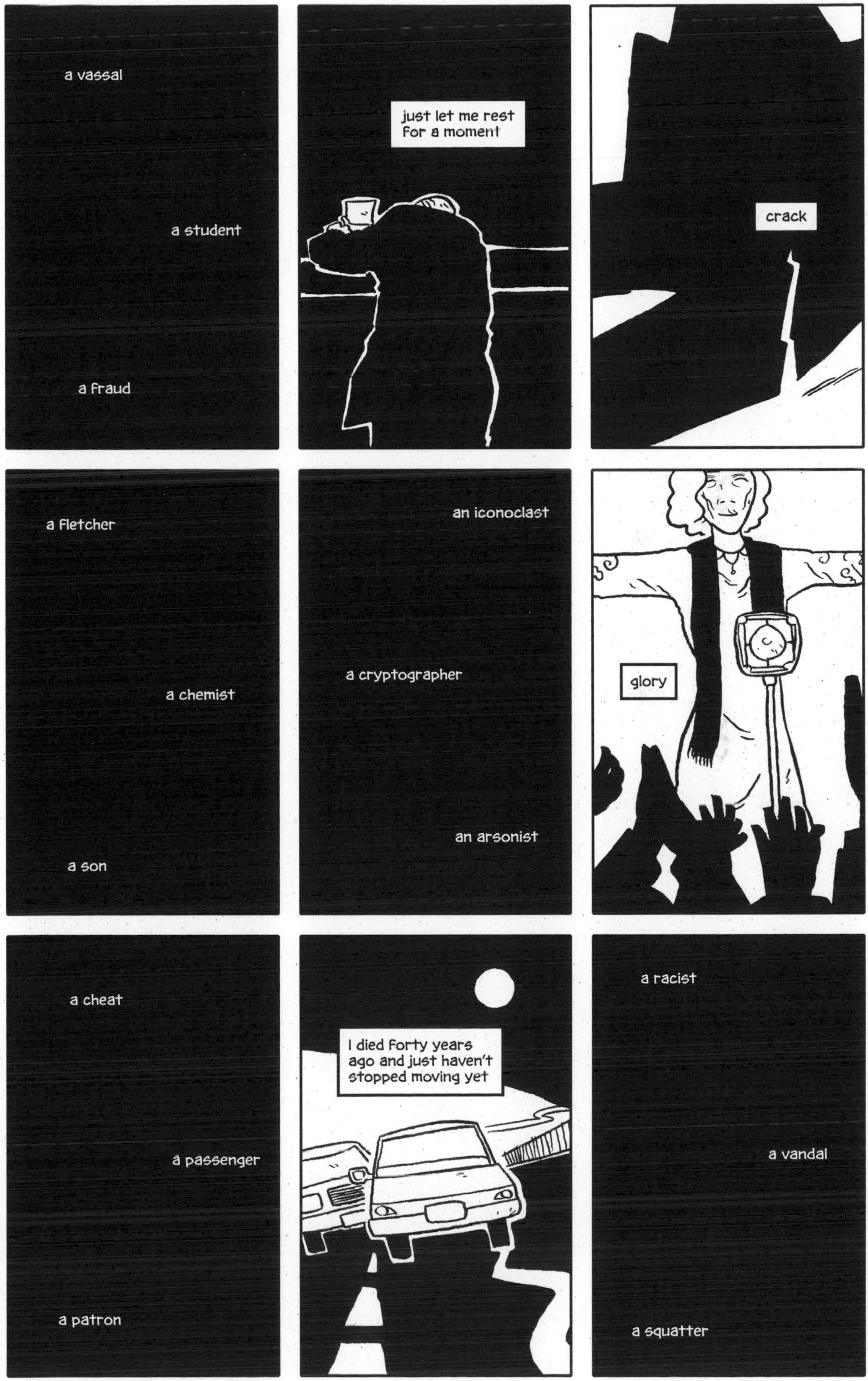

a vassal
a student
a fraud
just let me rest for a moment
crack
a fletcher
a chemist
a son
an iconoclast
a cryptographer
an arsonist
glory
a cheat
a passenger
a patron
I died forty years ago and just haven't stopped moving yet
a racist
a vandal
a squatter

an acrobat

an advocate

a prostitute

a penitent

a shepherd

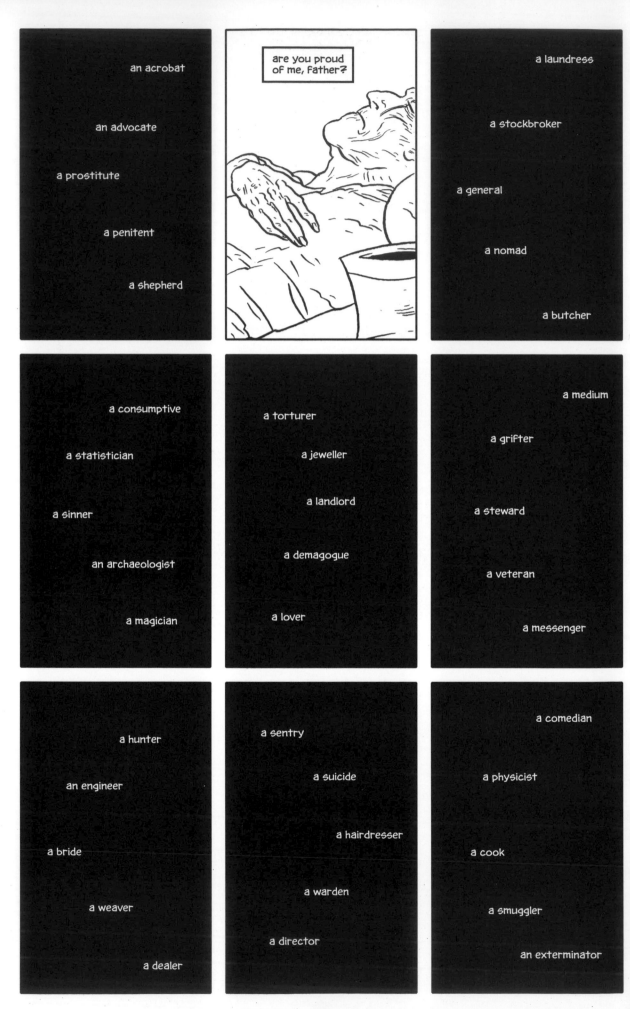

are you proud of me, father?

a laundress

a stockbroker

a general

a nomad

a butcher

a consumptive

a statistician

a sinner

an archaeologist

a magician

a torturer

a jeweller

a landlord

a demagogue

a lover

a medium

a grifter

a steward

a veteran

a messenger

a hunter

an engineer

a bride

a weaver

a dealer

a sentry

a suicide

a hairdresser

a warden

a director

a comedian

a physicist

a cook

a smuggler

an exterminator

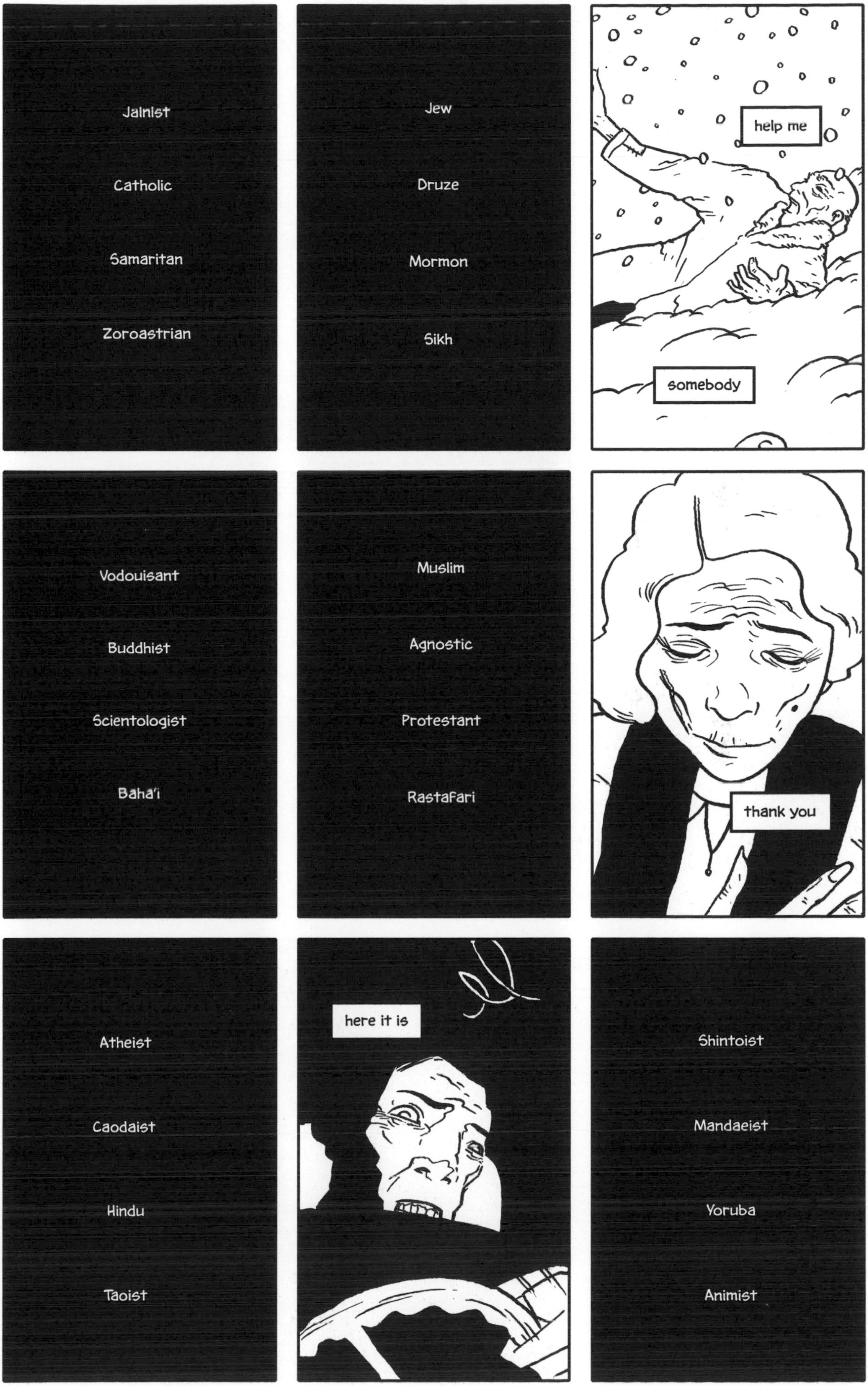
Jainist
Catholic
Samaritan
Zoroastrian
Jew
Druze
Mormon
Sikh
help me
somebody
Vodouisant
Buddhist
Scientologist
Baha'i
Muslim
Agnostic
Protestant
Rastafari
thank you
Atheist
Caodaist
Hindu
Taoist
here it is
Shintoist
Mandaeist
Yoruba
Animist

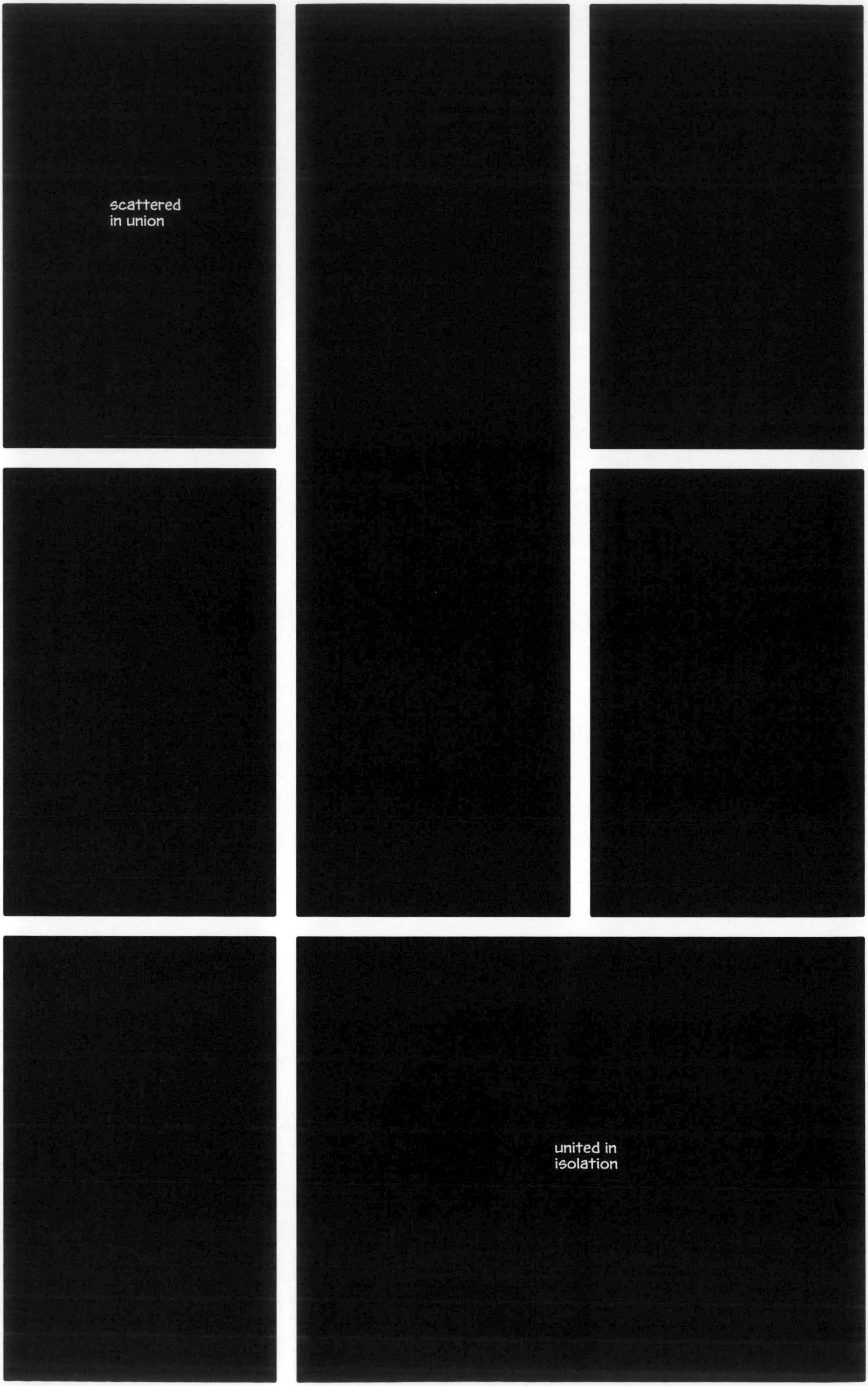
scattered
in union
united in
isolation

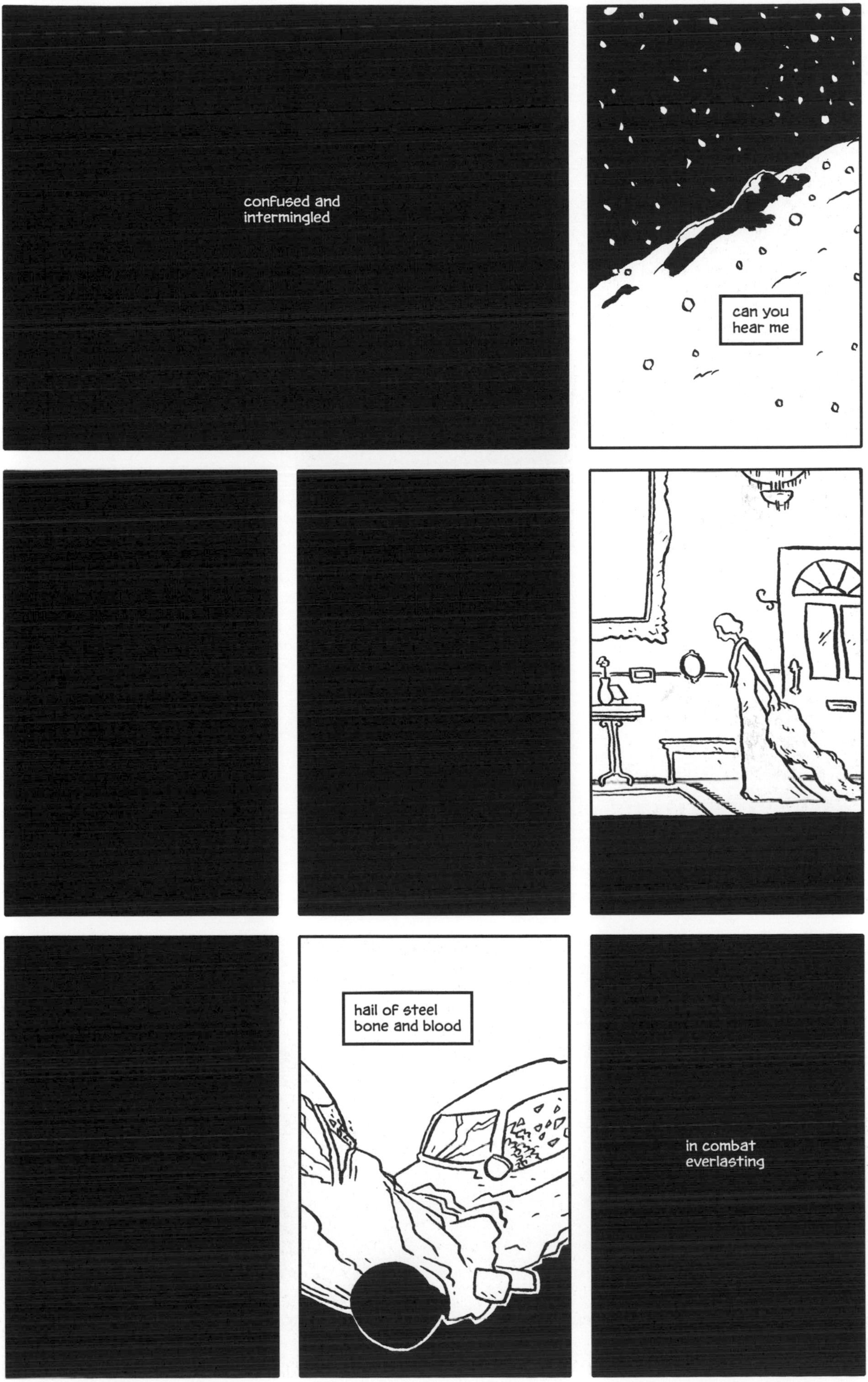
confused and intermingled
can you hear me
hail of steel bone and blood
in combat everlasting

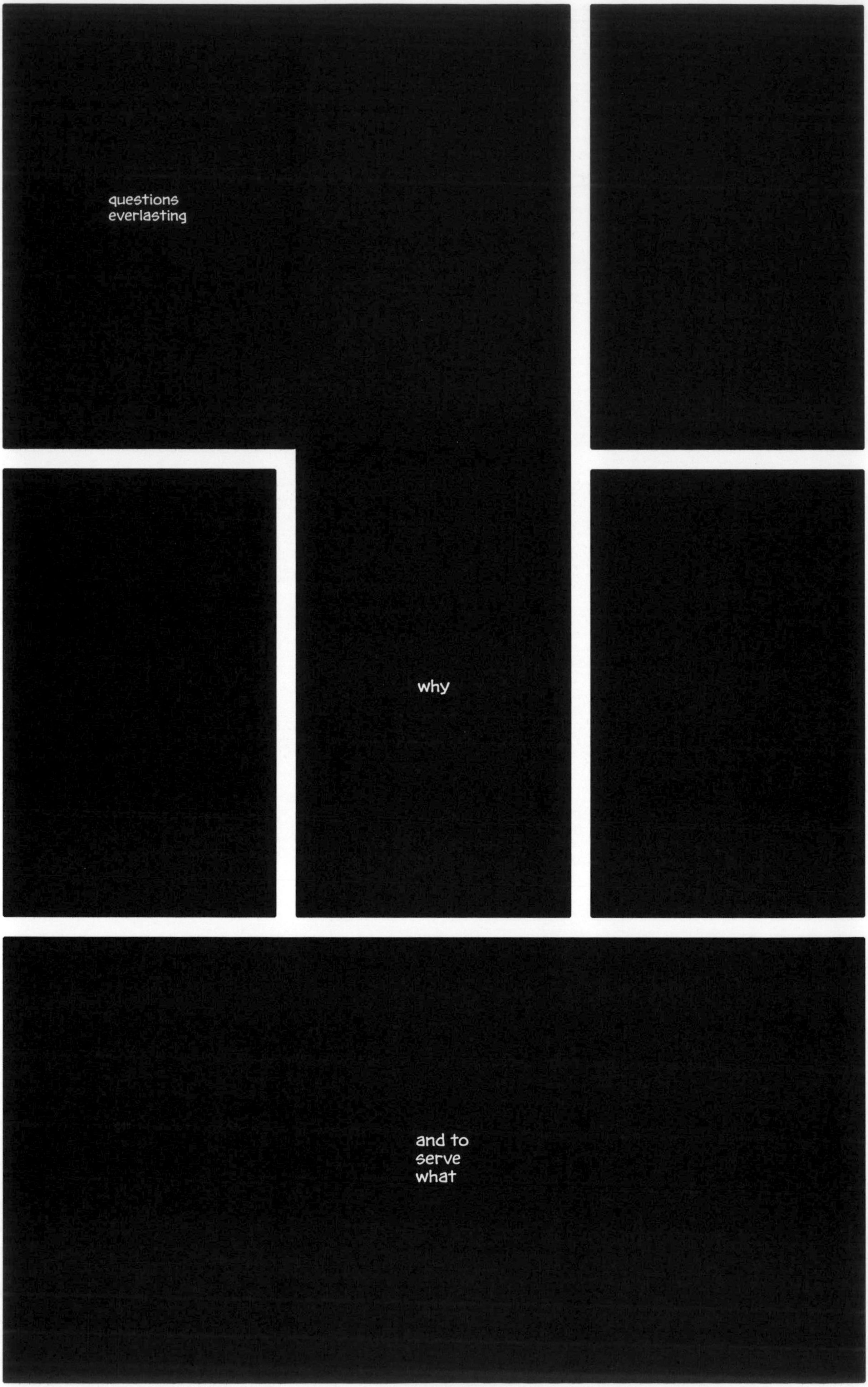
questions
everlasting
why
and to
serve
what

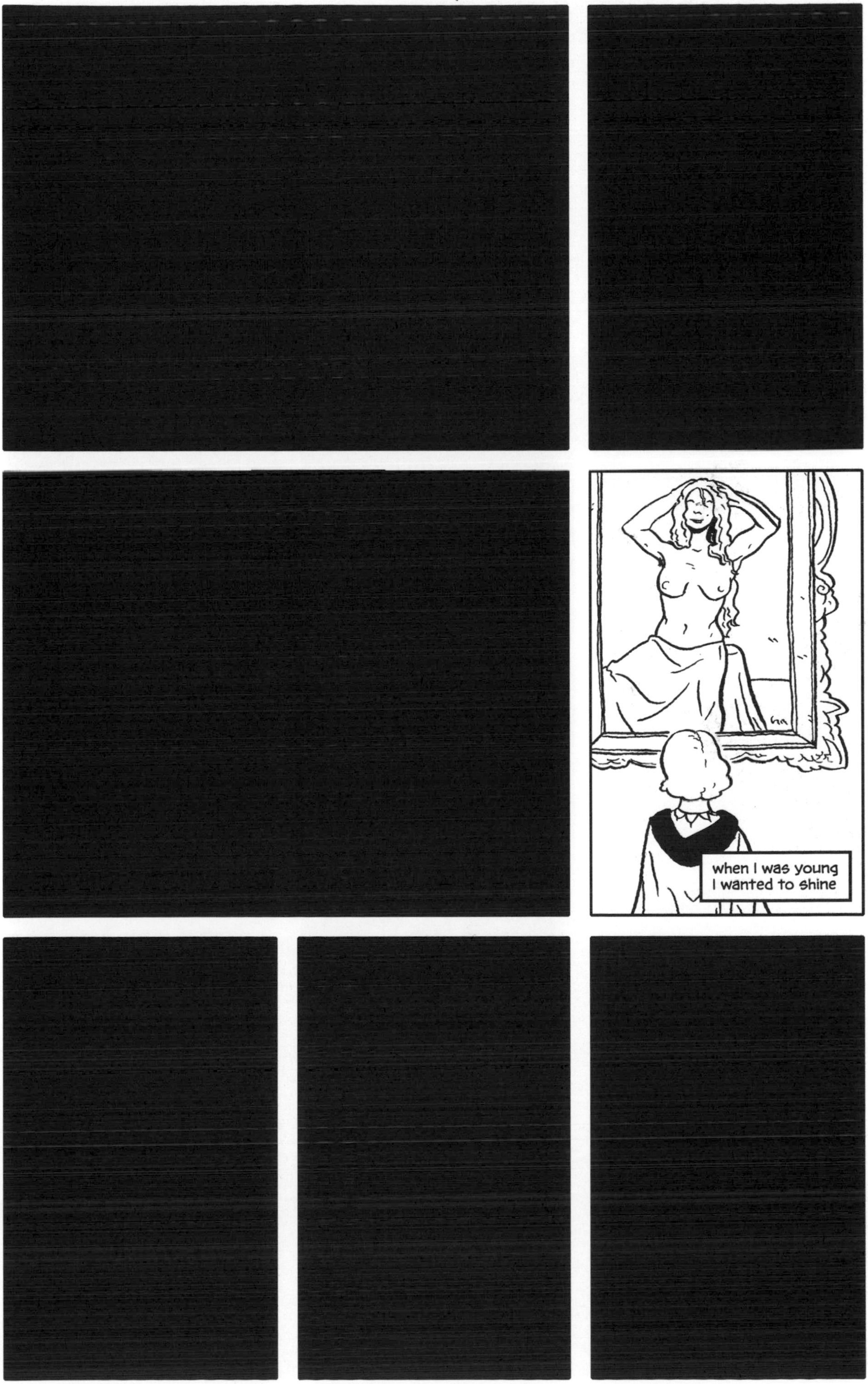
when I was young
I wanted to shine

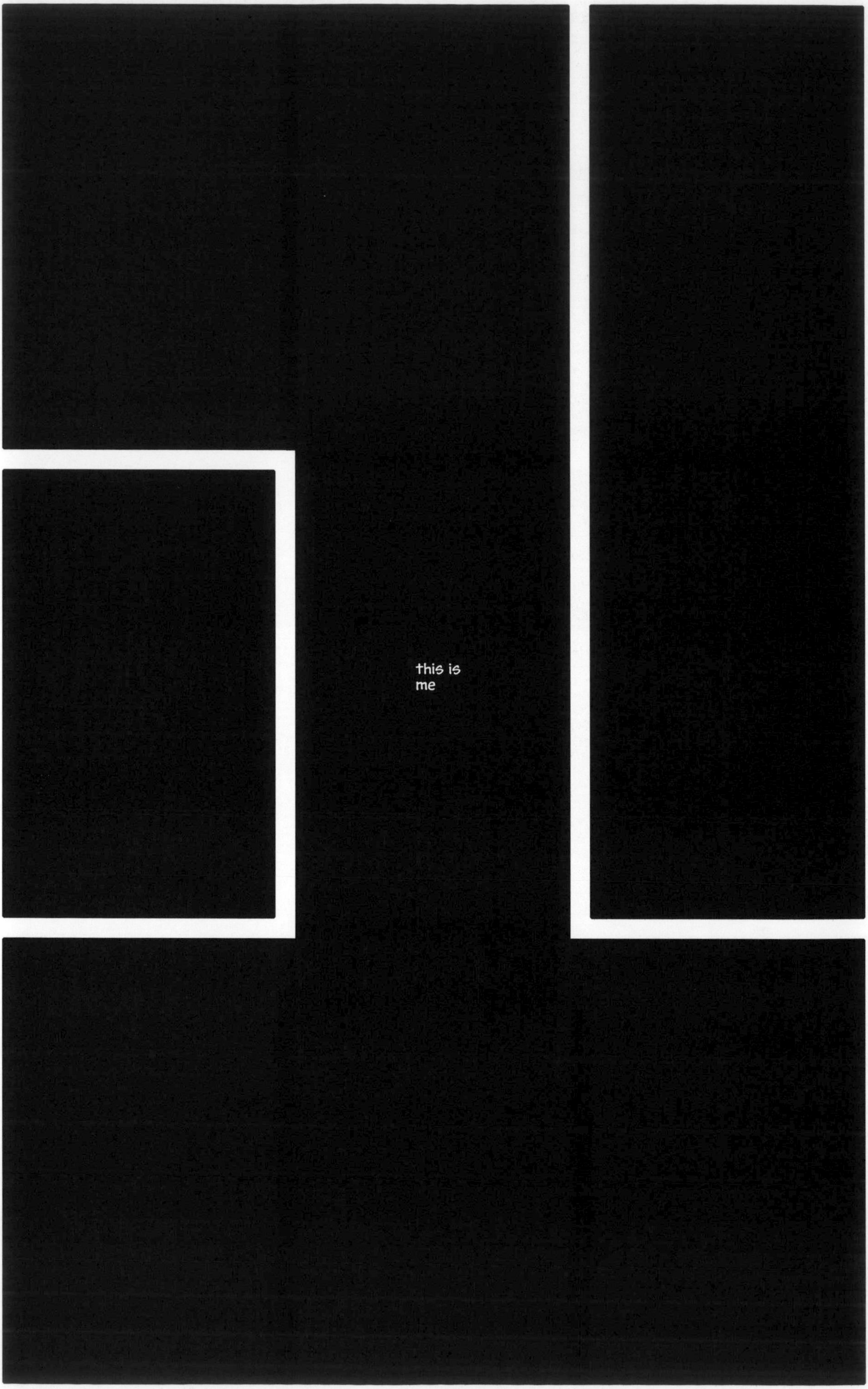
this is me

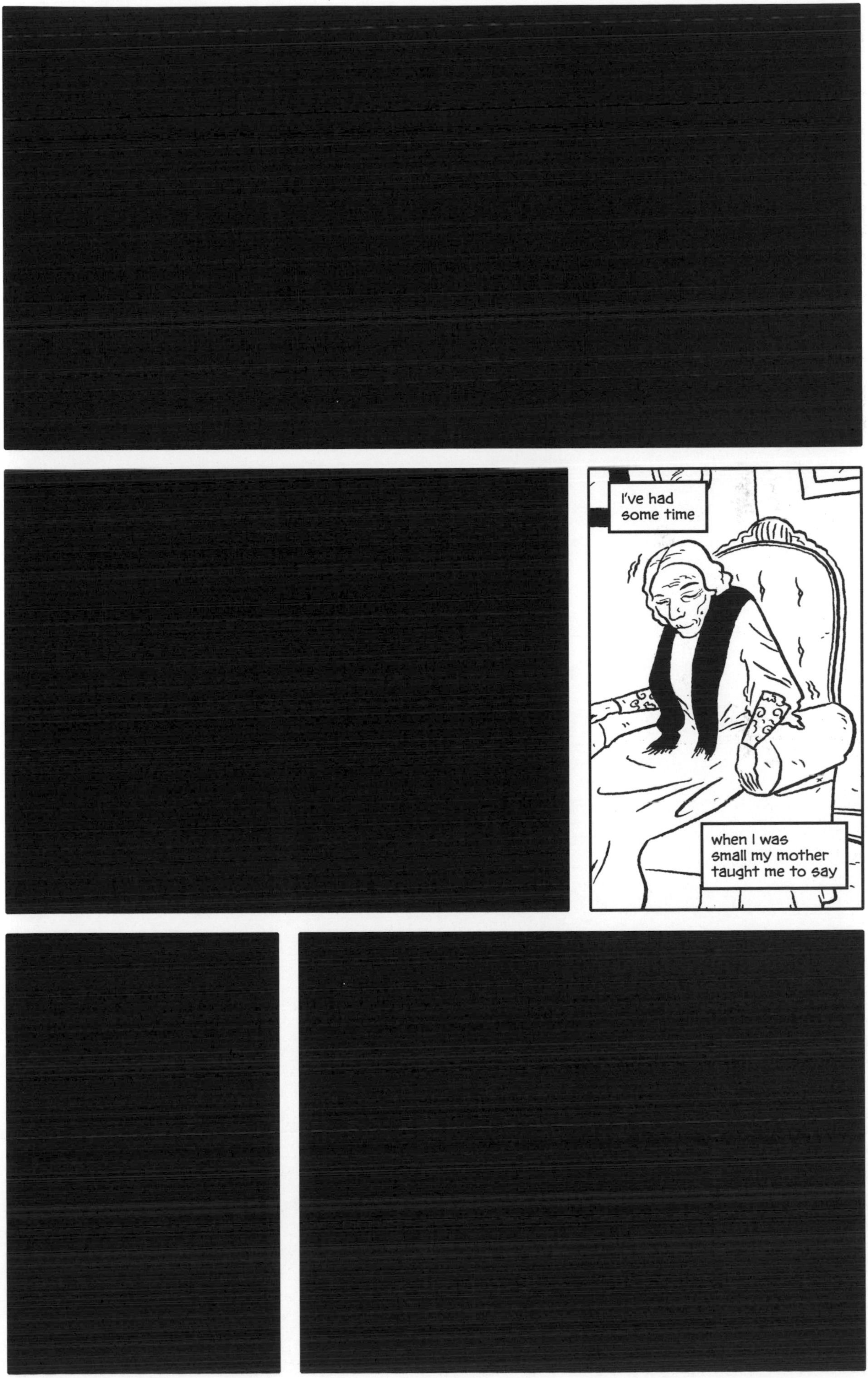
I've had some time
when I was small my mother taught me to say

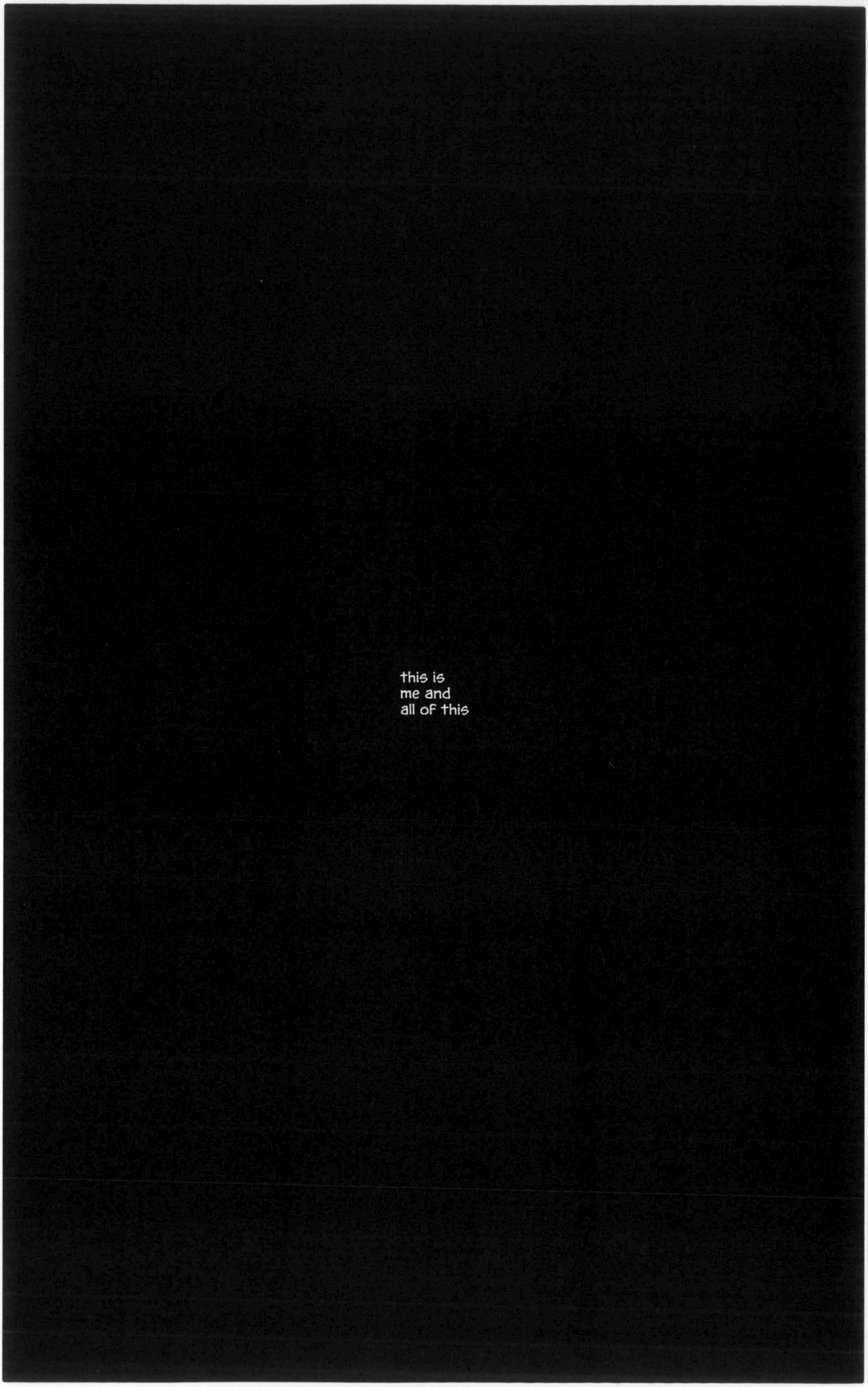
this is
me and
all of this

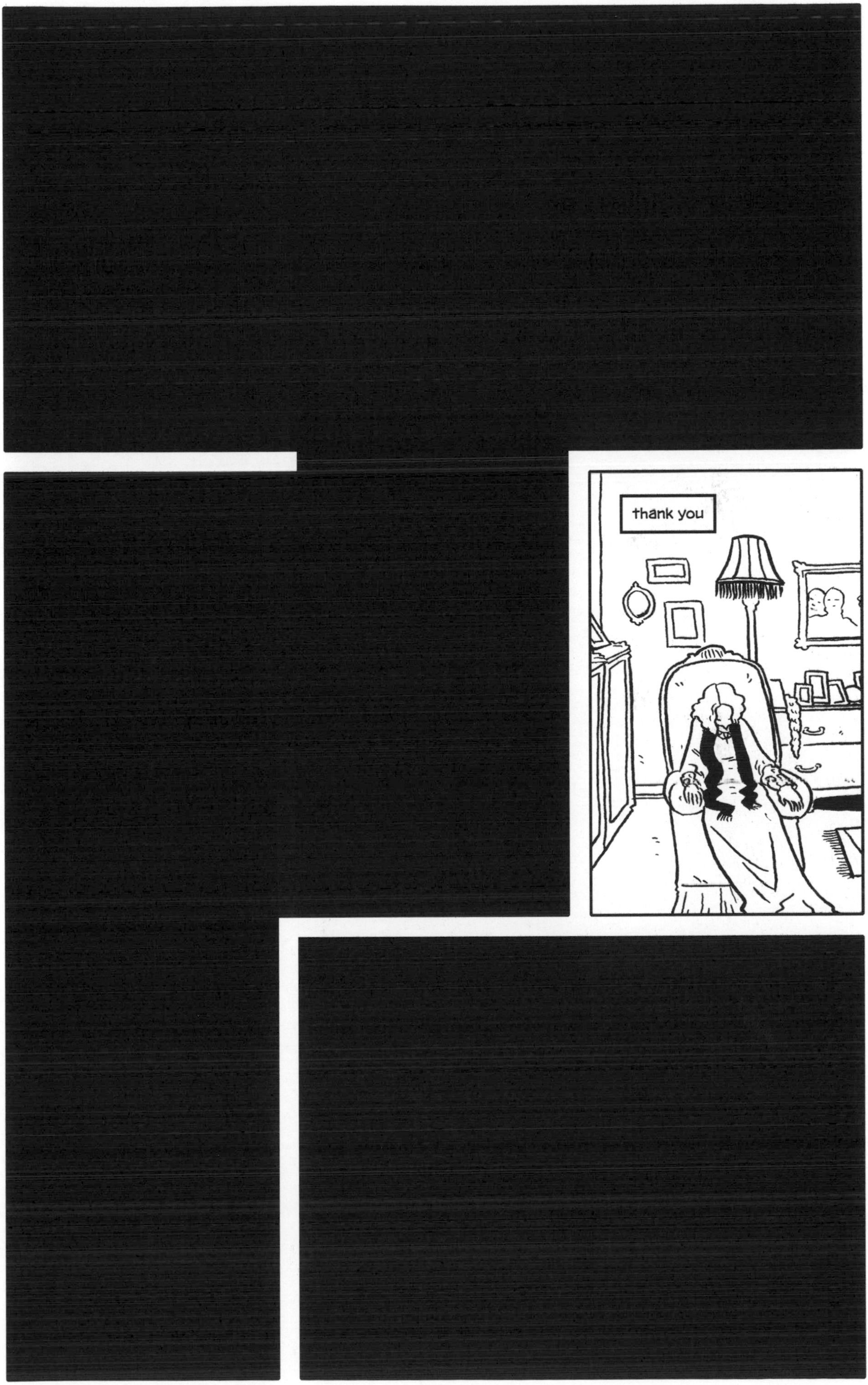
thank you

*Published by*
Oni Press, Inc.

*publisher*
Joe Nozemack

*editor in chief*
James Lucas Jones

*operations director*
George Rohac

*art director*
Keith Wood

*marketing director*
Cory Casoni

*editor*
Jill Beaton

*editor*
Charlie Chu

*production assistant*
Douglas E. Sherwood

ONI PRESS, INC.
1305 SE Martin Luther King Jr. Blvd.
Suite A
Portland, OR 97214
USA

onipress.com · rayfawkes.com

First edition: July 2011
ISBN 978-1-934964-66-8

Library of Congress Control Number: 2011922803

10 9 8 7 6 5 4 3 2 1

PRINTED IN CHINA.

Photo by Charlie Chu

**Ray Fawkes** is a Toronto-based fine artist and writer of graphic novels, prose fiction, and games. Ray's work ranges in styles from introspective, dreamscape horror to bombastic slapstick. He is a two-time Shuster Award nominee in the "Outstanding Canadian Writer" category, and his most recent publication, *Possessions Book One: Unclean Getaway* has been nominated for a YALSA award by the American Library Association.

# From Ray Fawkes & Oni Press...

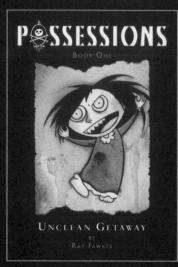

**POSSESSIONS™**
BOOK 1: UNCLEAN GETAWAY
88 pages • Digest
2-color • $5.99 US
ISBN 978-1-934964-36-1

**POSSESSIONS™**
BOOK 2: THE GHOST TABLE
88 pages • Digest
2-color • $5.99 US
ISBN 978-1-934964-61-3

**THE APOCALIPSTIX™**
with illustrator Cameron Stewart
136 pages • Digest
B&W • $11.95 US
ISBN 978-1-932664-45-4

# Also from Oni Press...

**GRAY HORSES™**
by Hope Larson
112 pages • 7"x9"
2-color • $14.95 US
ISBN 978-1-932664-36-2

**LITTLE STAR™**
by Andi Watson
160 pages • 6"x9"
B&W • $19.95 US
ISBN 978-1-932664-38-6

**LOCAL™**
by Brian Wood & Ryan Kelly
384 pages • Hardcover
B&W • $29.99 US
ISBN 978-1-934964-00-2

**LOST AT SEA™**
by Bryan Lee O'Malley
168 pages • Digest
B&W • $11.95 US
ISBN 978-1-932664-16-4

**PETROGRAD™**
by Phil Gelatt & Tyler Crook
264 pages • Hardcover
2-color • $29.99 US
ISBN 978-1-934964-44-6

**Available at finer comic book shops and booksellers everywhere!**

*For more information on these and other fine Oni Press titles, visit our website at www.onipress.com.*
*To find a comic book store near you visit www.comicshops.us.*